IMAGES
of America

MONROE

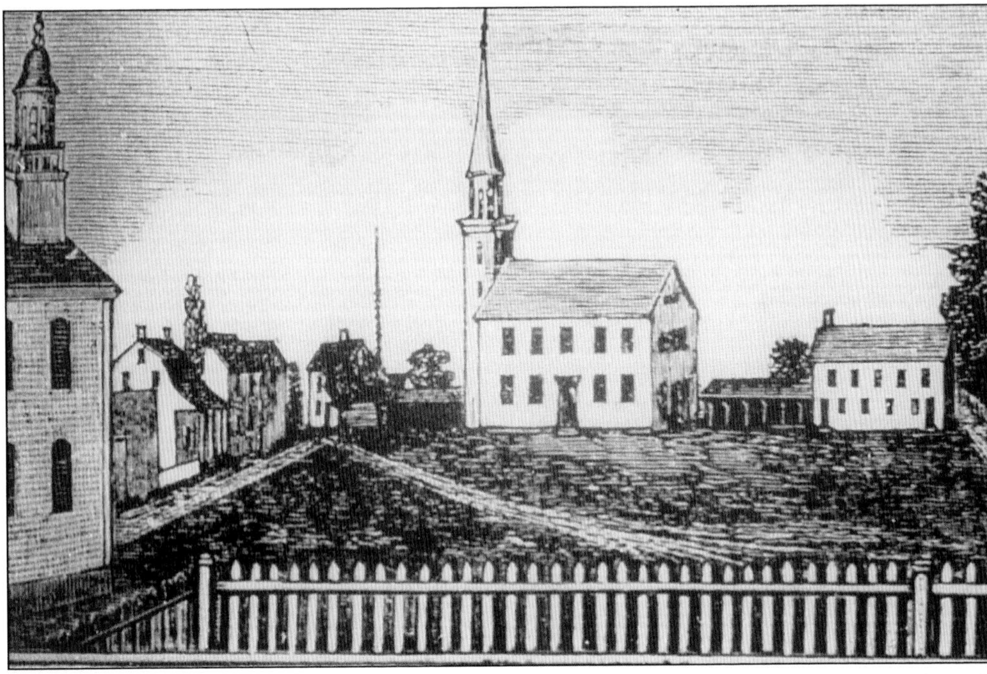

John Warner Barber depicted the Monroe Centre Green (*c.* 1836) in a woodcut. The tall church is the first Monroe Congregational Church, which was on the Green. It was torn down; the second church was built and placed across the road from the Green. Also shown in the woodcut are the deForest Tavern and St. Peter's Episcopal Church. To the right of the Monroe Congregational Church is the original town house.

IMAGES
of America

MONROE

Monroe Historical Society

ARCADIA
PUBLISHING

ISBN 978-0-7385-8739-4

Published by Arcadia Publishing
Charleston, South Carolina

Printed in the United States of America

Library of Congress Catalog Card Number: Applied For

For all general information contact Arcadia Publishing at:
Telephone 843-853-2070
Fax 843-853-0044
E-mail sales@arcadiapublishing.com
For customer service and orders:
Toll-Free 1-888-313-2665

Visit us on the Internet at www.arcadiapublishing.com

Dedicated to all the photographers,
past and present, amateur and professional,
who had the wisdom and foresight
to preserve their family history

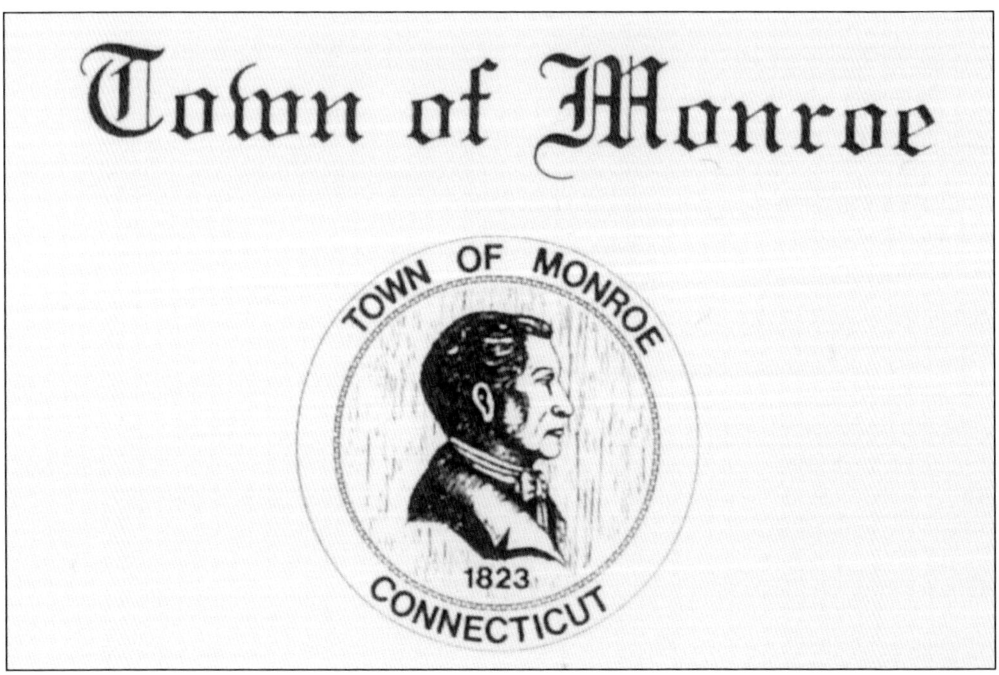

Contents

Acknowledgments

This book would not have been possible without the cooperation of many people who recognized the importance of a visual history of our town. We, the editors, have carefully chosen our pictures, seeking the charm and representation of a particular era, rather than presenting a definitive history. This is a pleasure book and not technical research, and in some instances, we have included pictures of individuals whose names, unfortunately, have been lost to history. In writing this book, we have tried to maintain a consistency, adhering to early spelling of names and places. We are indebted to Mickey Sciortino of Trumbull, whose photograph collection was truly a treasure trove in our early quest for pictures. The vast archives of the Monroe Historical Society provided us with a wealth of both pictures and vital commentary. Longtime resident Emma Johnson not only graciously allowed us to use well-documented vintage photographs, but also spent time with us relating Johnson family anecdotes. We thank Carolyn Adelman for sharing with us marvelous photographs and treasured citizenship documents of the Loss family. The late Robert Haller's picture collection of a more recent Monroe was invaluable to us, and we thank Audrey Haller for recognizing the importance of our project. Many townspeople provided us with hitherto unknown information and photographs: John Babina, Philip Jones, Lou Anthony, Marge Derle, Art and Maddie Young, Elma Jean Wiacek, Jane Chittick, Police Chief Robert Wesche, Lew and Bea Andrews, Sheila Kolesar, Bill Davin, and Edna Yanosy. At the town hall, Karen Burnaska and Kay Inderdohnen were always available to both lend support and provide needed factual information, as was Kathy Gossinger at North American Bank. Above all, we are grateful to Margaret Carpenter and owner Hank Banach of Minute Man Press in Monroe, who provided the expertise to reproduce these rare, original photographs. We cannot forget our committee members, Marge Tranzillo, Pat White, and Nancy Zorena, who made these pictures come alive through their colorful commentary, and to the members of the Monroe Historical Society, who proofread and checked our facts. A very special thanks to committee members Jane Preston and Barbara Waite, who, in addition to writing interesting, descriptive commentary, dedicated long hours to endless proofreading, fact checking, and general revision. Last, but certainly not least, we are indebted to Town Historian Ed Coffey, our final source on dates and names, and to Jean Loveland, our invaluable resource person, whose well-turned phrase often added the needed finishing touch. We, the editors, hope that this photographic chronicle of Monroe's past will inform and entertain those new to our town and will evoke warm memories for our longtime residents.

Gretchen Davison, Editor
Judy Standerford, Editor

Introduction

In early colonial times, the land which we now know as Monroe was mostly woodland, forest, and unexplored terrain, laced by brooks and streams and the mighty "Oosatonic" River as it flowed to the sea. An occasional hunting party found an abundance of wildlife in the area and fishermen plied their way upland—away from established villages and town—following the streams.

Native Americans, too, found profitable hunting here in the pure clean air of the wilderness. They fished the streams and established summer campgrounds along the great river. Those who came later found arrowheads, spearheads, and other tools, as well as piles of clamshells and the remains of other seafoods, near their campsites and even up into the hills such as Webb Mountain. History never recorded any unfriendly incidents.

In time, the families from the towns along the Sound pressed northward as they sought larger farms and more space. It was their desire to be closer to their churches that fostered the establishment of the hill towns. District schools were scattered about the area; Monroe eventually had seven. Blacksmith shops were soon thriving in every neighborhood.

Eventually, the railroads came to Stepney and Stevenson. Industrial development flourished for a time, and when industry in the cities drew the workers away from this area, a return to agriculture was the way of life. When, in 1823, the town of Monroe was chartered, a government structure soon evolved. The church played a prominent role in life and in government, but eventually the separation was realized, and taxes became necessary to pay the teachers, to build and repair the roads, to care for the indigent, and in later years, to build new schools. At least three post offices served the town. A bucket brigade fire company in Stepney signaled the need for the protection of the citizenry. New churches were established. The sleepy hill town awoke and was thriving, trying to keep up with its growing pains.

We are fortunate that the history of the town always claimed a role of importance as the years produced many changes. Three men who have played a crucial role in our history merit additional mention.

The first is the Reverend Elisha Rexford, the first pastor of the first church established here, a learned man with much wisdom. He served the longest of any clergyman ever in the town. In a quiet and orderly fashion, the Reverend Rexford was the guiding hand that helped shape the town's growth.

The Reverend Benjamin J. Swann was pastor of the Congregational Church for a much shorter time. In addition to his religious training and service, he was a born historian. He had a keen interest in that which needed to be recorded for posterity, and while he served as pastor of the church, he carefully researched the time in early church and town life when all the records were lost and/or destroyed. He then painstakingly recorded all his research directly into church records, a great accomplishment when one realizes the restraints on communications in those times. He left rich and abundant of information in his letters and writings, which are still available.

We would be greatly amiss if we didn't pay tribute to our present town historian, Edward N. Coffey, whose published book, *A Glimpse of Old Monroe*, is also a glimpse of his far-reaching knowledge of the town. He has assisted countless others in obtaining information about genealogy and family history, and in the discovery of ancestral homes, architectural facts, land sites, early names, information on the local Native American tribes, and educational facts about the historical development of New England life. Since the age of eight, a large share of Ed Coffey's life has been devoted to the advancement of our historical knowledge. The hunt goes on; he is ever-watchful to gain an old deed, an interesting folktale, or an old photograph if it sheds a small glimpse on what life in our town has been like. He has enriched this town, and we thank him.

Jean Loveland
September 1997

One

Pastimes in Times Past

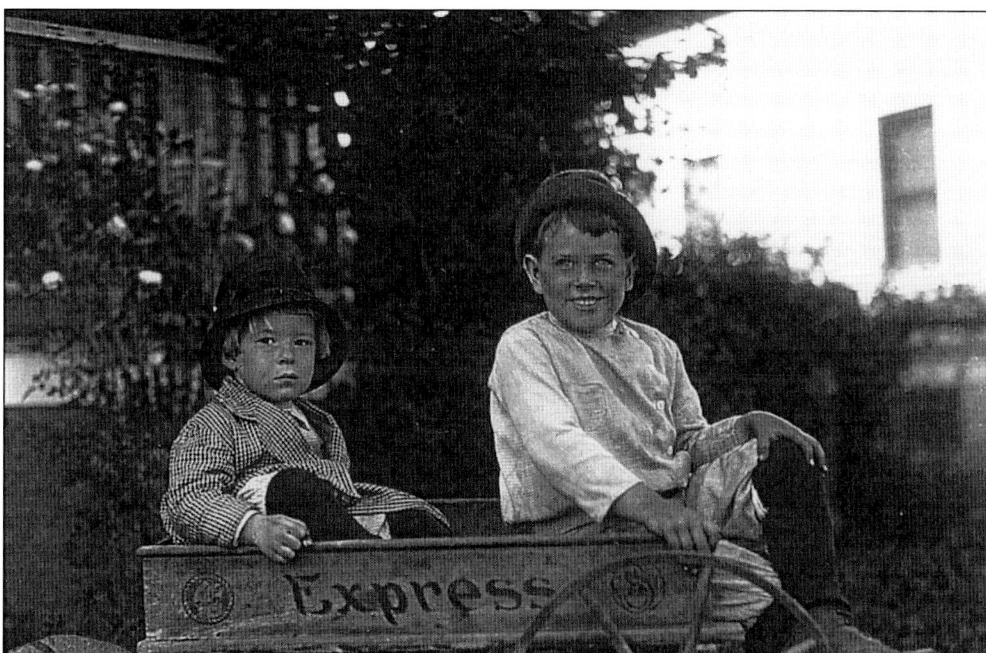

While admittedly not the most cosmopolitan of living spaces, Monroe has always offered many pleasurable moments to those with imaginations and a sense of fun. The names of these two boys have been lost to history, but the joy of sharing a ride in a wagon remains today.

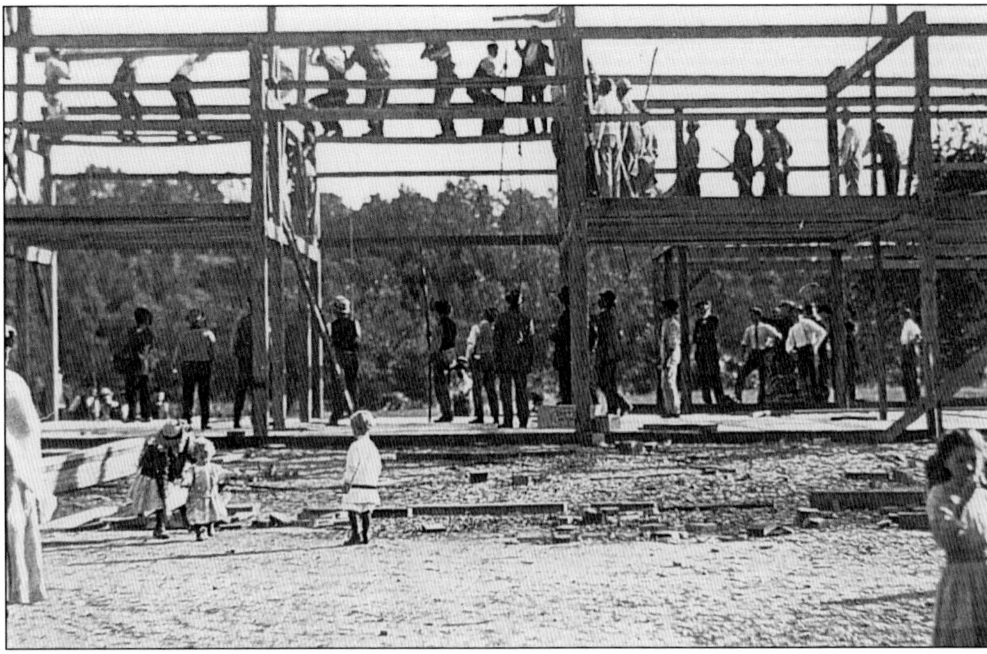

A town really became a community during a barn raising. Here, in this early 1900s view, the men brought tools, teams, and a good supply of neighborliness to raise the Burr Hawley barn as women and children watched. This barn stood at the intersection of Main Street and Stepney Road until the early 1970s. Today, the Monroe Supermarket is located here.

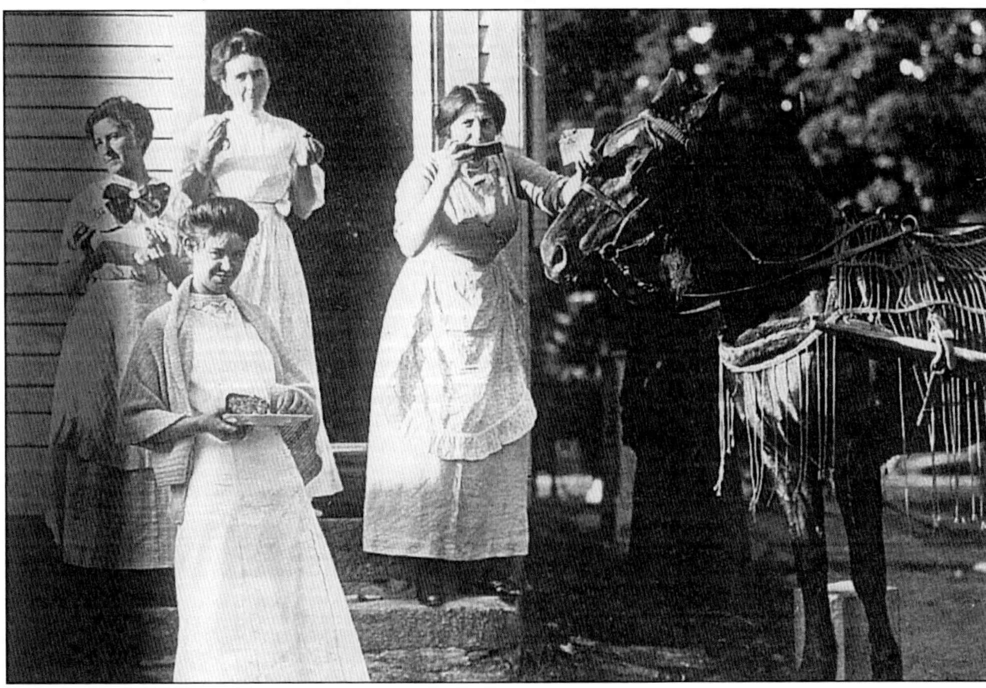

Barn raisings were anticipated social events which would last all day. These women are enjoying some of their bountiful food which would be shared at the gathering. The watchful horse is arrayed not in costume, but in a "fly flicker."

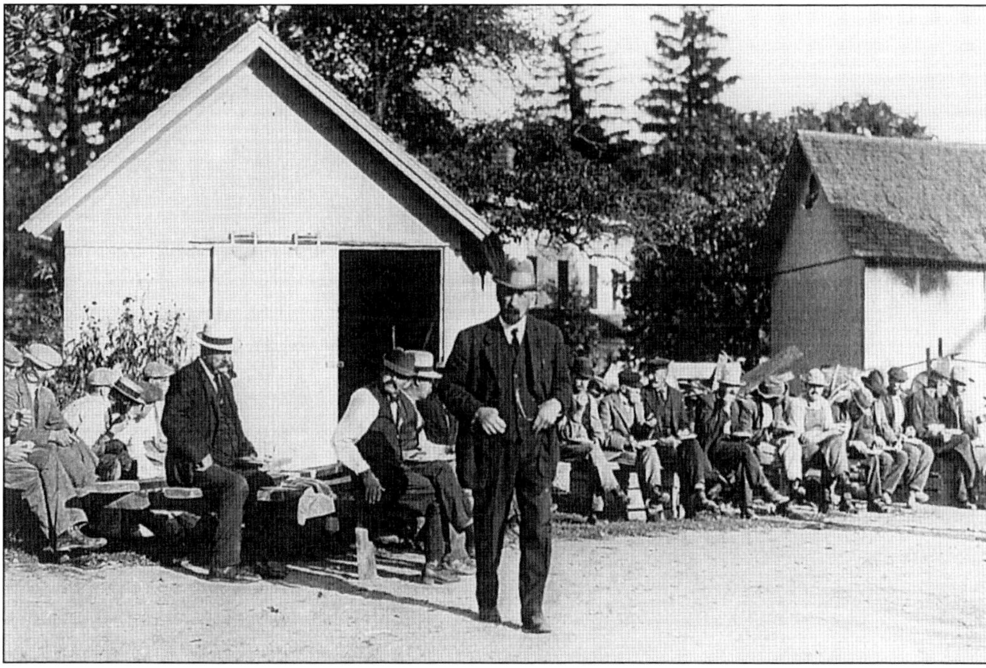

Lunchtime gave the men a break from toil as well as a chance to assess their progress, while more formally dressed spectators took pride in viewing the next generation's barn-raising skills.

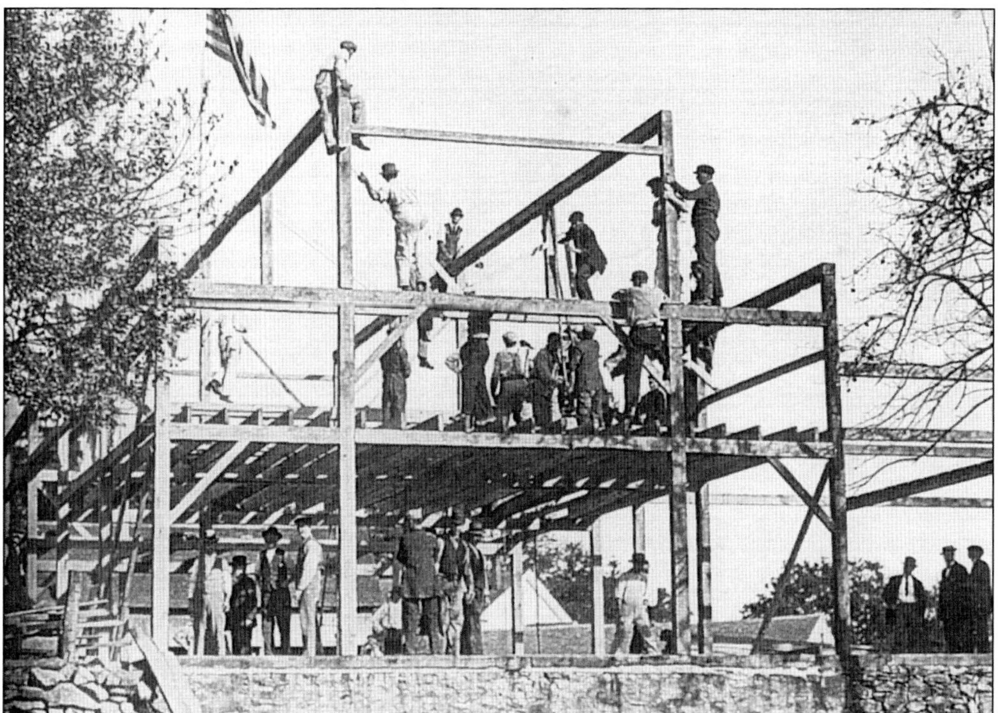

A master carpenter laid out the frame on the level ground and, with the help of neighbors, pegged it together. The various sides were raised by manpower with ropes, pulleys, and long push poles. With floor joists in place, the men expressed their satisfaction by raising the flag.

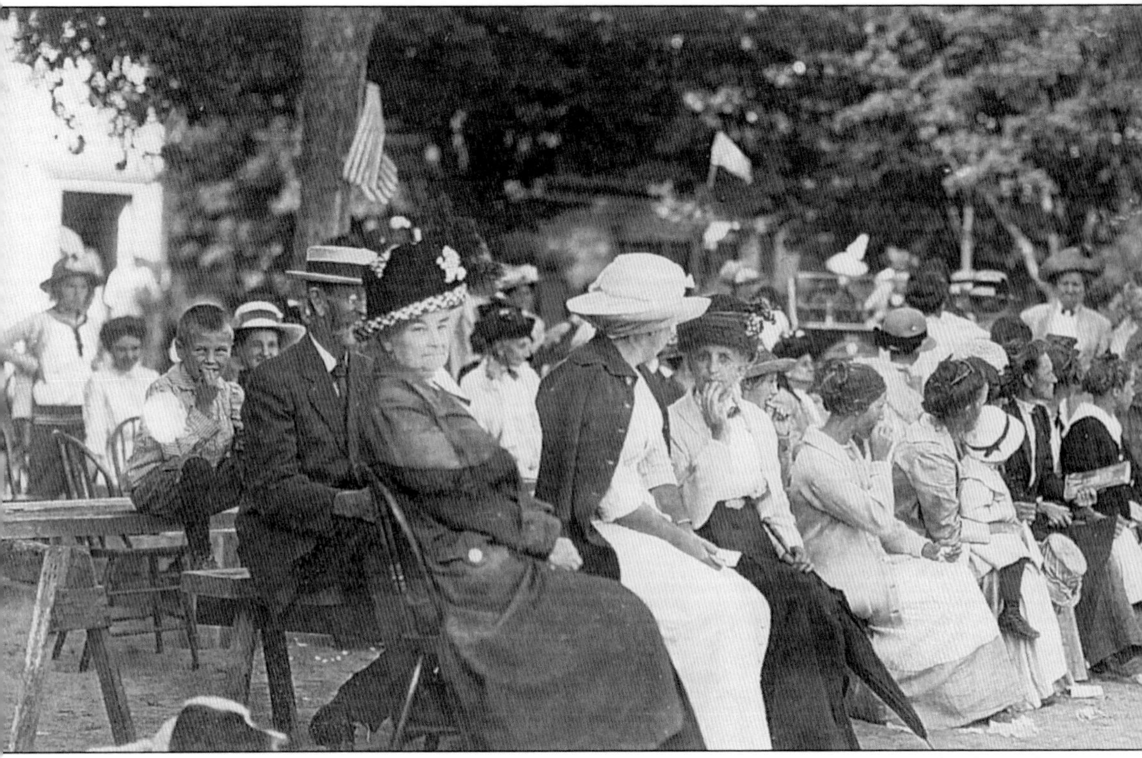

This event, identified as the Velie auction, seems to have attracted more people than chairs, but the young Louis Prevost appears content with his sawhorse and board perch (*c.* 1910).

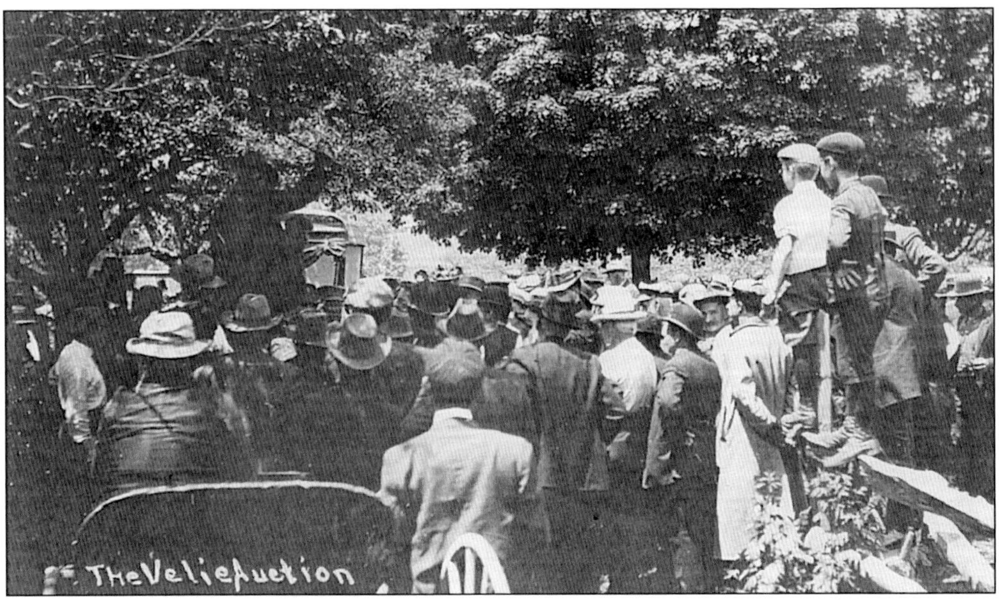

These men attending the Velie auction are certainly interested in the proceedings. Only one person has noticed the photographer!

AUCTION.

Will be sold at Public Auction to the highest bidder, on

Saturday, Feb. 14, 1885.

At 1 o'clock, P. M.,

at his late residence in Monroe, the personal property of Prosper Hurd, deceased.

This property consists of one Horse, two Sets of Harness, top Buggy, Wagon, Sleigh, Hay in barn, Joiners' and Farmers' Tools, etc.

JAMES BURR,

Executor.

Monroe, Feb. 5, 1885.

Townspeople looked forward to notices like this, since auctions were popular social gatherings.

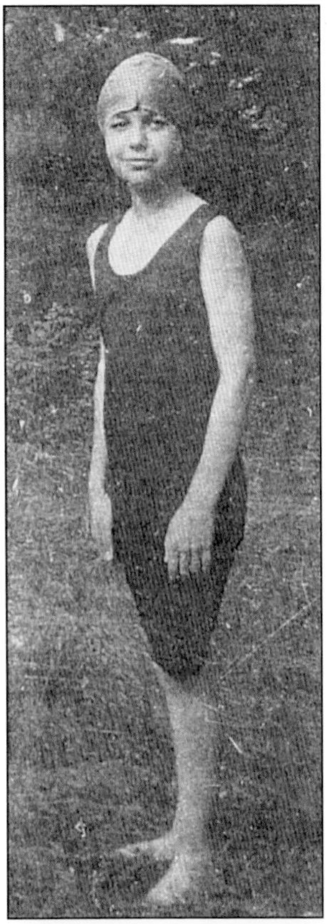

Proper attire was the order of the day. Even swimming required modesty. Note that the suit modeled by this local bathing beauty (on the left) is quite similar—top as well as shorts—to the boys in the bottom picture. These boys are "well suited" for their Camp Sherman boating experience at Loveland's Cove in the Stevenson area of Lake Zoar. Several summer camps flourished for many years along the lake (c. 1920).

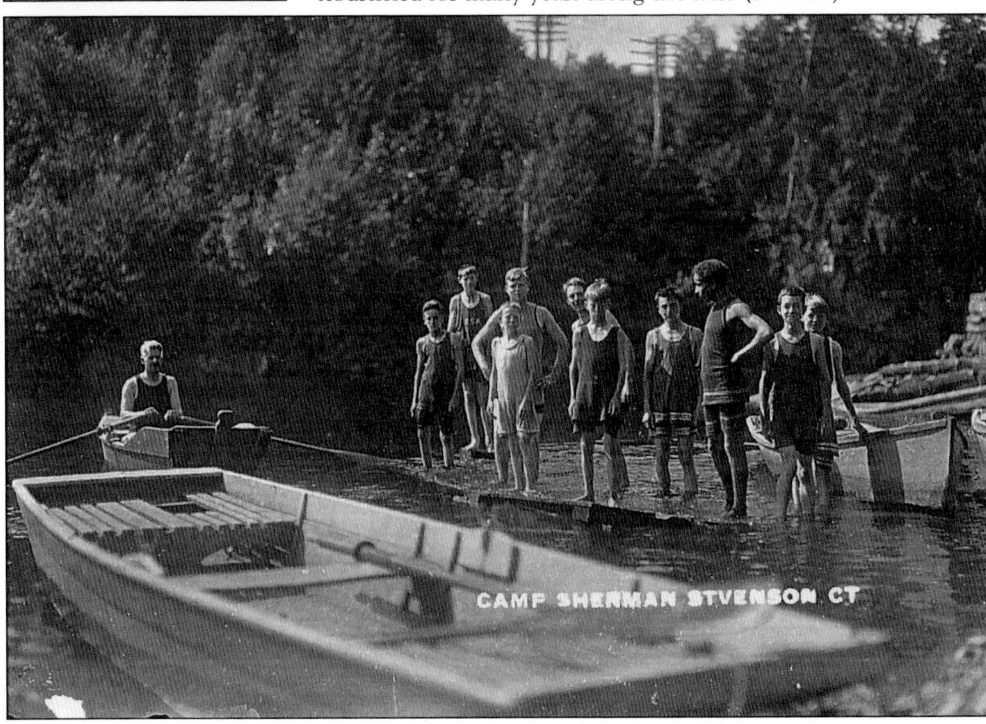

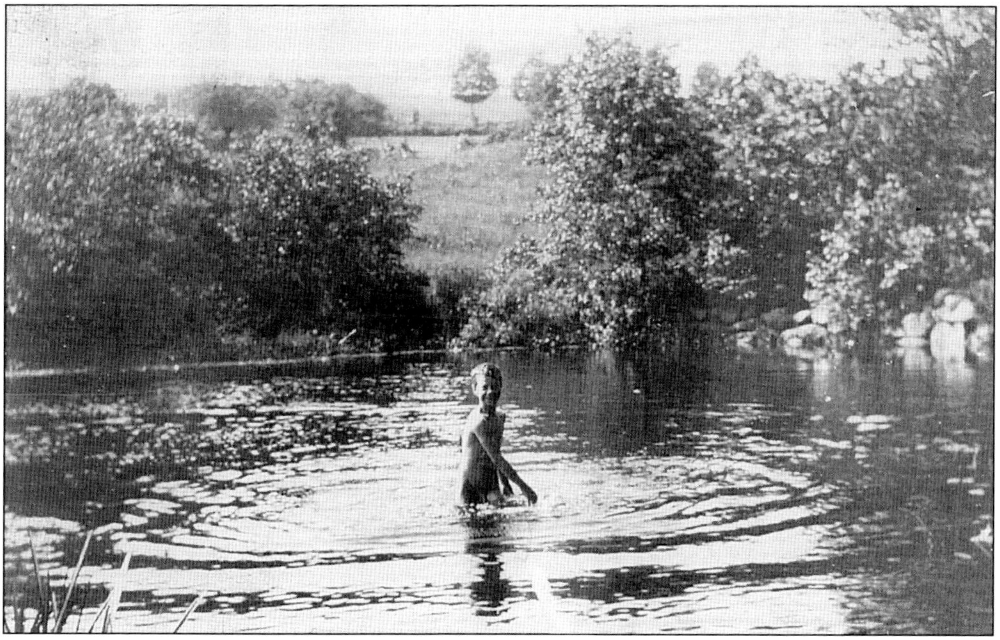

Summer in Monroe brought long, hot days. Young folks enjoyed cooling off in "the ole swimmin' hole." In a moment of solitude, who needed those cumbersome suits? Many farms had their own swimming holes where "skinny dipping" was permissible. This pond is off Hammertown Road.

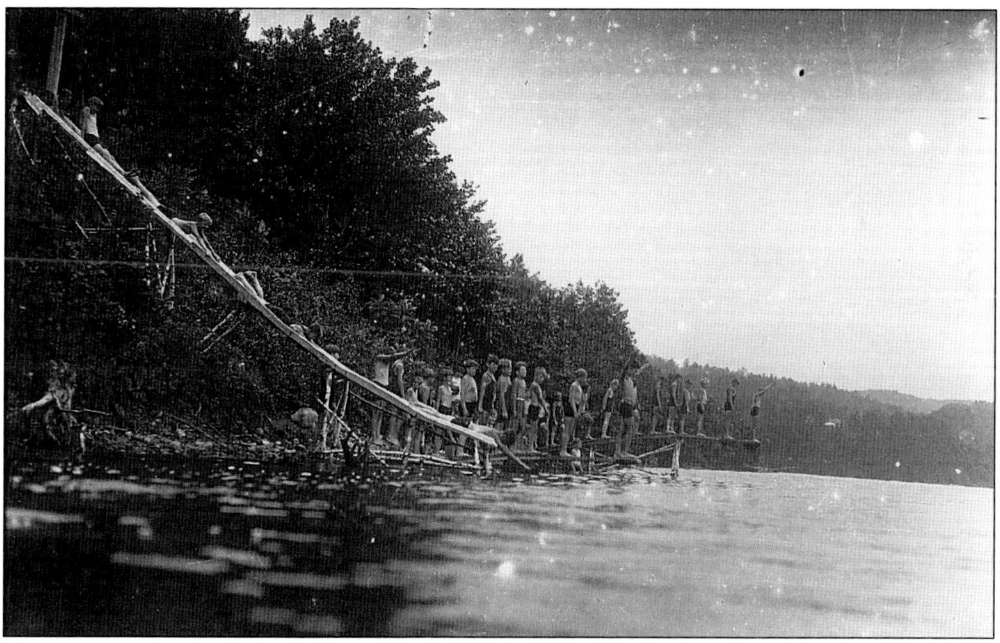

Hot summers called for cooling waters, and Lake Zoar was the favorite "watering spot" for young bathers. These boys at Camp Rippowam take a quick slide before joining the line for the diving board. Ouch! Imagine a slide made of native lumber—splinters and all. Ingenious campers at Camp Rippowam (the Stamford Boys Club) built this slide themselves on the shore of Lake Zoar (1922–25). No record was kept of the slivers the swimmers acquired.

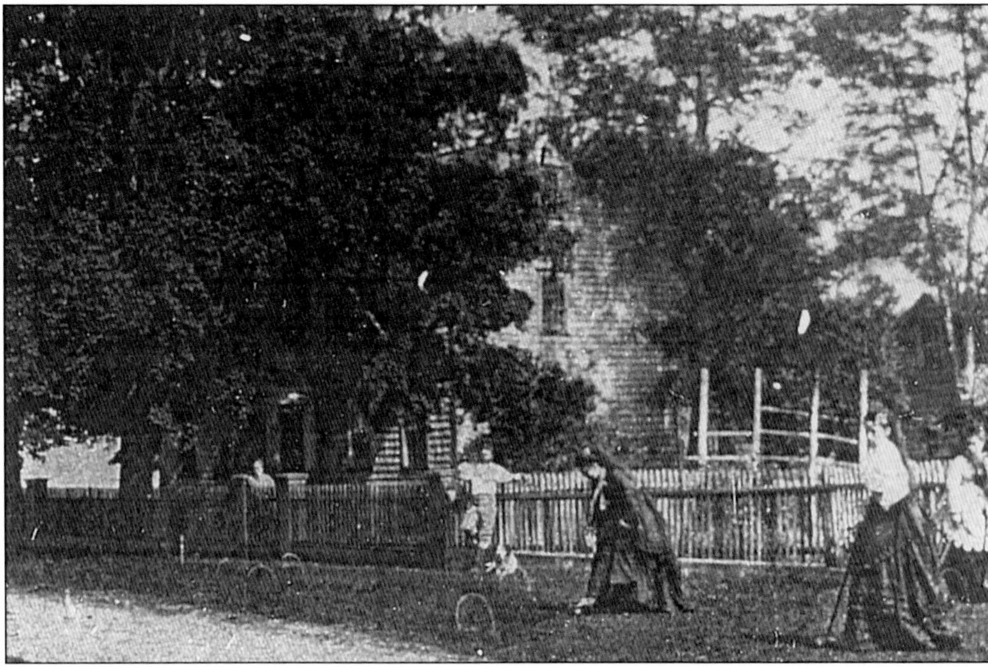

Even though it could be 100 degrees in the shade at the Hobart Beardsley homestead on Fan Hill Road, these ladies, because of propriety, could not shed any of their many layers of petticoats and skirts. No wonder croquet, with its minimal exertion, was a popular summer pastime in the 1870s.

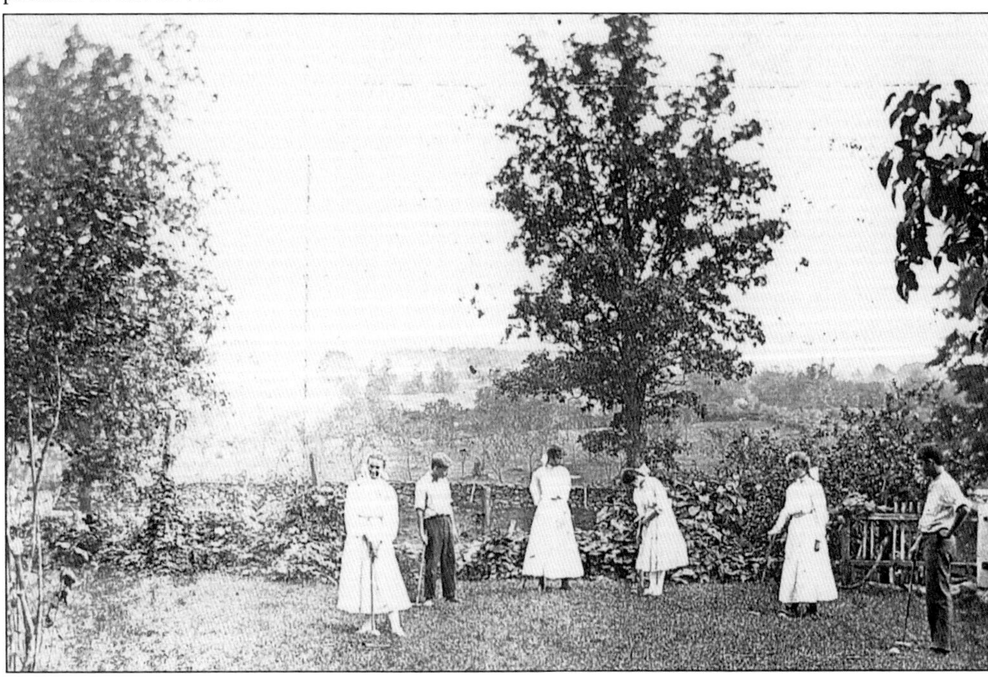

A few decades later (*c.* 1910) croquet was still popular, but the ladies were able to "lighten up." Skirts have risen, white has replaced black, and the men now join the ladies of the Smith family as they enjoy themselves on the Brick House lawn on Wheeler Road.

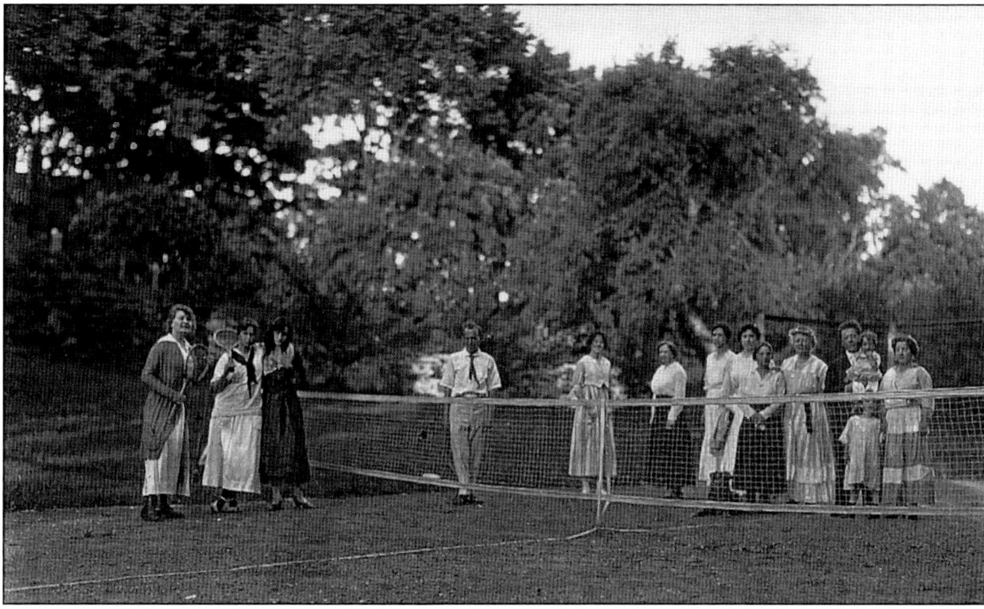

"Who wants to play me next?" Two young women challenge their friends to a game of lawn tennis at the Smith house. Wouldn't it be awkward to play in such cumbersome attire?

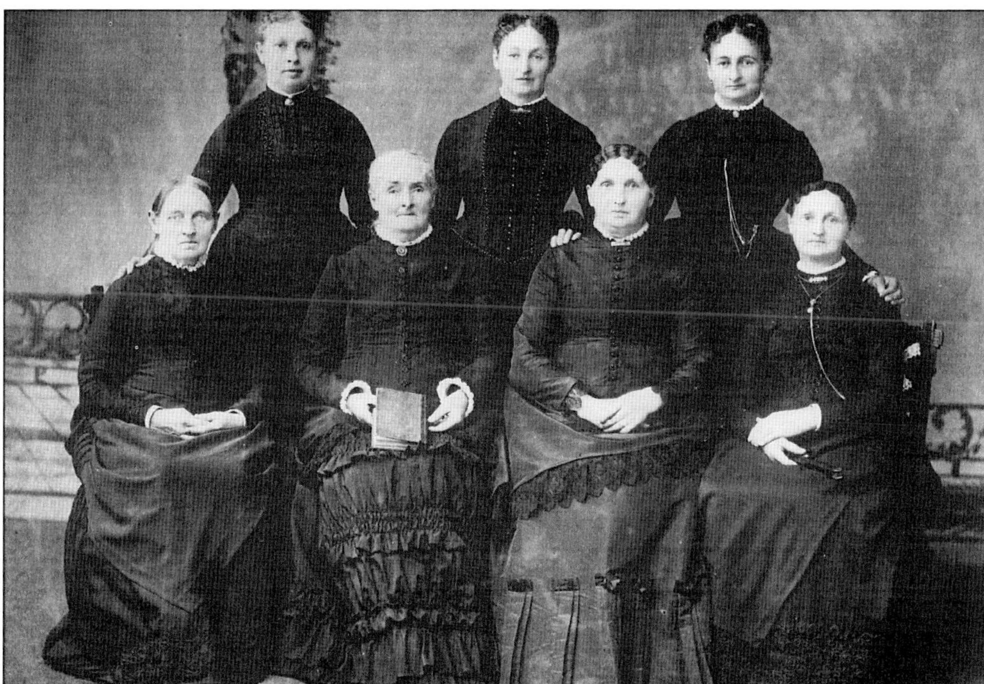

Wearing their winter finery, the seven Lewis sisters (Henriette Pierce, Delia Curtis, Eliza Jane Candee, and Julia Booth are in the in front; Laura Curtis, Elizabeth Beardsley, and Vine Sharp in the rear [listed from left to right]) await their New Year's guests. The family's pleasant gatherings were well known and eagerly anticipated.

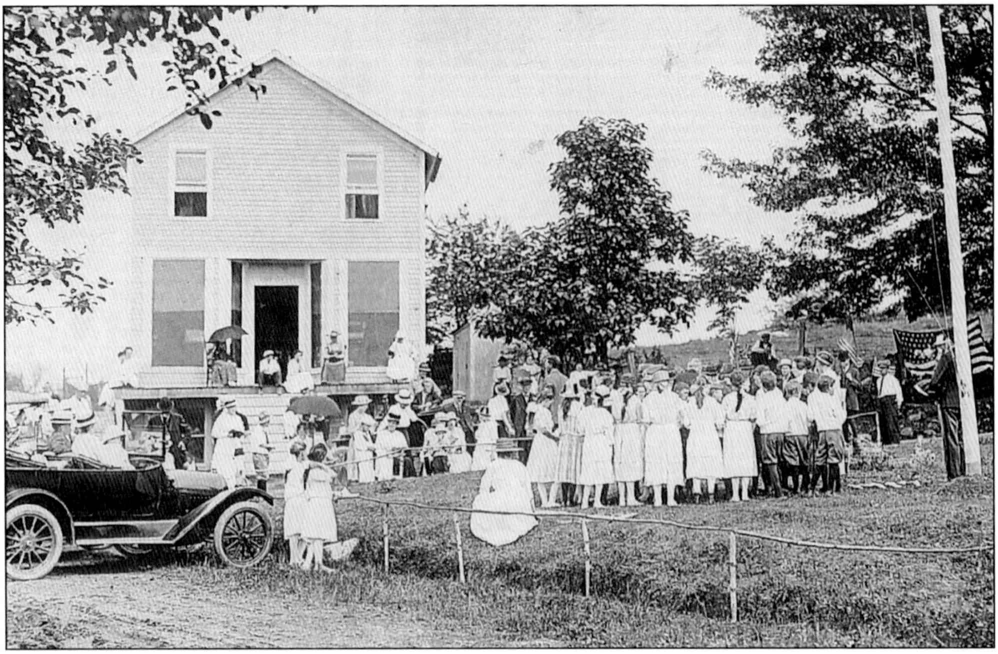

Any holiday such as the Fourth of July was a grand excuse for a gathering and for raising the flag. On this hot summer's day, this group gathered for a picnic and ceremony in front of the Burr-Twist General Store in Stevenson.

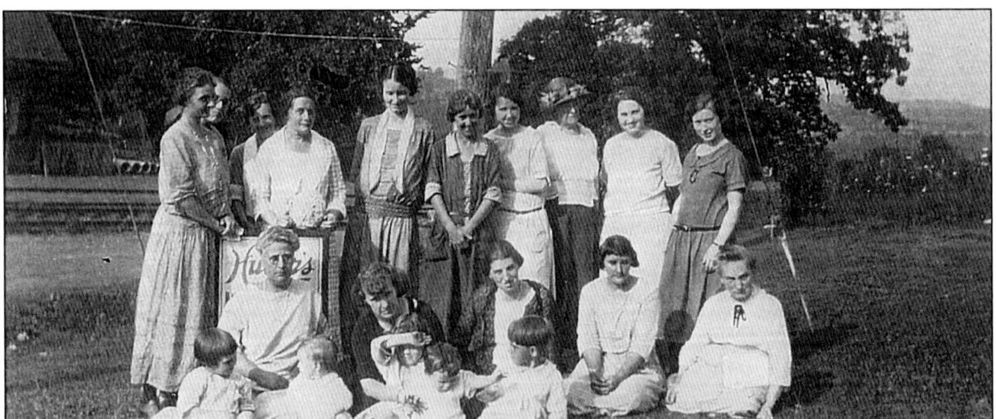

Ice cream was a special summertime treat. Members of the Stevenson Lake Zoar Ladies Club, with children in tow, pause for a moment in front of the Huber's Ice Cream sign before enjoying a cold and tasty delight. The Drings family across the railroad tracks had the first roadside stand in the area where ice cream was available, but only twice a week!

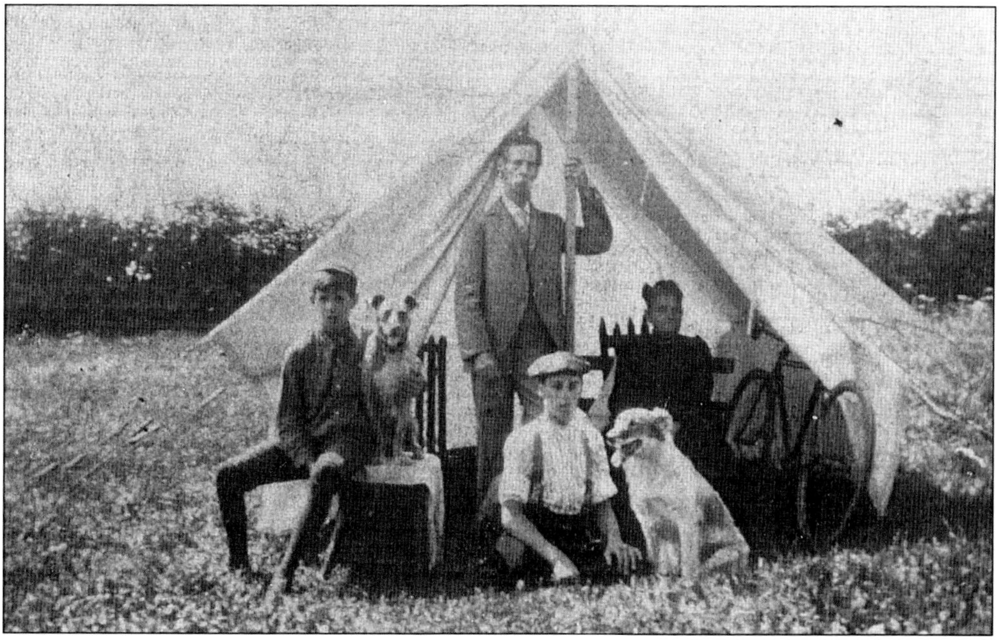

While family fun at the Stevenson campgrounds allowed the young boys to don casual attire, the parents maintained proper decorum in both their dress and behavior. They have even brought straight-backed chairs for their small tent.

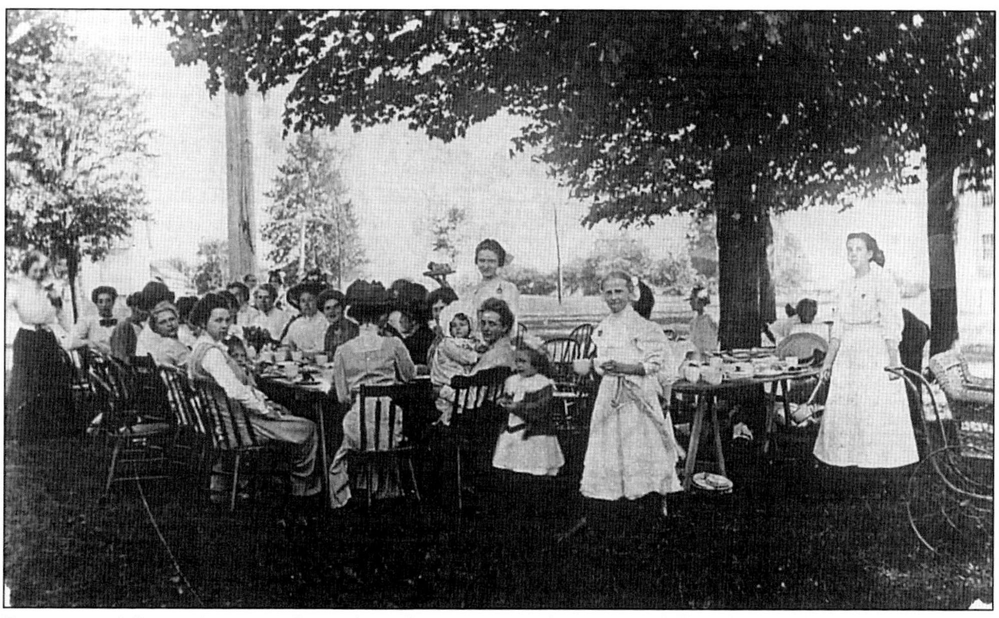

Picnics on Monroe's greens have long been a way of enjoying fellowship and the beauty of the New England seasons. These women and children share a repast on the Monroe Centre Green, c. 1913. The absent men and boys most likely had farm work to do.

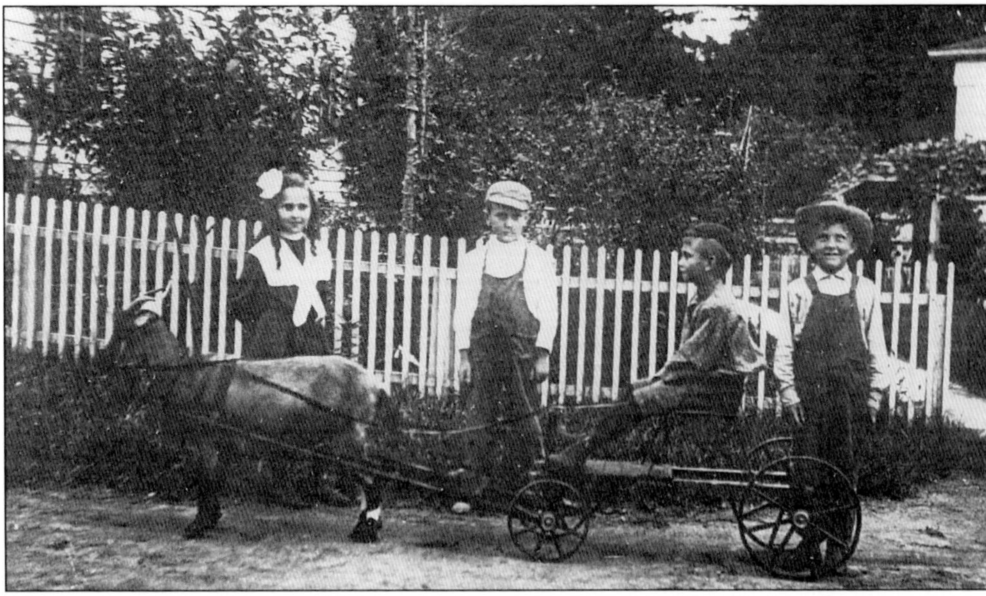

In the good old summertime—work's done for a while and it's time to play. Clayton Burr Hawley and several friends from Birdsey's Plain harness "Miss Goat" and get ready for the road.

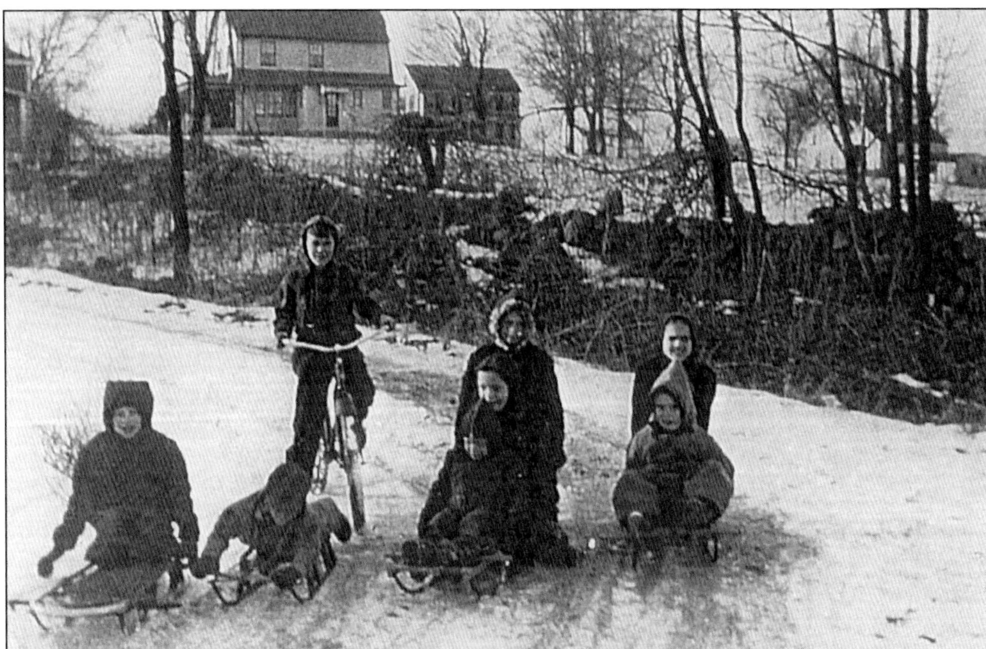

In times past, snow and sledding were major components of winter. In the late 1940s, Church Street, shown here, was often closed to traffic and became the domain of children. The children here are the Hurds (Carol, Billy, Bobby, and Helen), Marilyn and Lois Fisher, Jack Tramposch, and Eileen Richards. Streetlights made it possible for sledding parties to take place at night.

This gentleman is poised for a ringer as he practices before the weekly horseshoe competition. Horseshoes were an important part of the social life in early days, and competitions frequently lasted for an entire season. Area streams provided farmers with an abundance of clay needed to properly fashion horseshoe pits, which were a source of great pride to those who played.

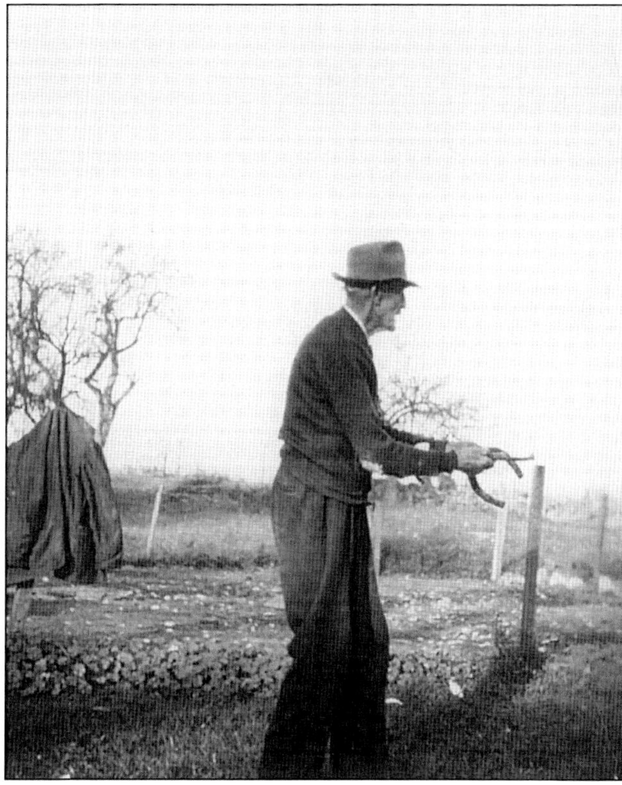

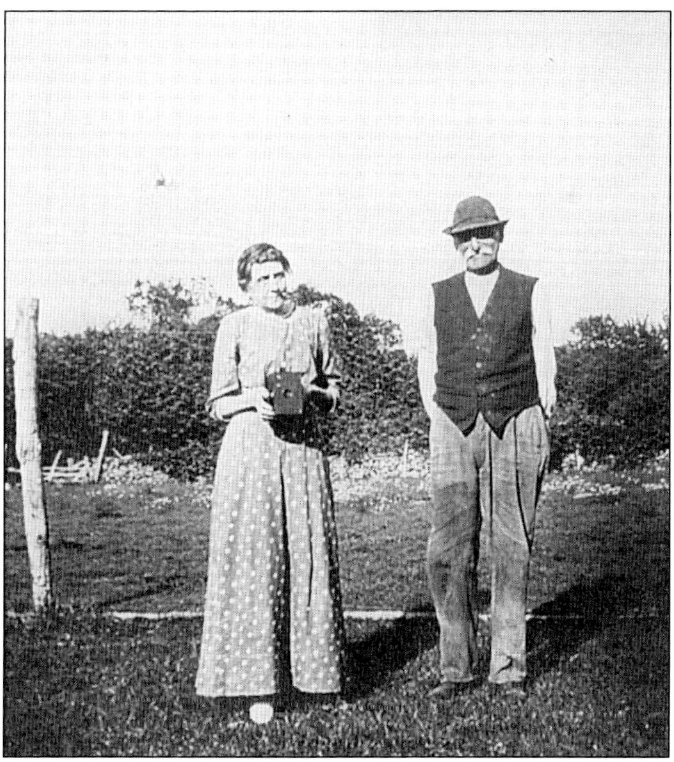

Say "Cheese!" Early box cameras, like the one held here by Gertrude Beardsley of Fan Hill Road (shown with Hobart Beardsley), helped preserve much of the pictorial history of the town.

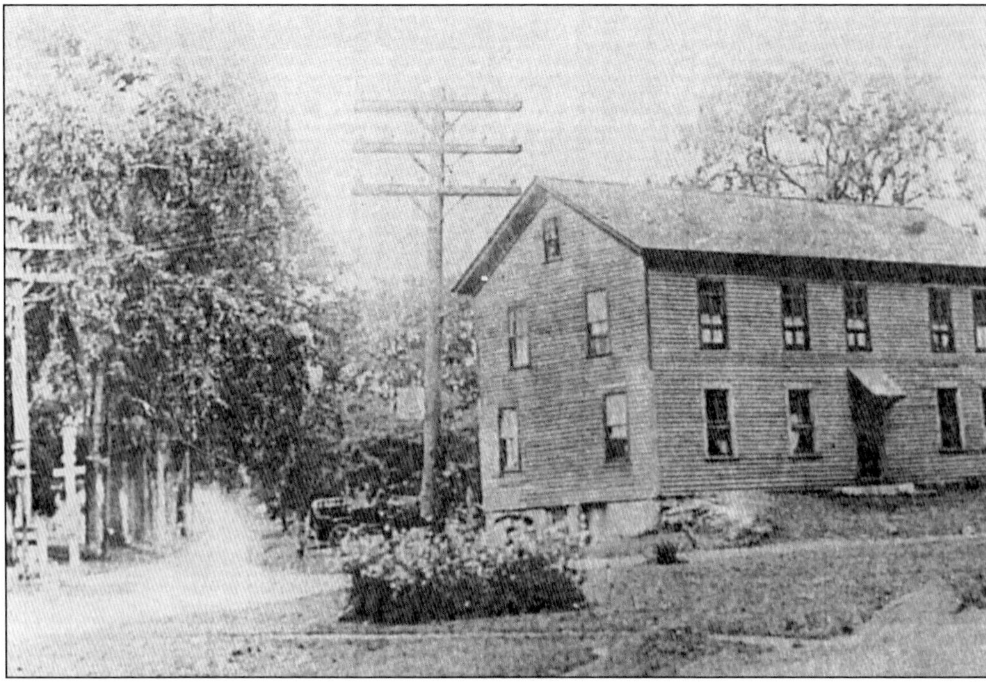

Leavenworth Hall was an important social gathering place in Birdsey's Plain. In the early 1800s, it served as a tavern and an inn. During the Civil War it was run as a store by Judson Curtiss, who eventually sold it to the Leavenworth family. There was a dance hall on the second floor, and many gala events were held here. The building was demolished in the 1980s to make way for the Monro Muffler and Brake Shop.

GRAND

SOIREE

—AT—

Leavenworth's Hall,

STEPNEY,

Thursday Ev'g, Nov. 25, '86.

Your company with Ladies is respectfully invited. This Card must be presented at the door.

MUSIC BY

BRADLEY'S BAND.

G. OSBORNE, Prompter.

Ladies, Refreshments. Gents, Music.

Two

Do I Have a Volunteer?

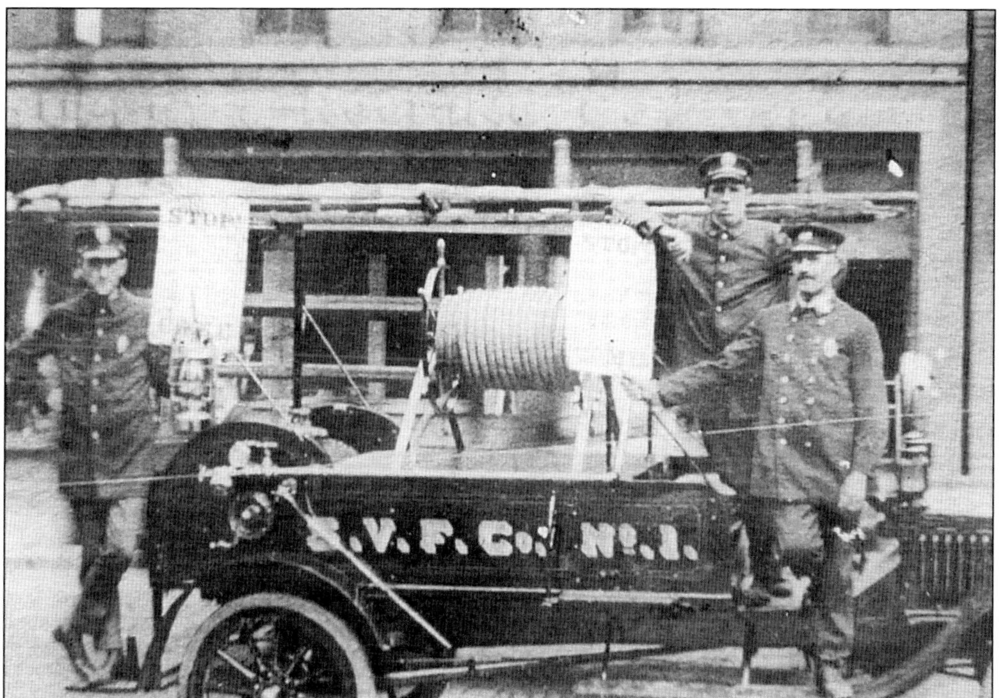

Volunteers have always been important to Monroe. Here, Stanley B. Joyce, Austin Dinkler, and Frank Keller of the Stepney Volunteer Fire Company (organized in 1916) pose proudly with their first firetruck, purchased second-hand from Bridgeport. The sign that the men held as they drove slowly from the city advertised the "Karnival," which would help pay for their new purchase.

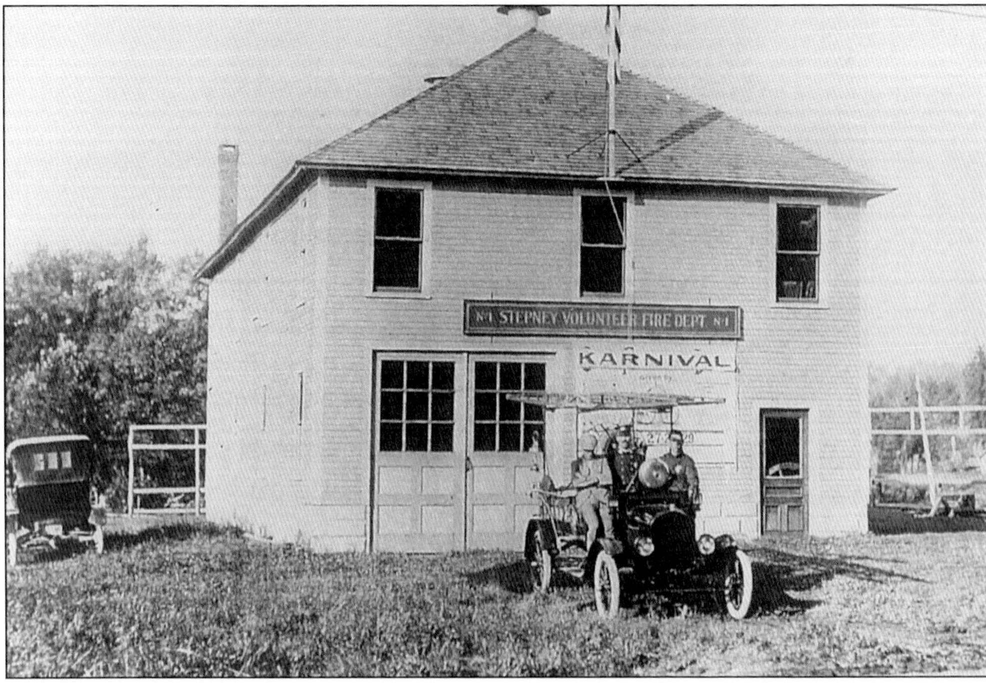

The "Karnival" is coming! The Stepney Fire House was the site of the yearly firemen's carnival in early days. Young and old alike eagerly anticipated this event. In the background, volunteers are erecting booths for the affair, which included a wooden dance floor, a popular attraction at early carnivals.

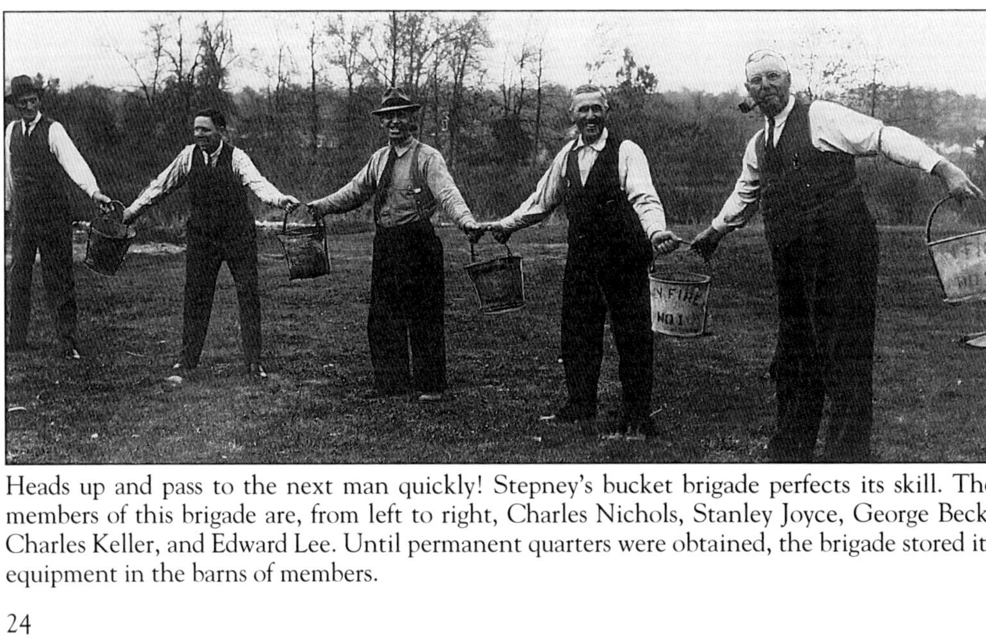

Heads up and pass to the next man quickly! Stepney's bucket brigade perfects its skill. The members of this brigade are, from left to right, Charles Nichols, Stanley Joyce, George Beck, Charles Keller, and Edward Lee. Until permanent quarters were obtained, the brigade stored its equipment in the barns of members.

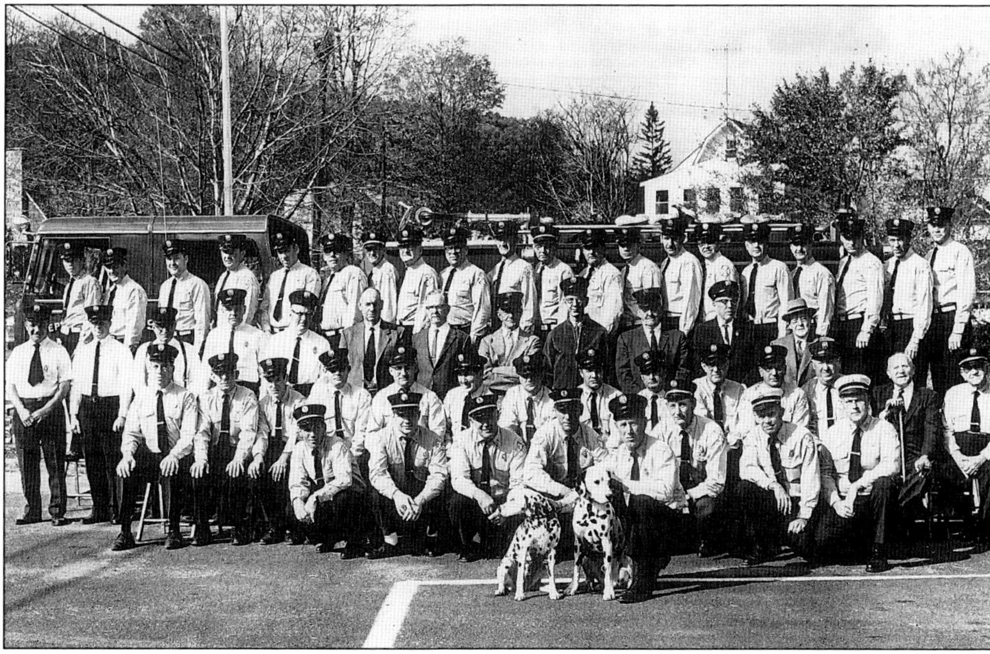

The beautiful Dalmatian dogs of fireman Bob Lederer add a special touch to this group of Stepney volunteer firemen in 1967. The Stepney Fire Company has at least one of the "fire dogs" raised by the Lederers in every parade.

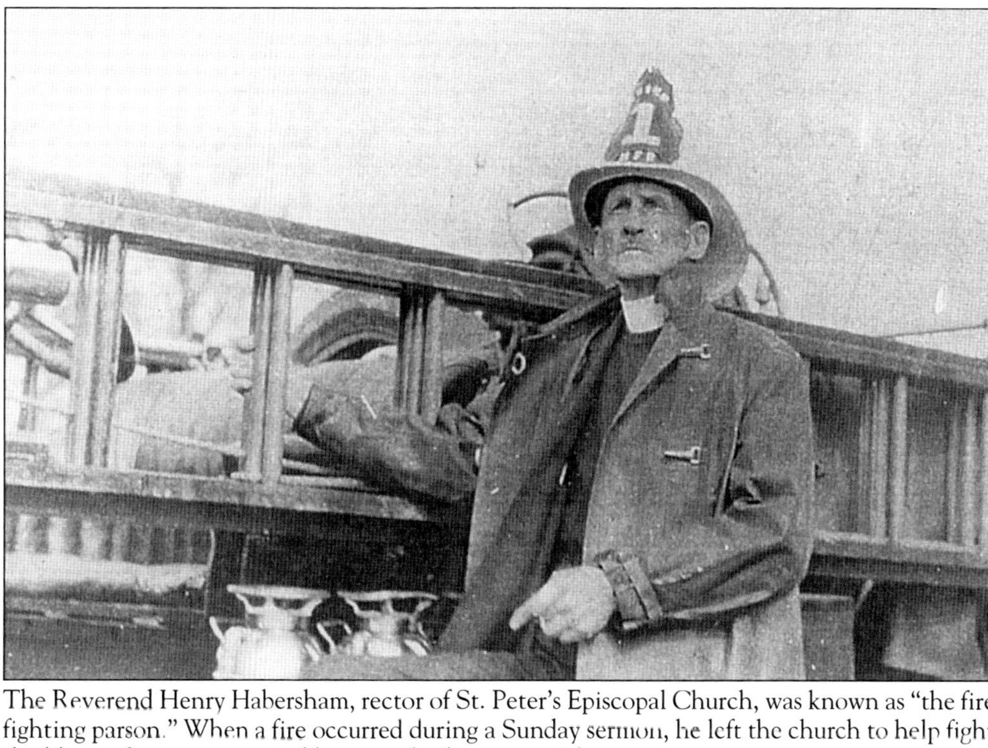

The Reverend Henry Habersham, rector of St. Peter's Episcopal Church, was known as "the fire fighting parson." When a fire occurred during a Sunday sermon, he left the church to help fight the blaze, often accompanied by several other men of the congregation.

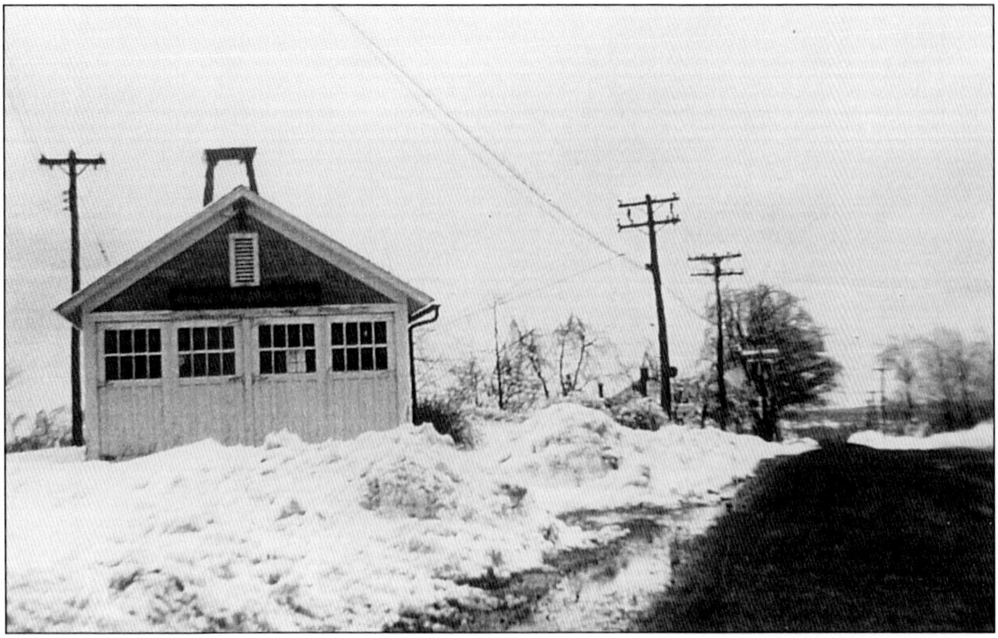

The junction of Monroe Turnpike and Moose Hill Road was the site of the Monroe Fire Company's first firehouse. This fire company was founded in 1923 as the culminating event of Monroe's centennial celebration.

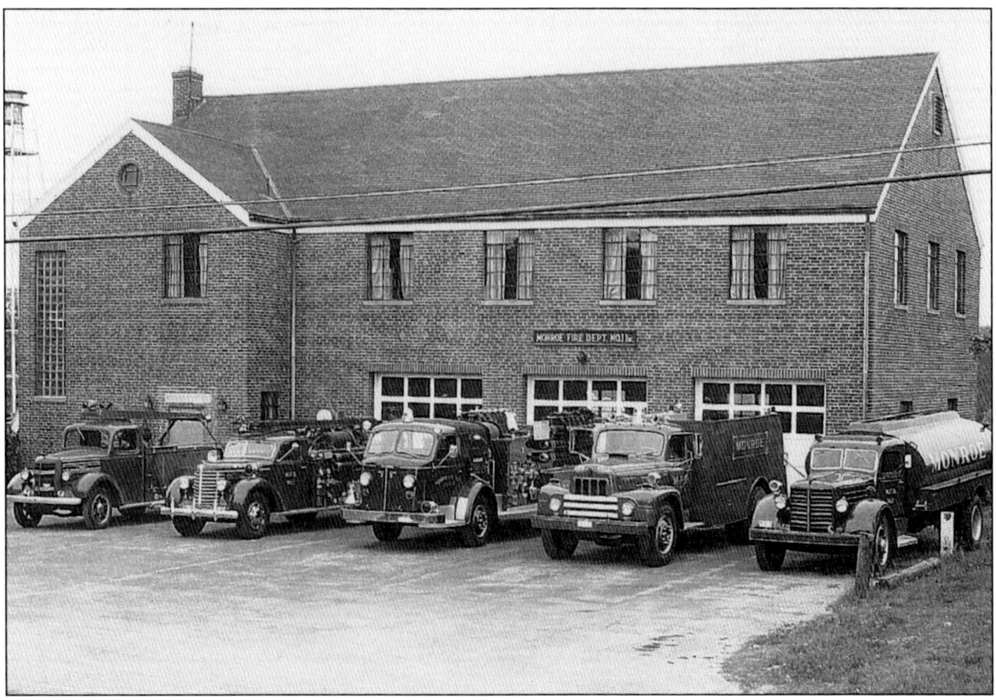

In the early 1950s, the two engines on the right had to sit outside because there wasn't room for them in the bays. In the winter, the tanker had to be drained so as not to freeze, making it necessary to fill the tanker every time there was a fire. An addition was put on in 1965 to alleviate this problem.

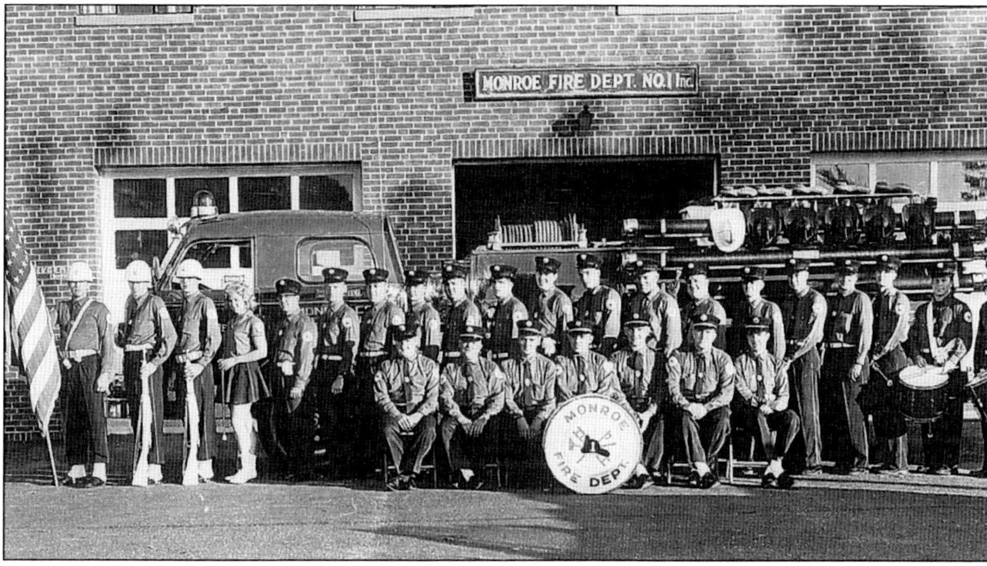

Progress is our most important product! By the late 1960s, the Monroe Fire Station motor fleet and volunteer firefighters had expanded to provide increased protection for a rapidly growing population. At the time of this picture, the department had just won the Best in State award at the state firemen's convention. Included in the picture are the officers (seated), the color guard (with helmets), and the drum line.

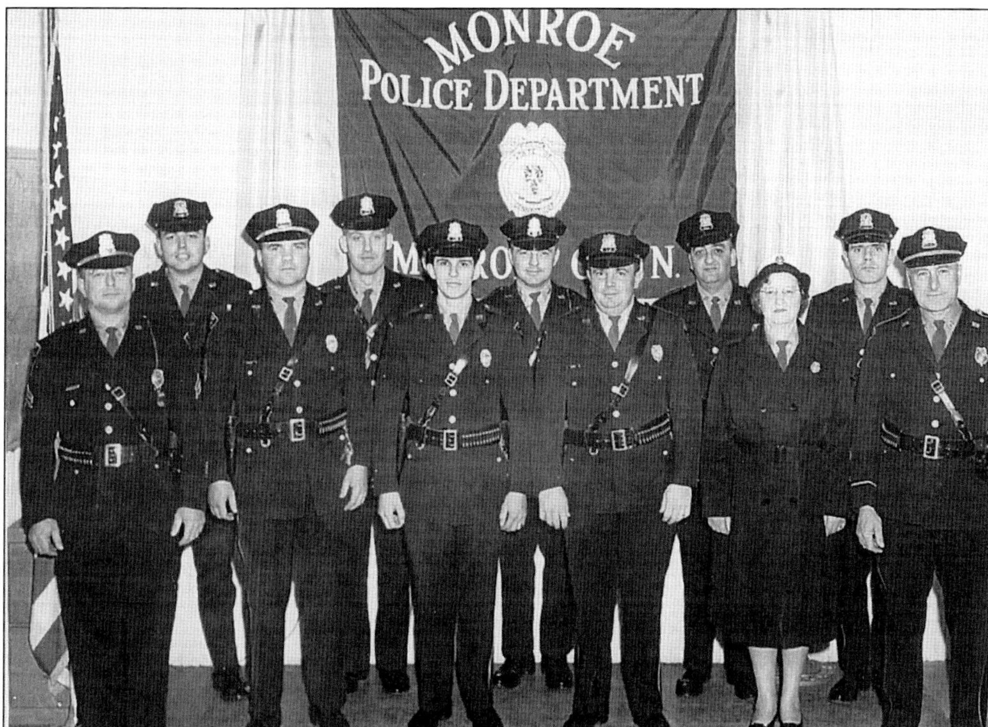

Monroe's entire police department of 1965 included Emilie Olson, the first policewoman in town, and next to her on the right, Jack Tufano, the first police chief. In the front row, second from the left, is Bob Wesche, the current police chief.

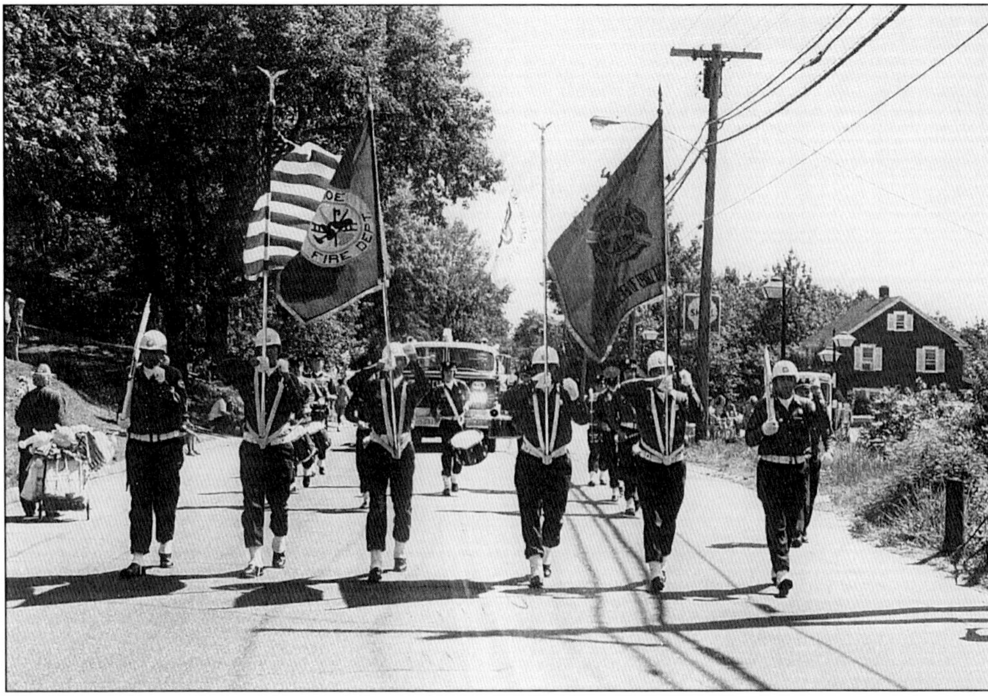

Left! Right! Left! For many years local firemen paraded on Monroe Turnpike before the opening night of the Monroe Firemen's Carnival. The carnival has survived, but the parade has marched on as a memory of the past.

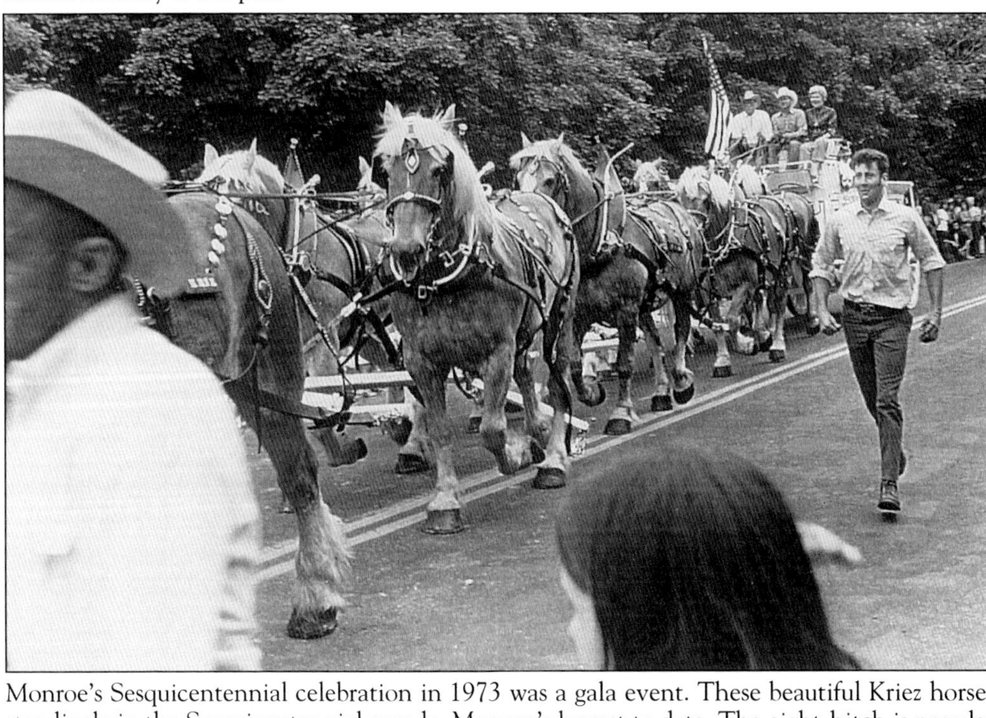

Monroe's Sesquicentennial celebration in 1973 was a gala event. These beautiful Kriez horses step lively in the Sesquicentennial parade, Monroe's largest to date. The eight-hitch is popular wherever it appears.

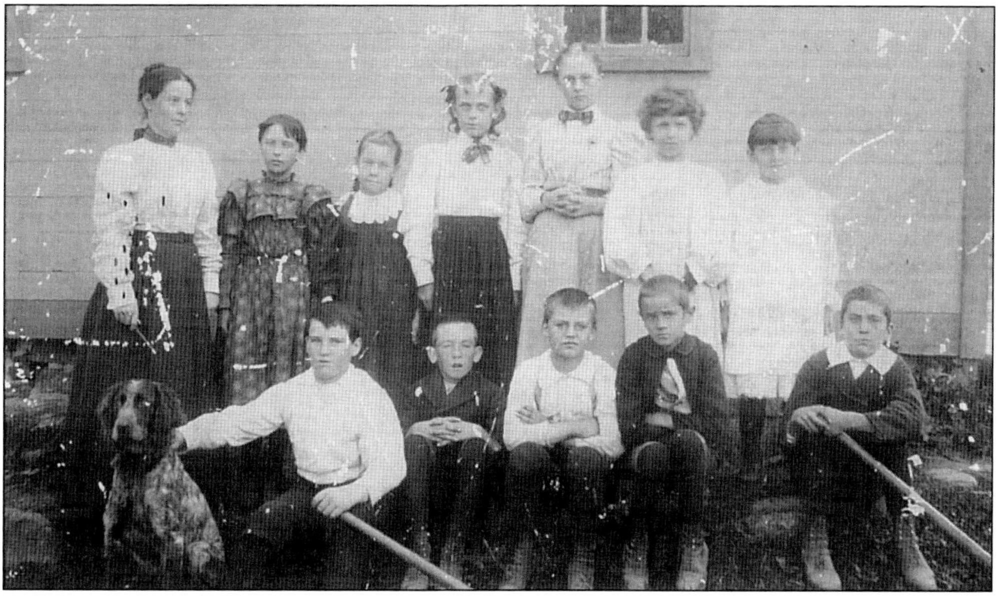

In 1896, Miss Hatch, her students, and Ernest Beers's dog posed for a class picture before playing a game of baseball at the East Village School.

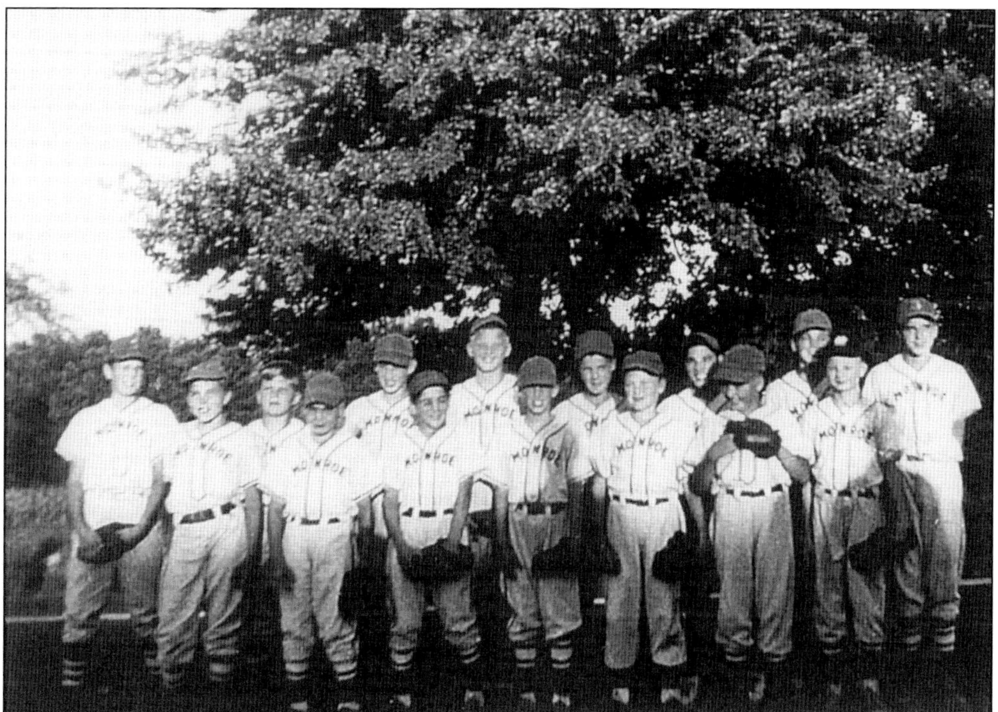

Take me out to the ballgame! In 1954, Monroe's first baseball team gave local residents the opportunity to root for the home team. The team was officially called the Monroe Clippers and was organized and coached by Robert Musante. Since that time, the Little League program has expanded as the town has grown.

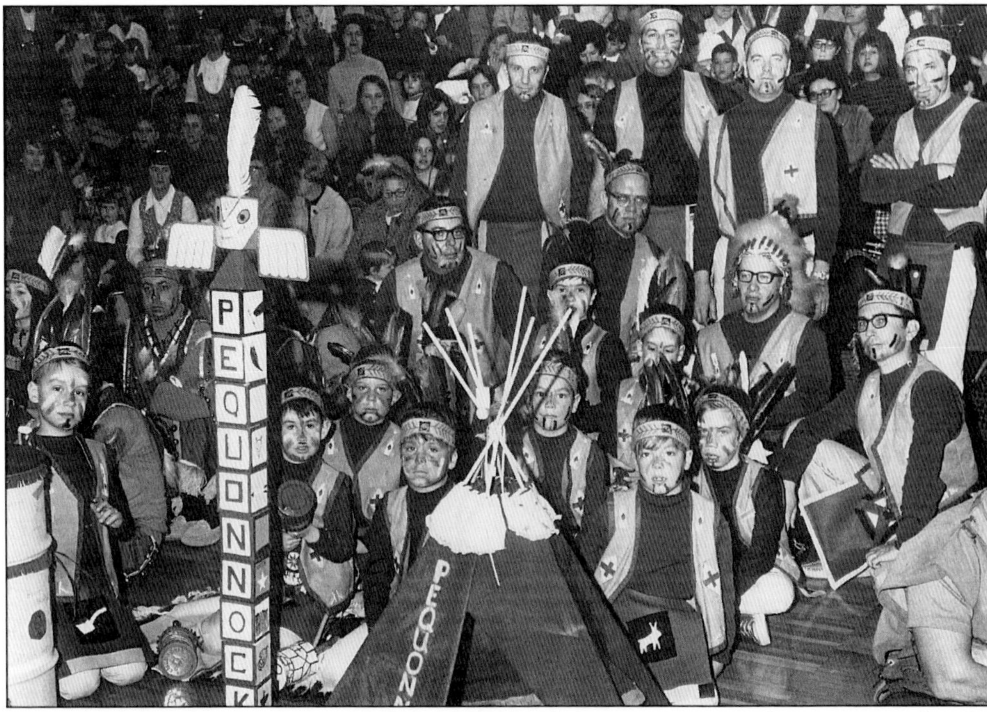

This group of Indian Guides (a YMCA program), fathers and sons of the Pequonnock tribe, attended a big pow-wow in the late 1960s. No scalps were taken.

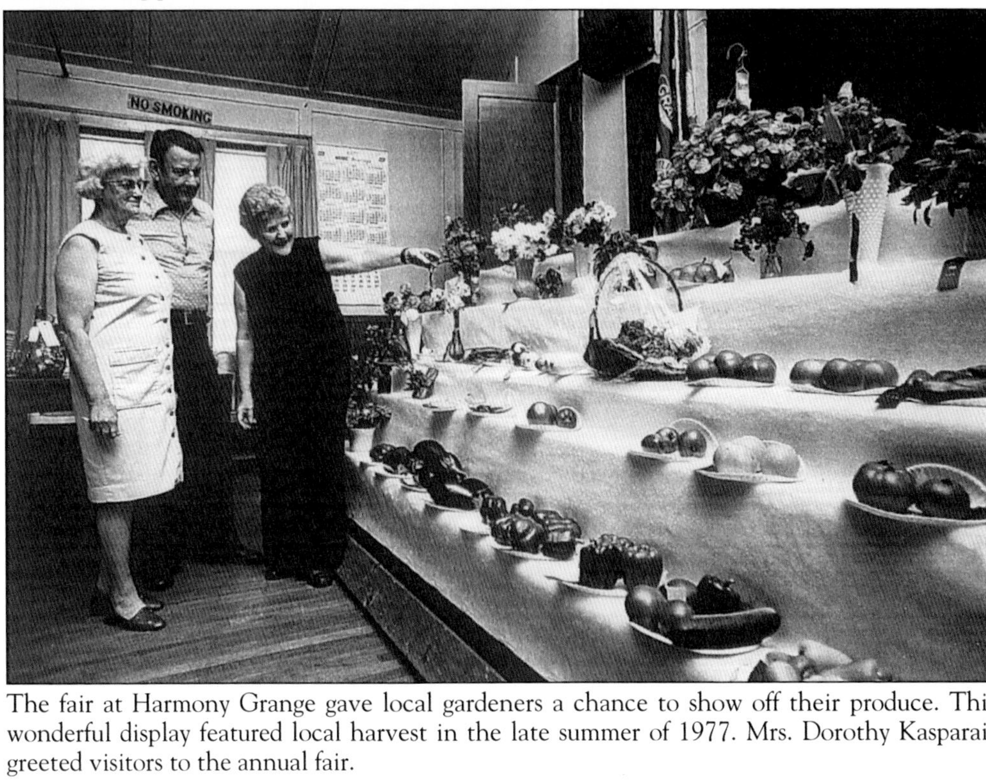

The fair at Harmony Grange gave local gardeners a chance to show off their produce. This wonderful display featured local harvest in the late summer of 1977. Mrs. Dorothy Kasparait greeted visitors to the annual fair.

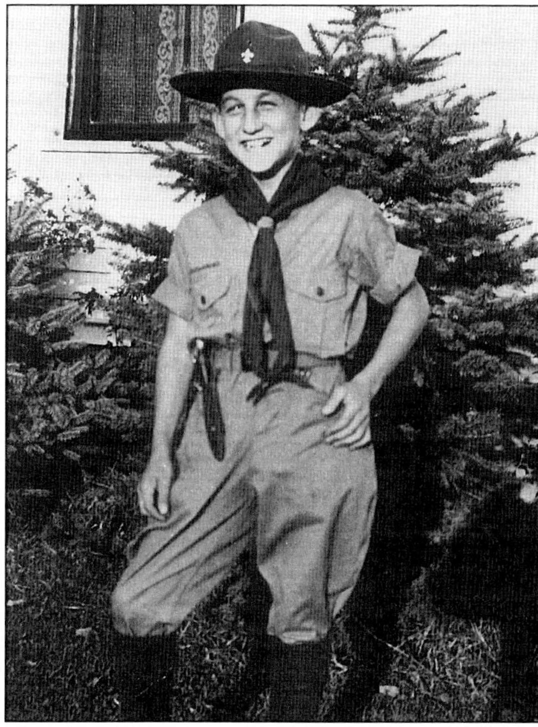

Bernard "Bernie" Sippin was certainly a perfect example of the Boy Scout motto "Be Prepared." What more did you need in 1942 than your uniform, your tools—and a smile?

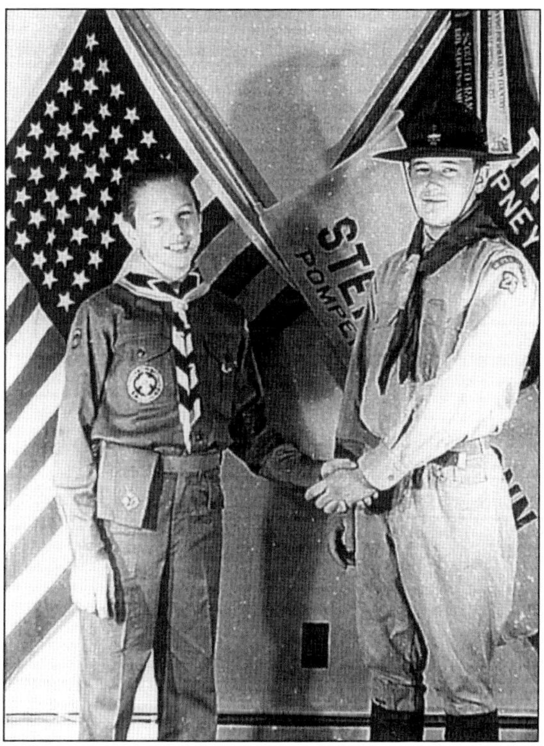

Twenty years after Bernie Sippin's scouting years, the uniform worn by Joseph Nemeth (on the right) hasn't changed much. David Elovecky is the other scout pictured.

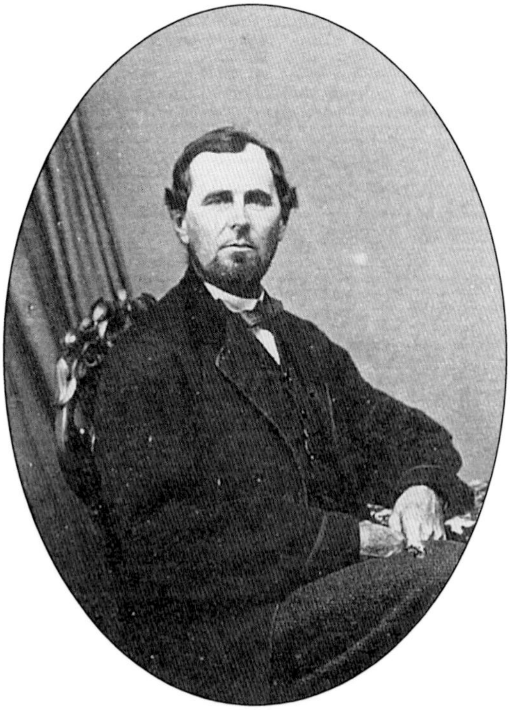

David F. Whitlock was a well-known resident of Monroe in the mid-nineteenth century. A member of the Congregational Church and Monroe's representative in the Connecticut General Assembly, he was the owner of a farm and store on Old Tannery Road, near the intersection of Williamsburg Drive, and was very active in civic affairs.

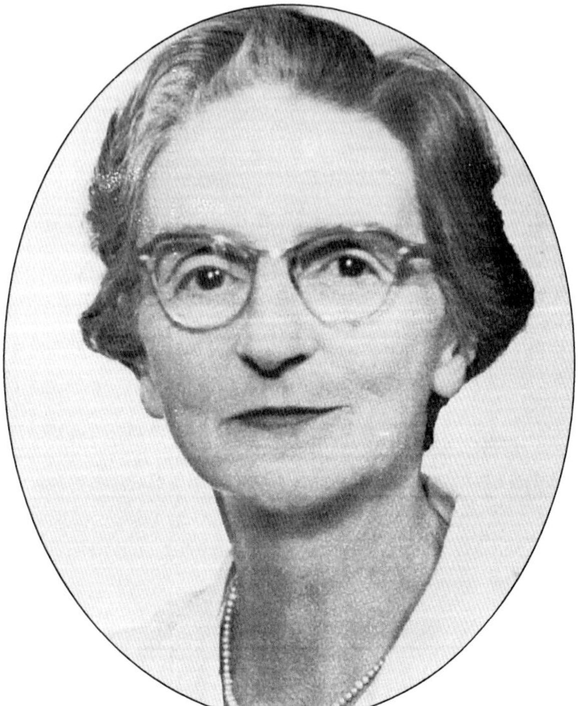

Pat Saxton is a warmly remembered Monroe resident of this century. As a dedicated volunteer, she organized Bundles for Britain during World War II, helped to restart the League of Women Voters in Monroe in the 1950s, and was always an advocate of education. She was named Woman of the Year by the Monroe Mothers' Club in 1973 and is remembered by her daughters as "very much a mom."

Three

The War Effort

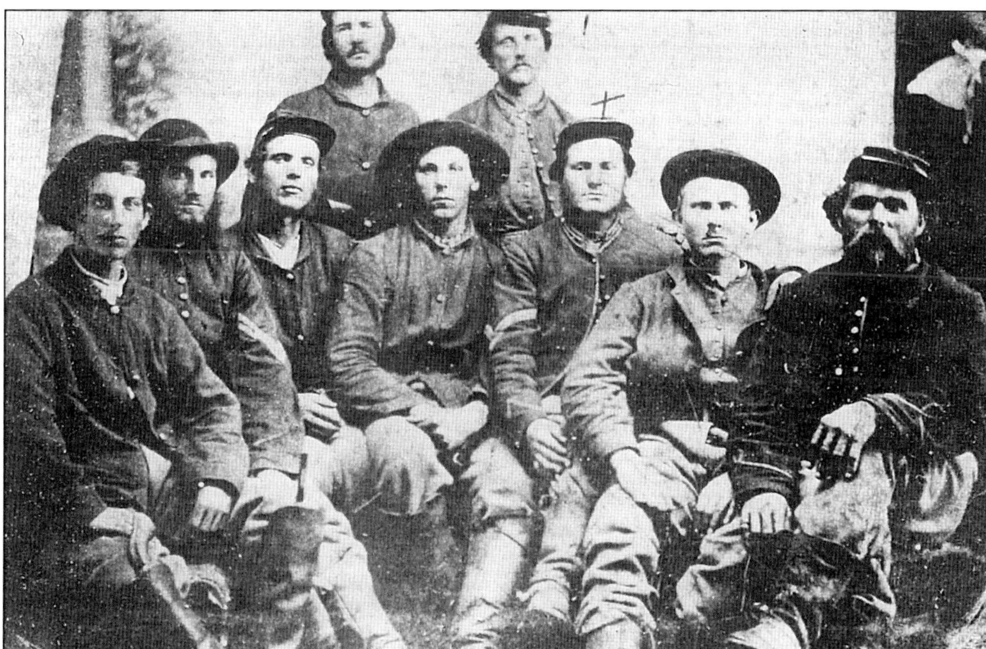

Home from the Civil War! Andrew Lewis Burr (third from right), with a group of his fellow soldiers, poses for this portrait. The soldiers are wearing the usual garb of the War between the States.

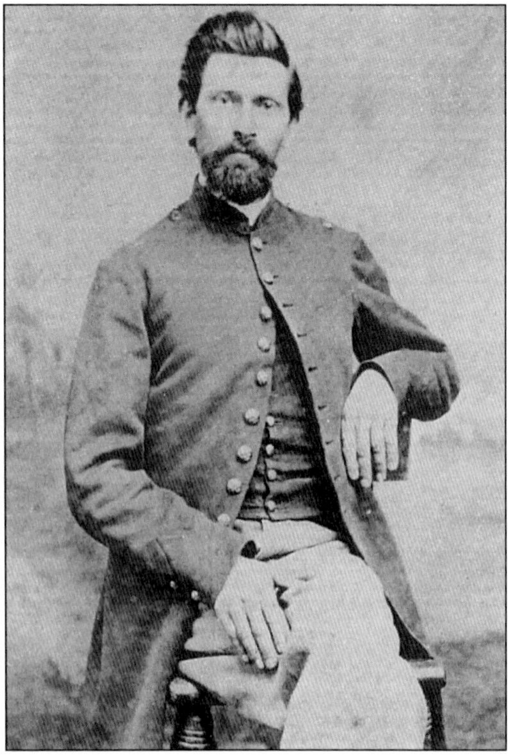

Little did Henry Dunning Burr realize, as he posed in full uniform for the photographer, that he would be severely wounded at Antietam.

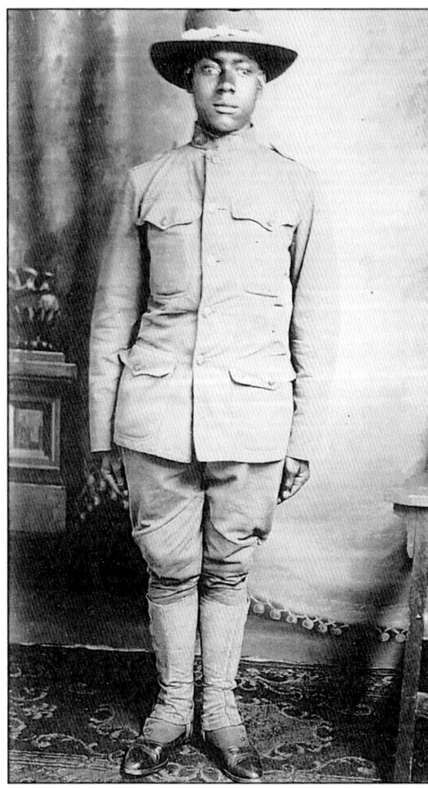

Samuel Baskerville, resplendent in a uniform of the period, was a proud World War I soldier from Monroe. His family lived on Elm Street and for many years worked on the Burr Berry Farm.

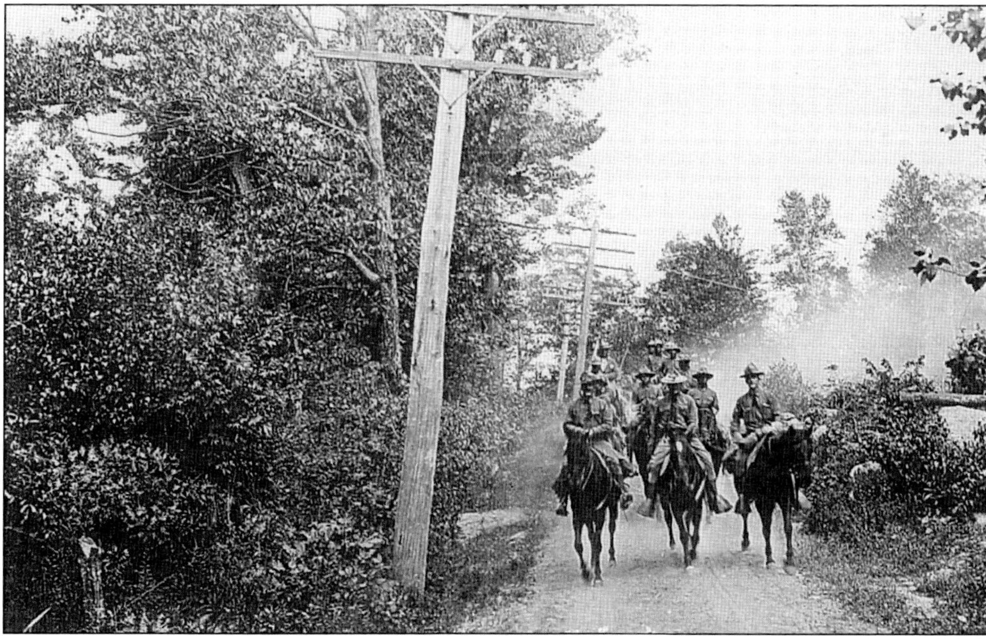

They passed this way! In August of 1912, field exercises, known as the War Maneuvers, were held throughout this area. These New Jersey guardsmen were a part of the Blue Team who were charged with "protecting" New York's water supply from the invading Red Team.

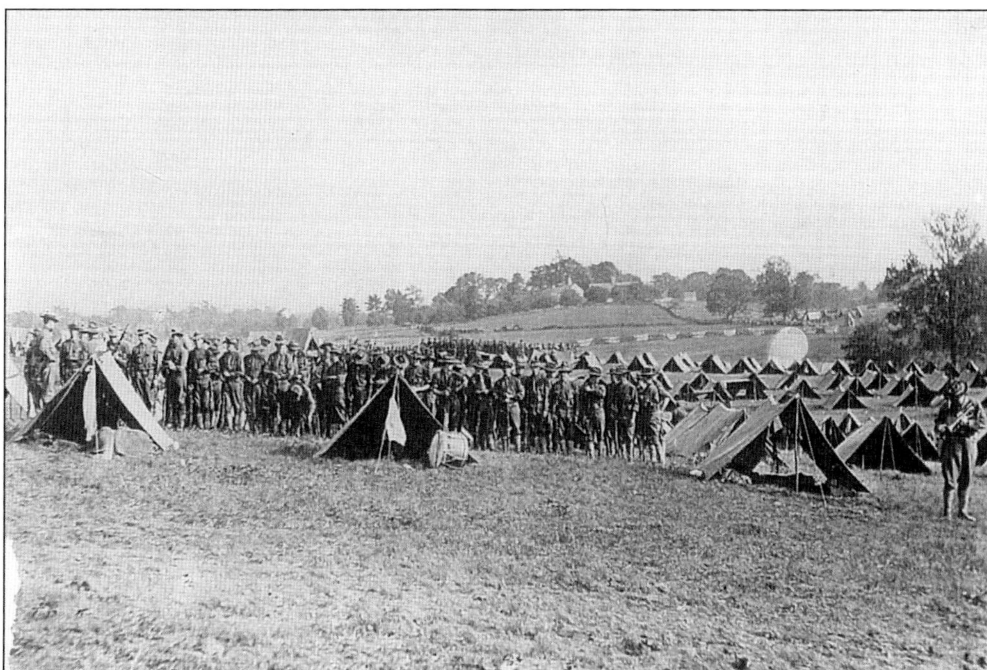

During the War Maneuvers of 1912, soldiers from many military divisions were encamped throughout this area. Monroe residents commonly refer to this time as "the encampment."

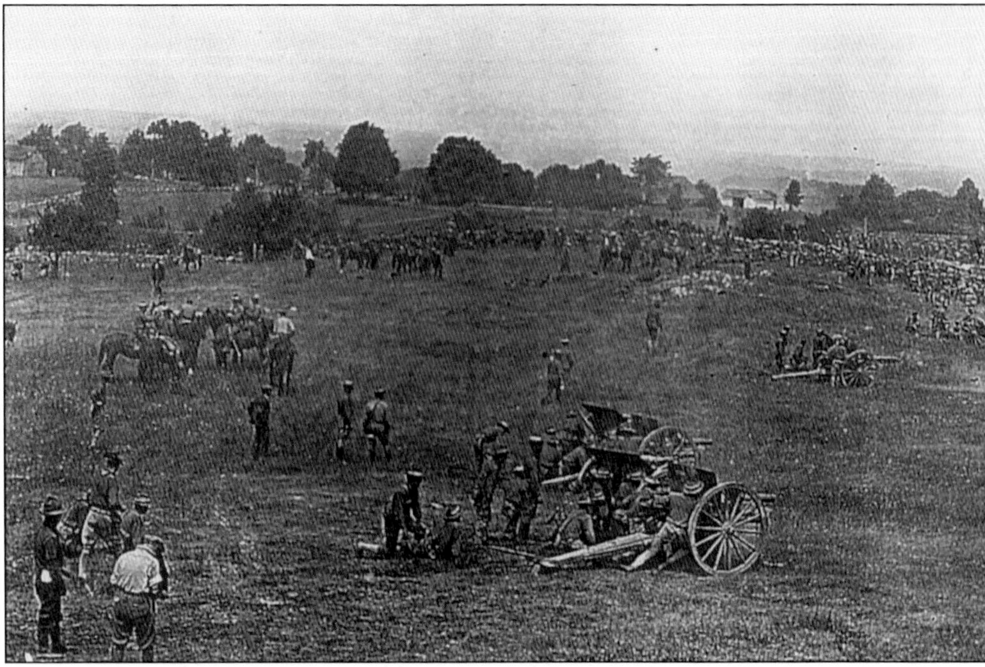

Battles of the War Maneuvers of 1912 were held throughout Fairfield County, culminating on August 19 in Newtown. Monroe served as a thoroughfare for these troops.

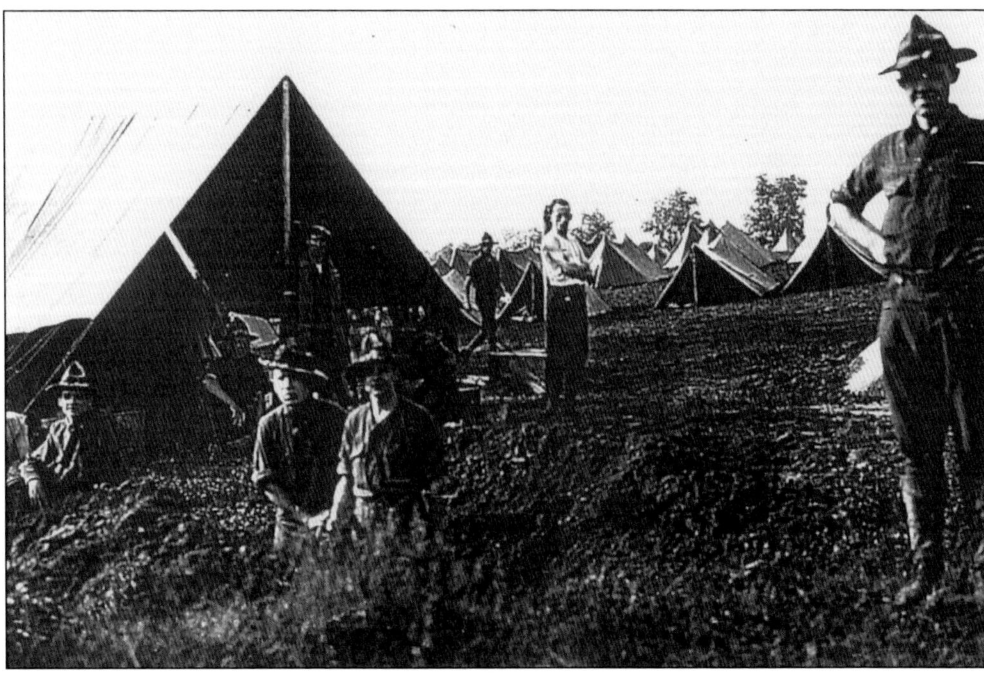

"Tenting tonight on the old campground." In this photograph, soldiers enjoy a brief respite from the war games.

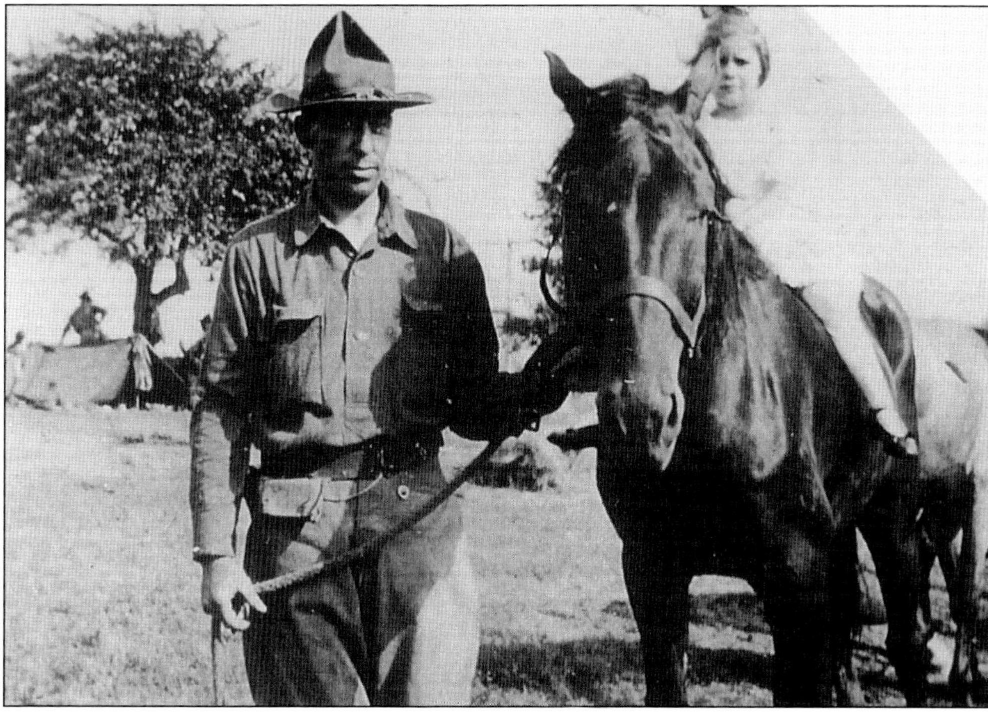

What a treat for this youngster to have a ride on the soldier's horse! The troops' maneuvers provided entertainment for the local townspeople. This picture was taken on visiting day at the tent sites of the Red and Blue Armies in 1912.

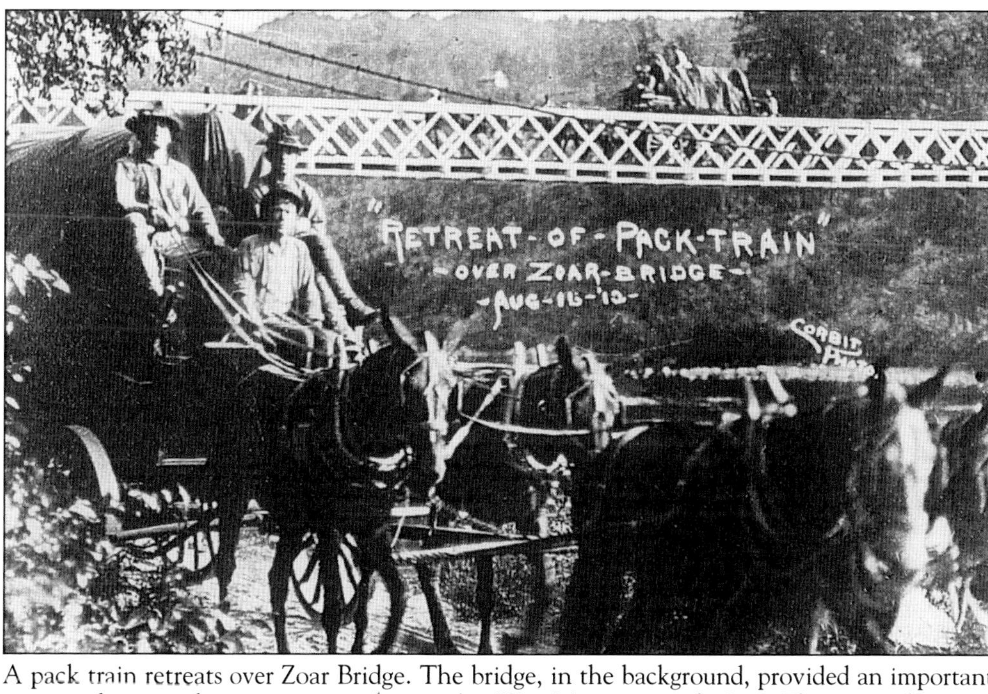

A pack train retreats over Zoar Bridge. The bridge, in the background, provided an important means of transit for army troops during the War Maneuvers of 1912. This was taken "on location" in the town of Oxford..

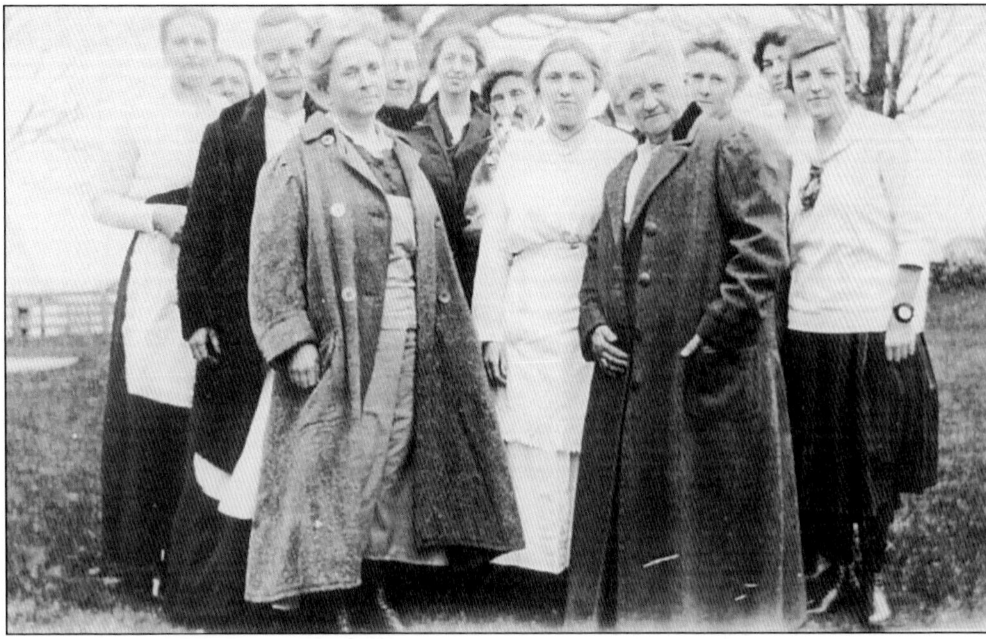

World War I was a time for these ladies of the Red Cross to organize themselves. They met at town hall to make bandages and to sell peach jam (homemade, of course), in order to raise money for their projects. Included here are Sadie Simmons, E. Curtis, Emma Opper, Grace Wales, Ida Jacot, B. Hurd, Elizabeth Beardsley, and A. Curtis. The names of the others have been lost to history.

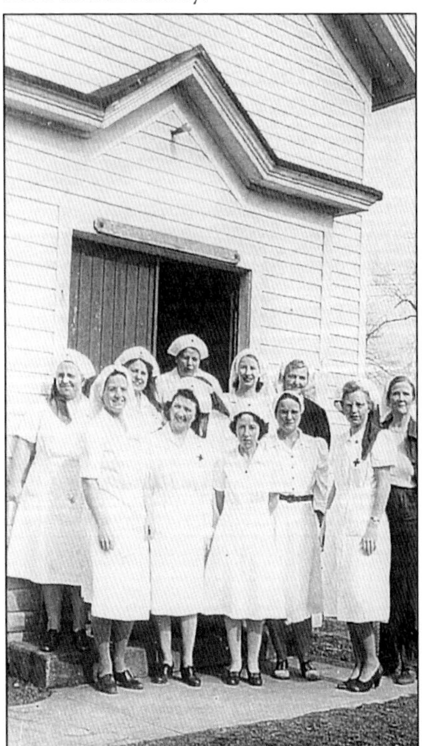

These World War II Red Cross workers pose in front of Beardsley Hall in their uniforms before starting their projects to aid the war effort. Our town was known for its support of our troops in all the wars.

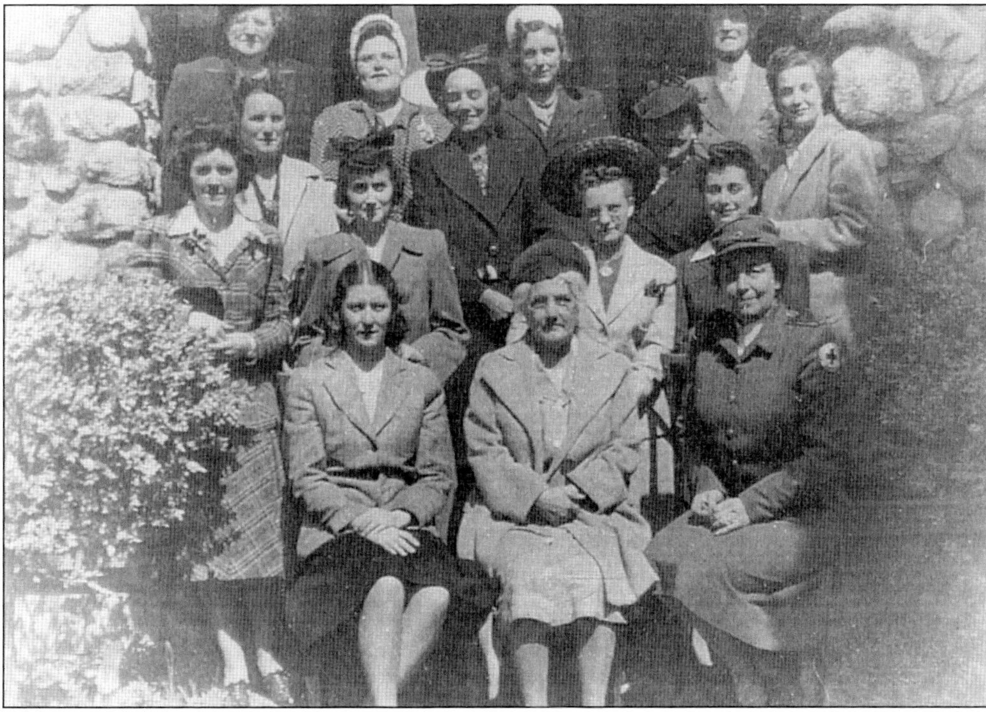

The American Red Cross provided help on the home front during World War II. Monroe's men and women volunteered at the William Mix home (the Red Cross headquarters) on Monroe Turnpike.

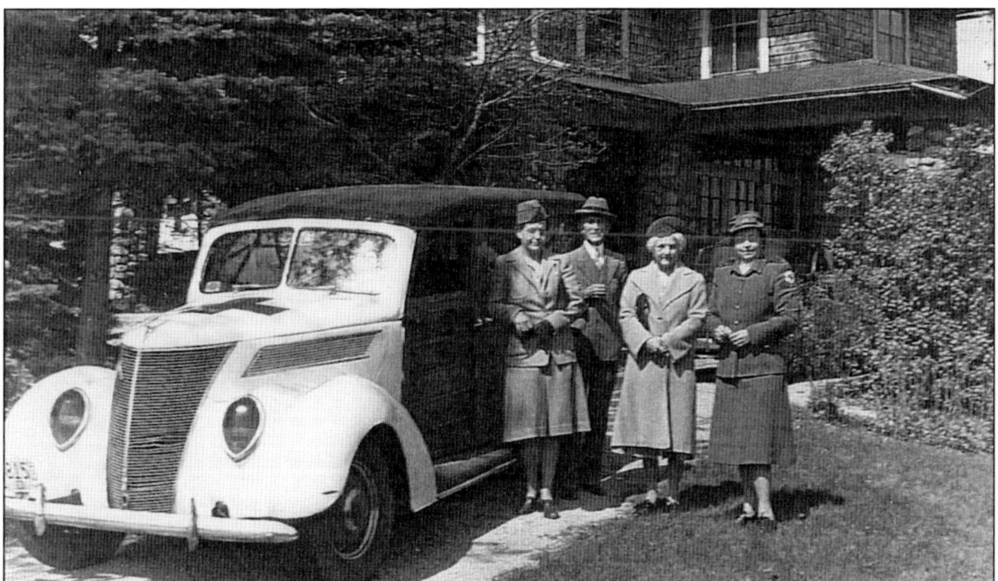

William Mix (second from left) is shown with his daughter, Clara Lewis (far right), who was chairperson of the local Red Cross branch. Mrs. Charles T. Cooper Jr. is on the left, and Mrs. Daisy Beck is second from the right. A publication, *Our Town*, was sent to men and women overseas informing them of local supporting activities. These mimeographed hometown newsletters were a lifeline for our servicemen in World War II.

WEATHER FORECAST
TREMENDOUS FORCES MOVING FORWARD ON ALL FRONTS. CONTINUING IN FULL INTENSITY.

OUR-TOWN

MONROE CONN.

FALL EDITION
NEWS AND VIEWS OBTAINED DIRECTLY BY POST – BY HEAR-SAY AND PARTY LINE —

VOL. 1. OCTOBER 1944 NO. 6

PUBLISHED BY THE MONROE BRANCH of the BRIDGEPORT CHAPTER - AM. RED CROSS

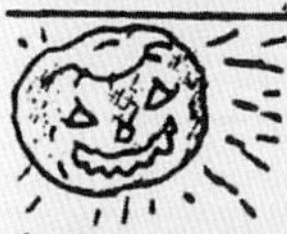

AUTUMN — THE CROPS ARE IN – THE CHILDREN ARE BACK AT SCHOOL. THERE IS FROST IN THE AIR – AND WHEN THAT OLD HARVEST MOON COMES UP OVER THE HOME TOWN, THE WHITE SPIRES OF THE CHURCHES RISE TO MEET IT. THE LIGHTS ARE ON IN THE HOUSES AND THE SUPPER DISHES ARE DONE. THERE IS SMOKE RISING FROM THE CHIMNEYS AND THE SMELL OF THE BURNING HICKORY LOGS MINGLES WITH THE FRAGRANCE OF PUMPKIN PIES AND THE RED CHEEKED APPLES IN THE KITCHEN.

IN MANY A HOME, LETTERS ARE BEING WRITTEN TO LOVED ONES, AND IN EVERY HOME, A PRAYER IS BEING OFFERED FOR EVERY BOY AND GIRL IN THE SERVICE OF OUR COUNTRY – OF COURSE WE CAN'T HELP FROM ASKING A SPECIAL BLESSING ON THOSE NEAREST AND DEAREST TO US, WHO ARE OUT THERE FIGHTING SO VALIANTLY FOR US ALL –

IN ANSWER TO THE MANY BOYS WHO WRITE US THAT WHEN THEY START OUT ON A NIGHT RAID OR HAVE TIME TO RELAX, THEY WONDER WHAT IS GOING ON IN THE HOME TOWN AT THE SAME TIME – WE'VE TRIED TO GIVE YOU THE PICTURE –

NEW FLASH!!

WORD HAS BEEN RECIEVED THAT WILLIAM SANDONE, REPORTED MISSING IN ACTION, IS A PRISONER OF WAR IN GERMANY.

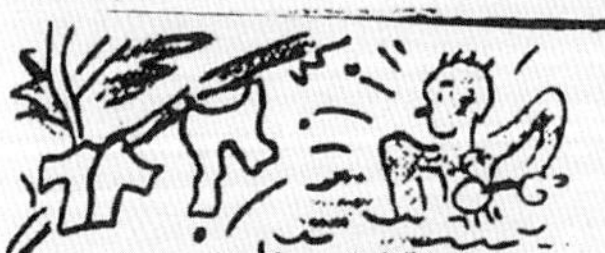

WATER'S FINE — HE JUST HAS TO GO ABOUT 100 FEET FOR A GOOD SWIM, SAYS GEORGE BLAKE, IN NEW GUINEA, BUT HE'D RATHER TAKE A DIP IN THE STEVENSON DAM POND ANY DAY –

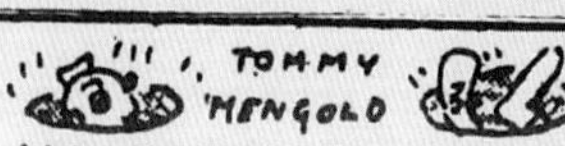

TOMMY MENGOLD WRITES FROM FRANCE, THAT HE'S BECOME INTIMATELY ACQUAINTED WITH ALL TYPES OF FOX HOLES.

→ DONALD JOYCE WITH PATTONS ARMY SAYS HE ALSO HAS TO DIG UP HIS OWN LIVING QUARTERS.

→ CLARENCE WAGNER IN FRANCE WITH THE FAMOUS 29th INF DIVISION, SAYS THINGS ARE BEGINING TO LOOK BRIGHTER OVER THERE

It looks the same way to LEWIS ANDREWS, SINCE CENSORSHIP HAS BEEN LIFTED ENUF FOR HIM TO WRITE AT THE TOP OF HIS LETTERS ADABAN, IRAN

ERNEST HILTON ALSO IN IRAN IS STILL SHOVING FREIGHT CARS AROUND CONTAINING GOODS FOR RUSSI

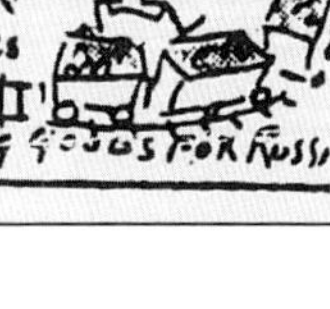

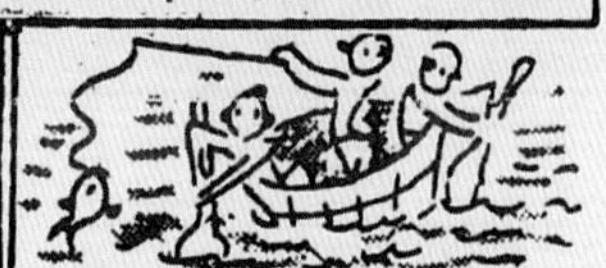

Rub-a-dub-dub – ? men in a tub!

STEVE TINGLEY – ON ONE OF THE ISLANDS IN THE MARSHALLS SAYS THAT HE AND A COUPLE OF OTHER GUYS, GOT AHOLD OF ENUF WOOD TO BUILD A LITTLE BOAT – we thought private yachts went out with the war.

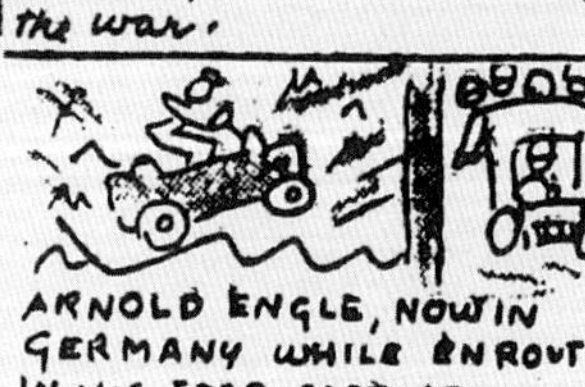

ARNOLD ENGLE, NOW IN GERMANY WHILE ENROUTE, IN HIS JEEP, CAPTURED A TRUCK WITH 5 GERMANS – SAID HE USED THE SAME OLD TRICK YOU BOYS USED ON THE COPS AT HOME.

REPORT FROM THE HOME FRONT

RED CROSS HEADQUARTERS ARE AGAIN OPEN THRUOUT THE WEEK AND A FULL SCHEDULE IS PLANNED FOR THE COMING SEASON.

A CLASS IN HOME NURSING WAS STARTED LAST WEEK.

THE LADIES ARE STILL BUSILY WORKING ON SURGICAL DRESSINGS AND CONVALESCENT GARMENTS

THE TOWNSFOLK CONTINUE TO CONTRIBUTE BLOOD PLASMA MANY FOR THE 5th and 6th TIMES.

THERE IS A FINE DISPLAY OF THE HANDWORK OF THE JUNIOR RED CROSS, IN THE WINDOW OF THE STEPNEY FOUNTAIN.

OUR RED CROSS IS ON THE ALERT TO RENDER AID IN ANY EMERGENCY.

To our Correspondents

BY THE TIME OUR NEXT ISSUE REACHES YOU, THANKSGIVING DAY WILL HAVE COME AND GONE — BUT EVERYDAY IS THANKSGIVING DAY FOR US AND YOUR LOVED ONES WHEN WE GET A LETTER FROM YOU BOYS - LETTERS WERE RECIEVED FROM THE FOLLOWING - THANK-YOU BOYS —

MARCEL GRISIER — SAMUEL SMITH
JOSEPH GUERNSEY — FRED STOWE
JESSE LUCKNER — SAM SWENDSON
CLARENCE WAGNER — GEORGE BLAKE
HOWARD BRAINARD — ALFRED BLAKE
ERNEST HILTON — HENRY SIMOKAT
GEORGE ANDERSON — LOUIS WHASEL
ORLEN BEARDSLEY — PHILIP GREGORY
BERNICE LUCKNER — MYLA MAC EWAN
LEWIS ANDREWS — JACK TUFINO

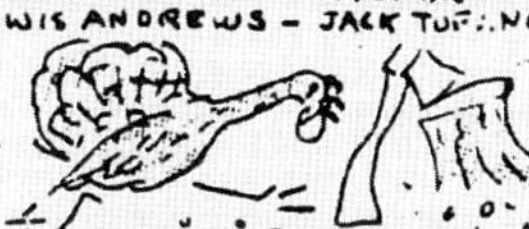

DON'T BE TIMID ABOUT ASKING OUR HOME SERVICE FOR ANY INFORMATION CONCERNING RELATIVES OR FRIENDS IN THE SERVICE — THEY WILL TRACK DOWN YOUR REQUEST

JESSE LUCKNER, JR. IS OUT THERE HELPING TO CLEAN UP THE ISLAND OF SAIPAN

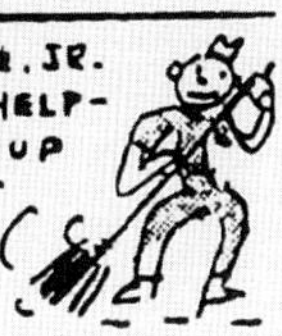

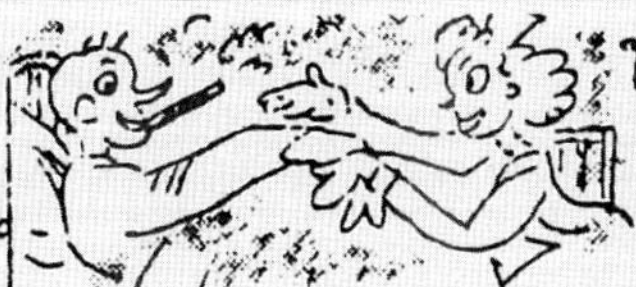

THE CADET NURSING CORPS HAS JUST GAINED TWO NEW MEMBERS — JOAN BULKELY OF STEPNEY IS AT THE EASTERN MAINE GENERAL HOSPITAL, BANGOR, ME. AND GLORIA STEPHENS OF MONROE, IS AT THE MC LEAN HOSPITAL - WAVERLY, MASS.

MYLA MAC EWAN IS STATIONED AT THE U.S. NAVAL HOSPITAL NEWPORT, R.I. SHE IS HELPING TO LIGHTEN THE HOURS OF THE MEN IN THE WARDS.

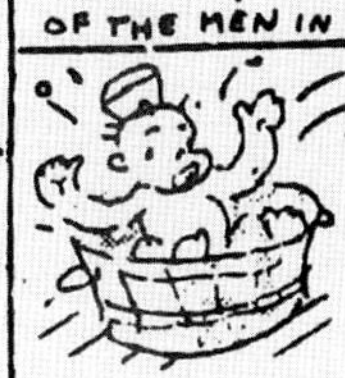

ENSIGN BERNICE LUCKNER. SAYS THE NAVY HAS A GREAT JOB FOR HER THESE DAYS. HELPING TO LAUNCH THE FUTURE NAVY — (newborns of NAVY Families)

LEWIS ANDREWS NOW BOASTS A GOOD CONDUCT MEDAL

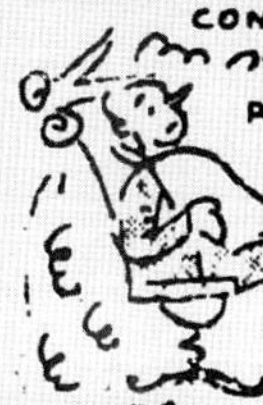

PVT. ROBERT COOGAN JUST GOT HIS FIRST G.I. HAIRCUT Boo-Hoo- THOSE BEAU-TI-FUL CURLS

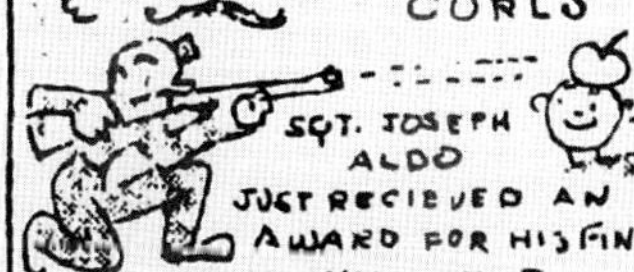

SGT. JOSEPH ALDO JUST RECIEVED AN AWARD FOR HIS FINE MARKSMANSHIP — LOOK OUT — YOU — JAPS AND GERMANS

This is a composite issue of OUR TOWN extracted from the October, 1944 issue.

THE $64.00 QUESTION

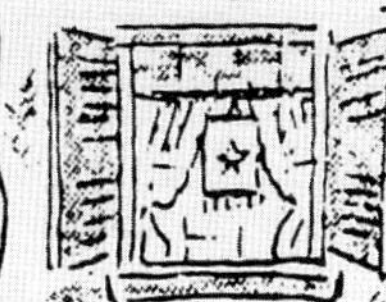

IF YOU HAD A FURLOUGH WHERE WOULD YOU LIKE TO SPEND IT? (me too)

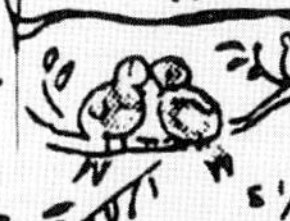

ENGAGEMENTS ANNOUNCED —

S 1/c VIVIAN KENT OF PEPPER ST. TO SGT GEORGE FRASIER OF SCOTT DEPOT WEST VA

WALTER LUCKNER OF THE NAVY TO GERTRUDE WYCINOWSKE OF BRIDGEPORT

LT. JACK EDWARDS ARMY PILOT, BROUGHT HIS BRIDE, UP FROM GEORGIA, TO VISIT THE OLD HOME TOWN — YUM - YUM — THOSE — GEORGIA PEACHES

SAYS THE G.I. "THAT'S WHAT I LIKE - A GIRL WITH A GOOD HEAD, ON my shoulder."

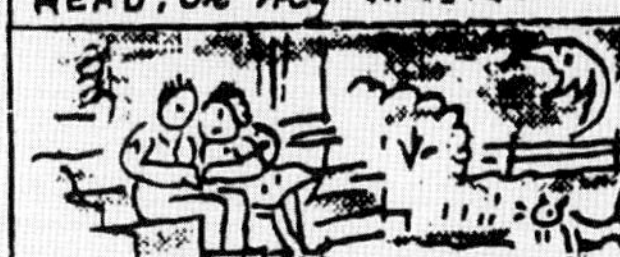

CHARLES CORNUT, HOME AFTER 2 1/2 YEARS IN THE SO PACIFIC SPENT TWO HAPPY WEEKS IN STEPNEY WITH HIS WIFE — "Seems good to be home" HE SAID.

THEY ARE STILL GOING — BOB HALLER - TO CAMP STEWART GEORGIA FOR ANTI AIRCRAFT - TRAINING - EDWARD S BEARDSLEY JR - to CAMP DEVENS, MASS WILLIAM BLAKE TO CAMP DEVENS - MASS -

WRITE in care of — AMERICAN RED CROSS MONROE BRANCH - STEPNEY DEPOT CONN

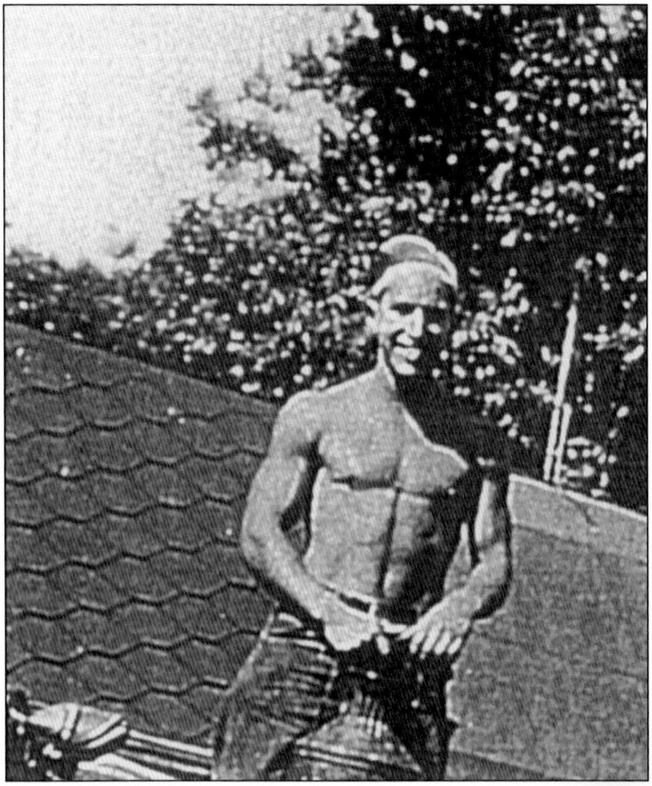

Victor Sippin smiles for the camera in happier days before World War II. American Legion Post 176 was named for him and for David Winspur (below), both of whom lost their lives in service to their country.

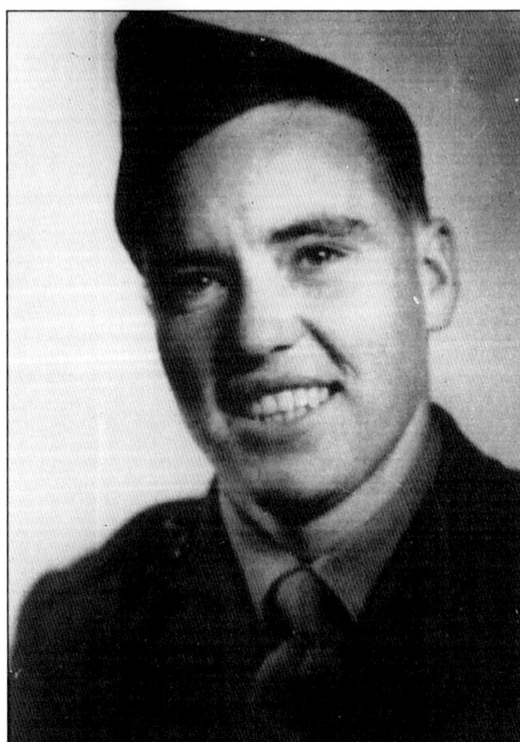

Victor Sippin died in the south of France on August 24, 1944, while liberating the French. His PT boat, with all five aboard, went down in Port de Bouc near Marseilles. Douglas Fairbanks Jr. was his commanding officer. Sadly, less than a year later, David Winspur was shot and killed during combat on Iwo Jima on March 13, 1945.

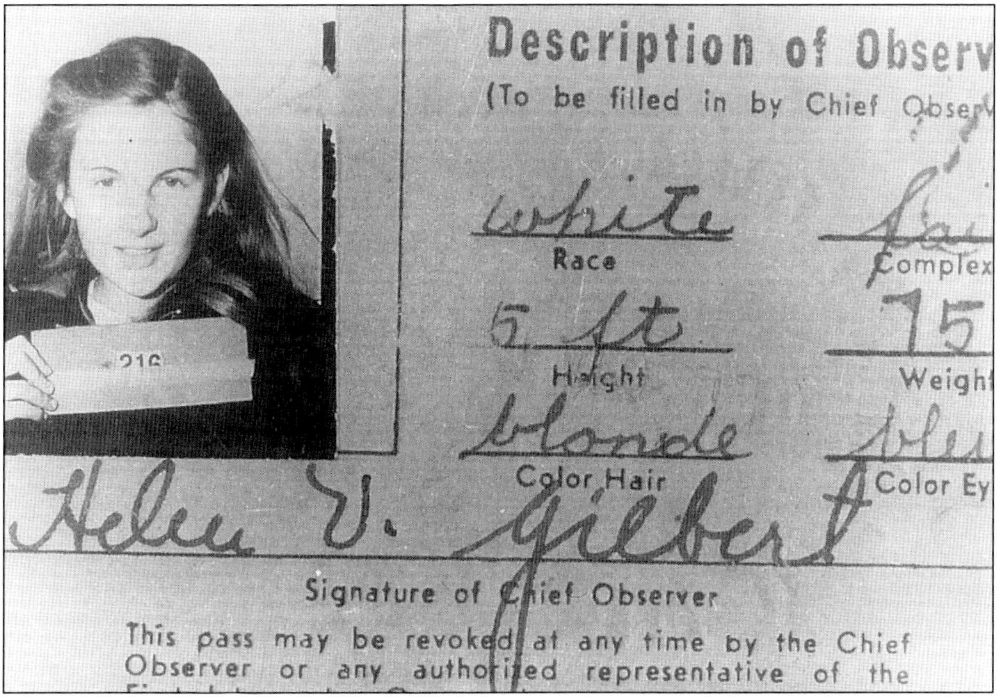

To guard our land from foreign invaders by air, many citizens volunteered their time during World War II as aircraft spotters and carried cards like this to identify themselves. This card identified young Joy Standish of Barn Hill Road. Volunteers spent many lonely hours at the spotters shack on Barn Hill Road.

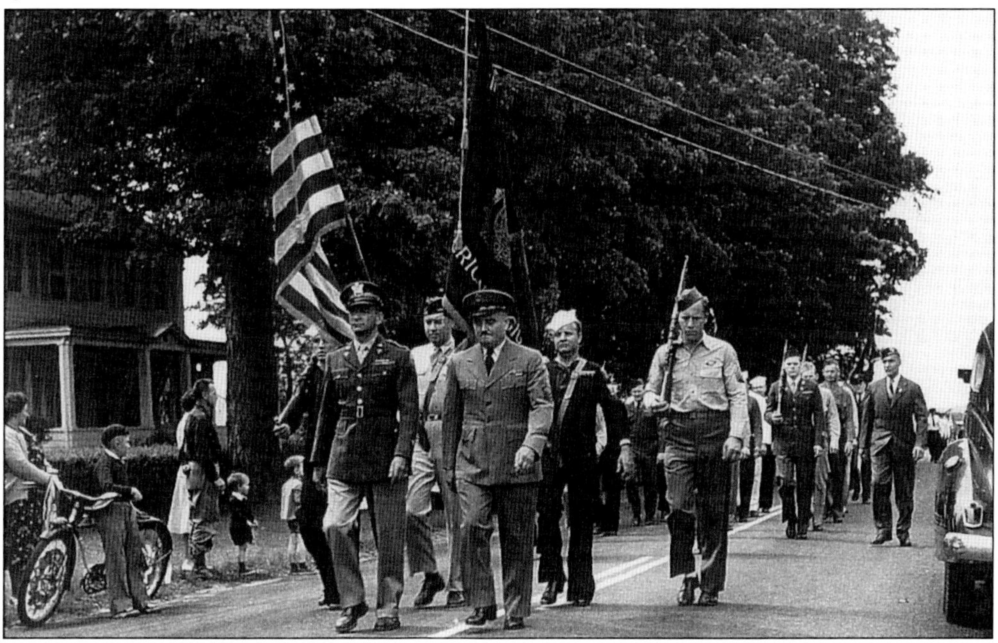

The Memorial Day Parade of 1949 included in its line-up many of Monroe's finest who had served in World War II. From left to right, Dr. John Rosenfeld, Peter Spada, Bradley Swendsen, Robert Haller, and George Wolf are pictured here.

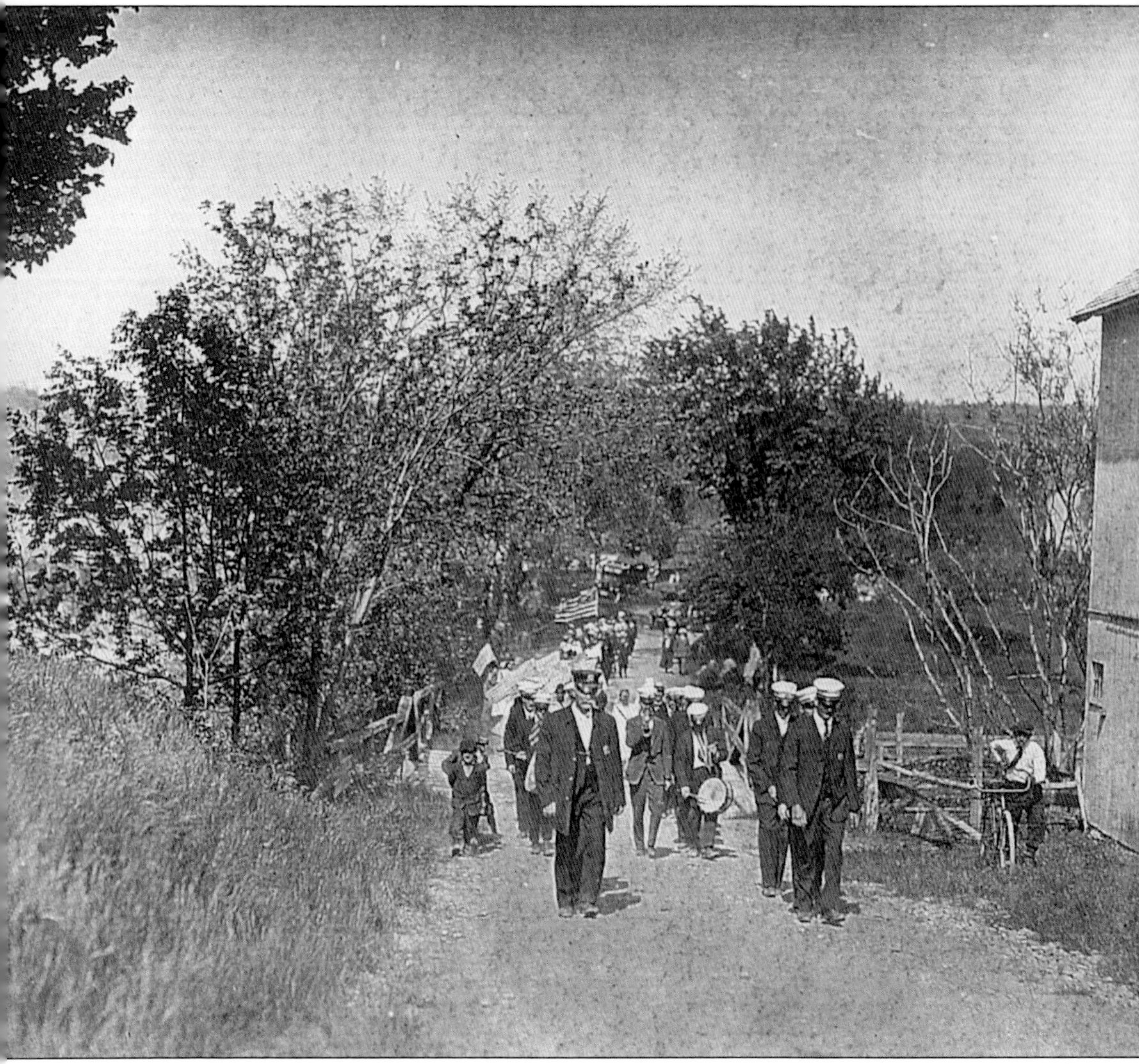

No matter where Monroe holds its Memorial Day parade, there's always an uphill climb! This early parade in Stepney was no exception. The parade included many former servicemen and always culminated in laying wreaths at the graves of the veterans.

Four

Getting Around

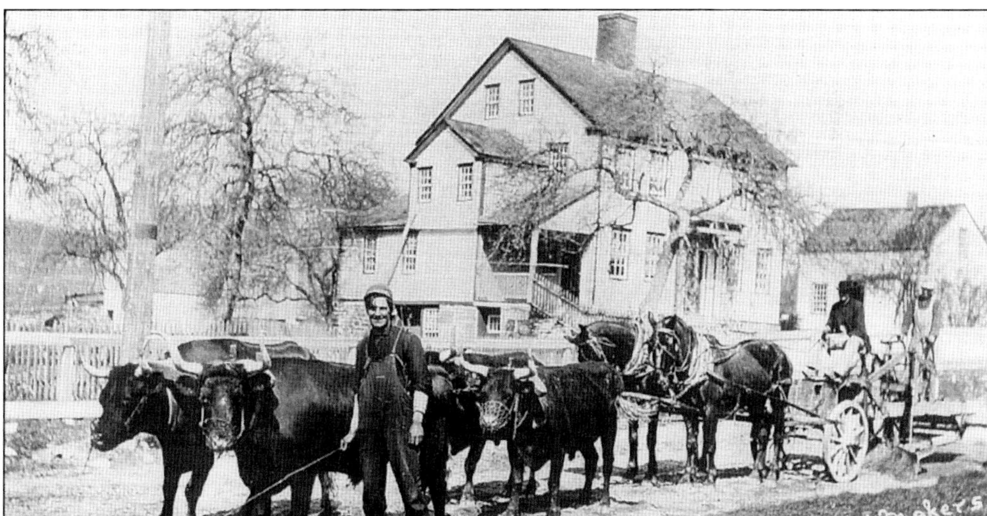

The frost is out. Now it's time to regrade and tidy up rutted, bumpy roads. Two horses and four oxen power the four-wheeled road grader on what is now Main Street near the intersection of Purdy Hill Road. The Bond farmhouse in the background still sits there today.

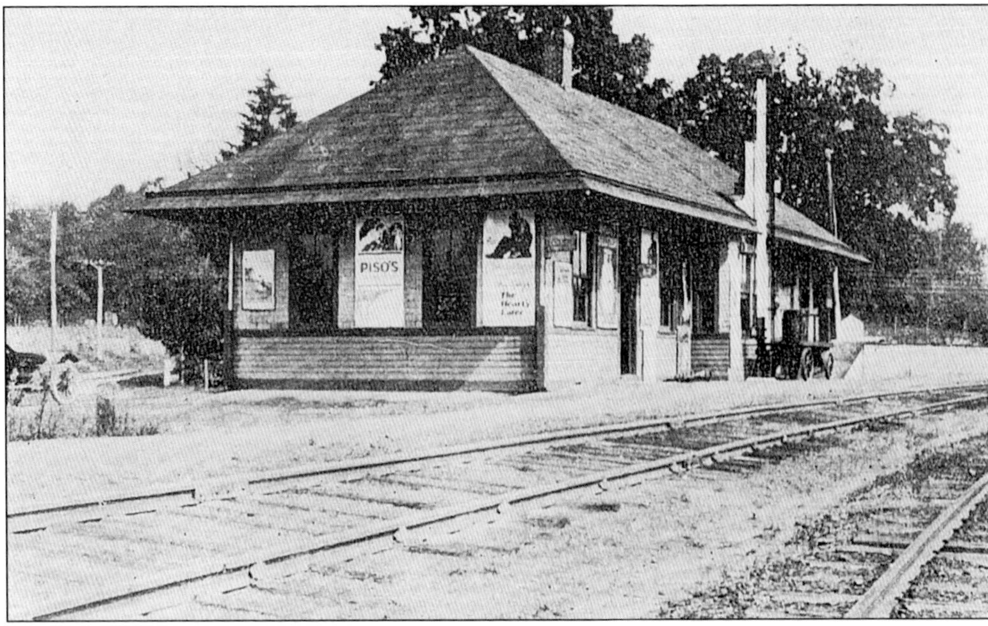

The Stepney Depot on Maple Street was one of two stations in Stepney. This line connected Monroe to Bridgeport, where Monroe citizens could find shopping and services not available in their "rural paradise." In 1940, the cost of this trip was 30¢, and it took at least an hour. The building is still being used today by a local construction company.

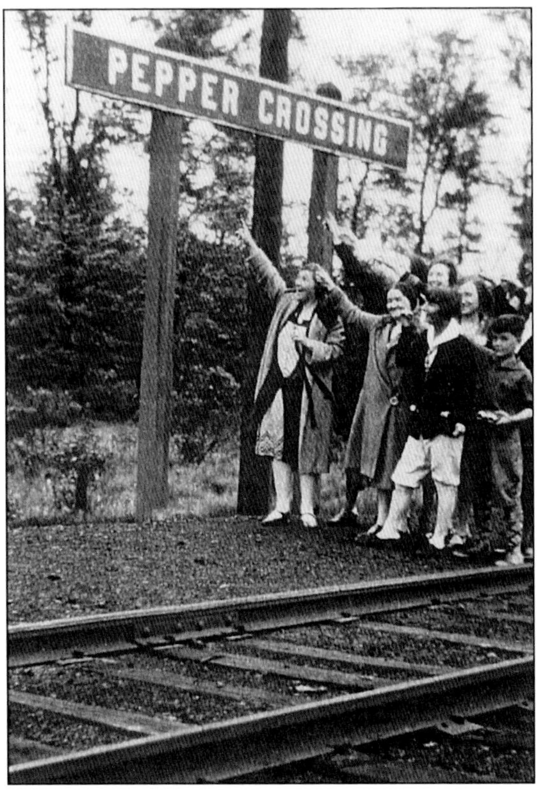

Mildred H. Fagan and friends are "flagging down" the train for a special day in the "big city"—Bridgeport. Here Pepper Street crosses both the railroad and Cutler's Farm Road, and travelers could flag down the train. The nearby Harry Garder family entertained boarders in the summer, many of whom came via train (c. 1921). Pepper Crossing was recently eliminated during road construction.

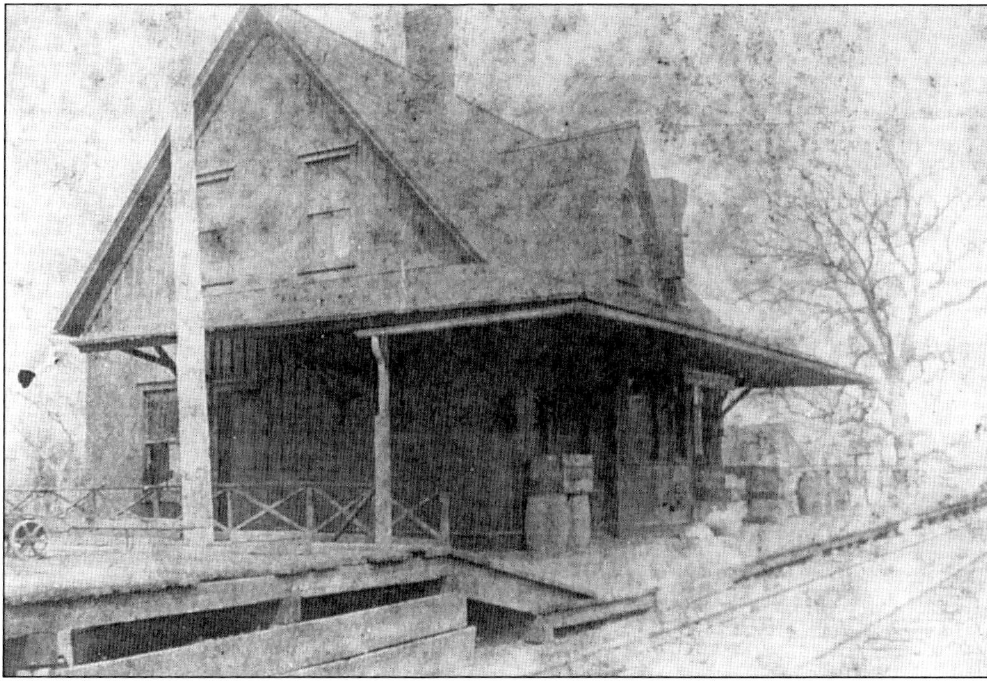

The Derby Extension, a part of the Berkshire railway line, was put through the northeastern village of Zoar Bridge and opened officially in October 1888. The president of the railroad, Colonel William H. Stevenson, was honored by the community when his name was given to the depot. This old Stevenson Railroad station burned down and was replaced by the station pictured below.

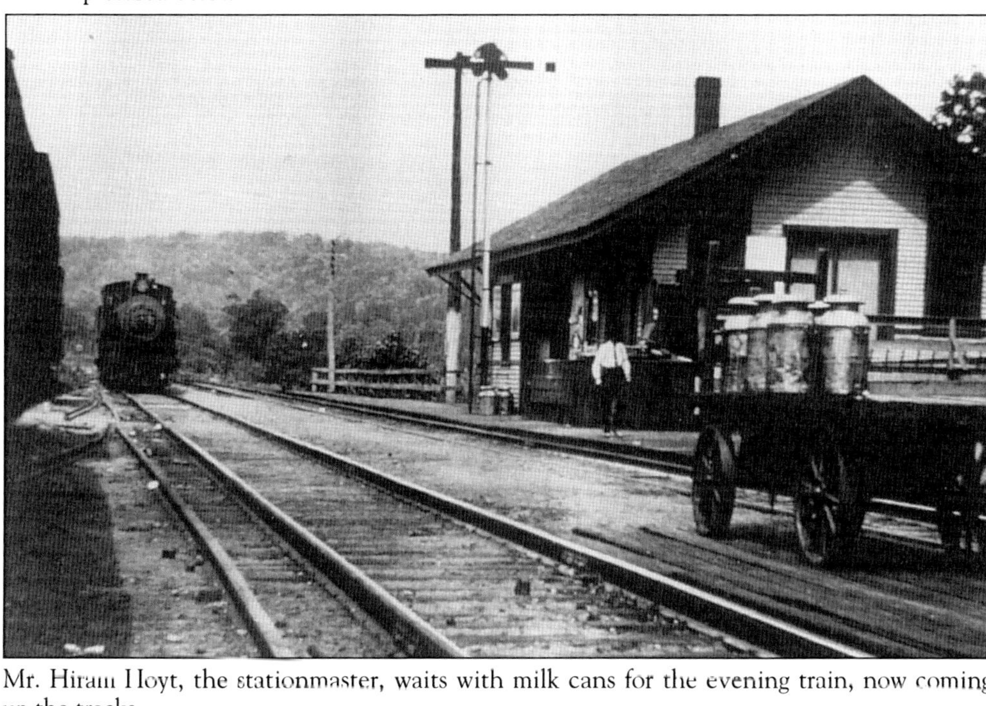

Mr. Hiram Hoyt, the stationmaster, waits with milk cans for the evening train, now coming up the tracks.

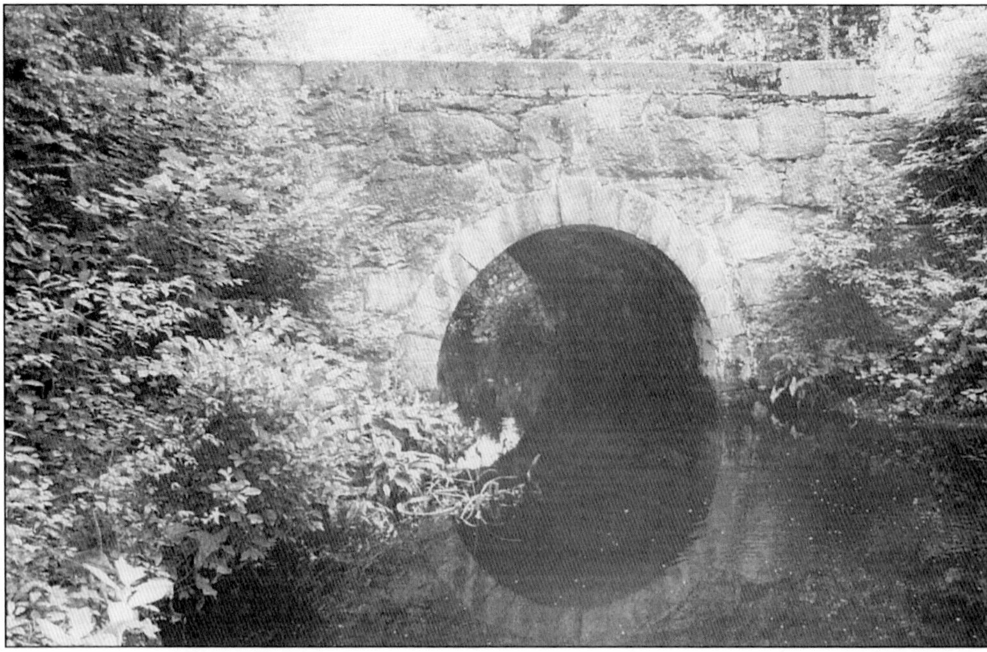

Located off Grant Road, this single-track Housatonic Railroad bridge (*c.* 1870) is on the Connecticut List of Historic Sites.

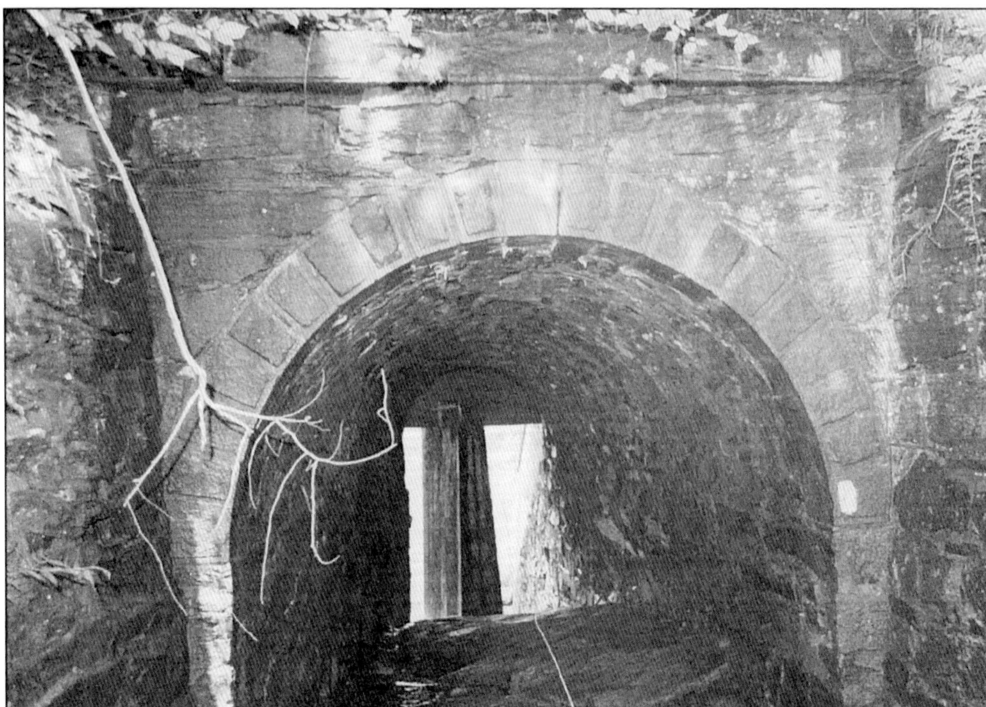

This railroad bridge between Route 34 and Cottage Street (*c.* 1888) served the Stevenson branch of the Housatonic Railroad, before being taken over by the New York–New Haven–Hartford line. It is still visible on the hill opposite Zoar Beach.

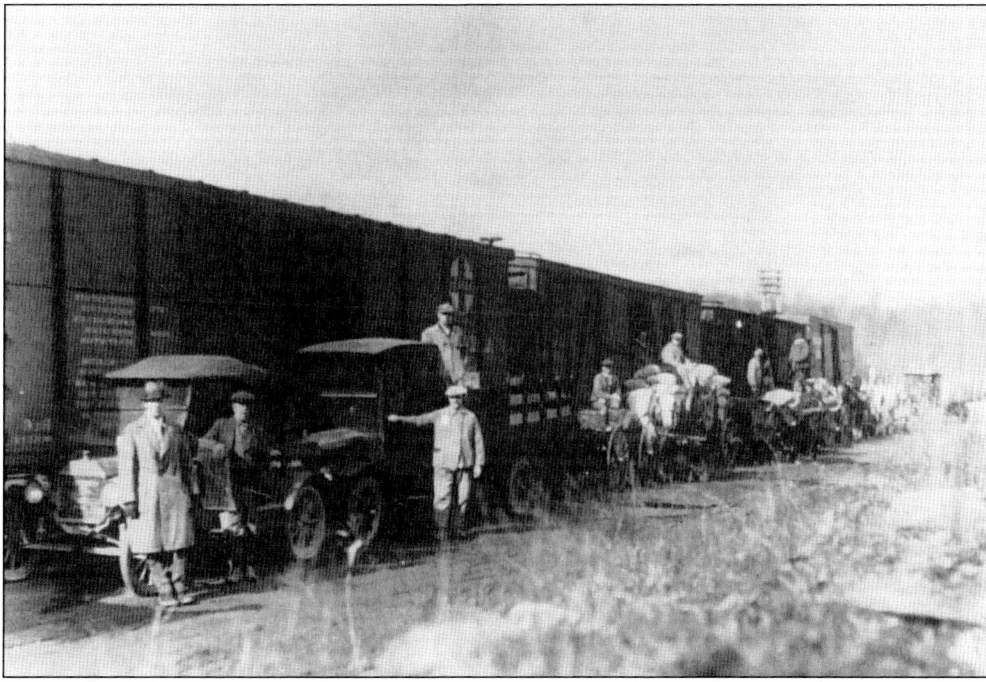

Horses, oxen, trucks, and trains were all important means of transporting goods in the early twentieth century. These men are waiting at Stepney Depot to pick up supplies for area merchants and farmers.

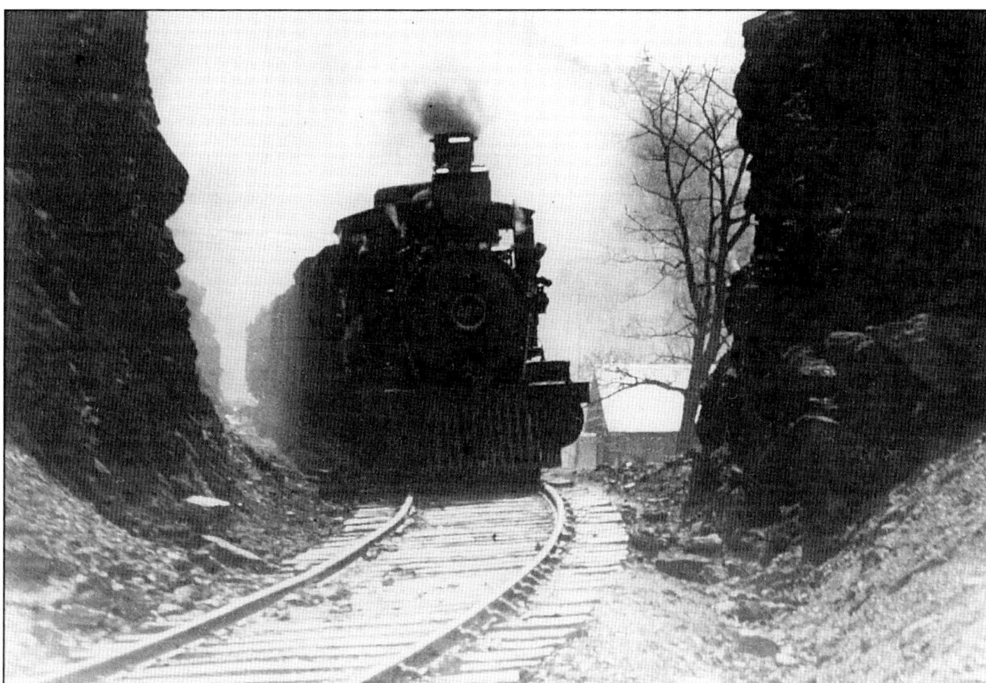

The New York–New Haven–Hartford Railroad steam engine chugs through Stevenson along this heavily traveled main route (*c.* 1910).

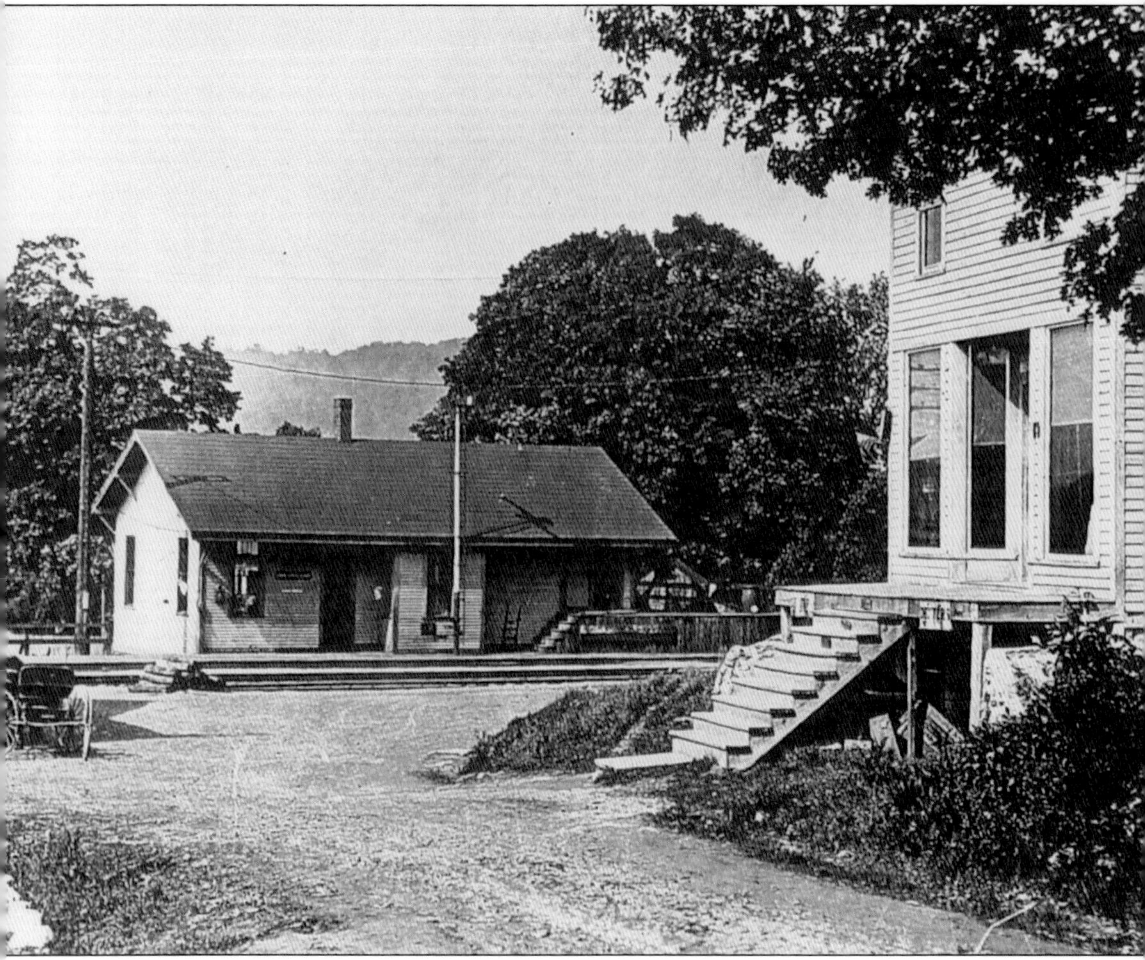

The Burr-Twist Store and the Stevenson station are pictured here in 1905. The store housed the Stevenson Post Office for many years until the post office moved across the street. The buggy pictured is parked outside a large feed mill. The store, no longer in operation, is now a private residence.

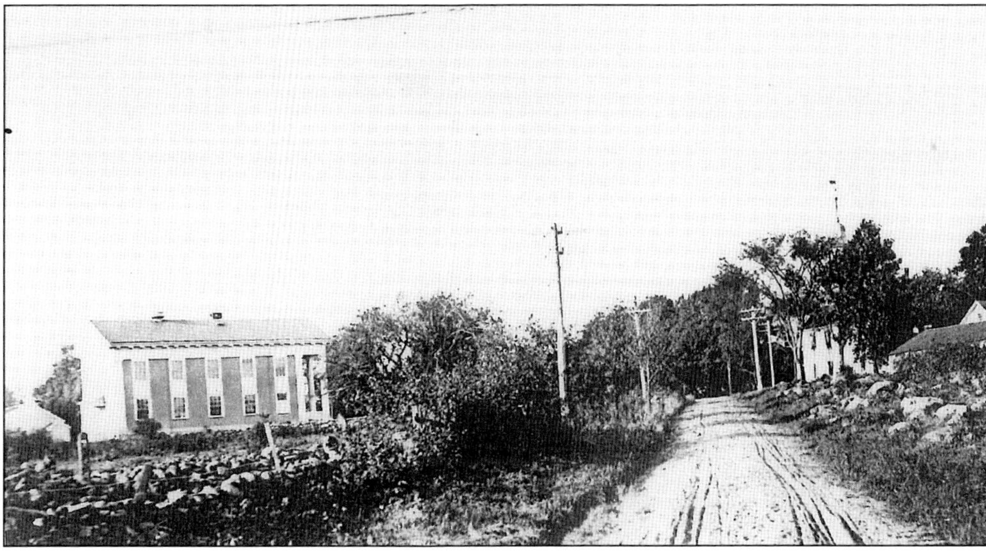

Monroe Turnpike was often muddy and full of deep ruts. The Masonic temple, on the left, and St. Peter's Episcopal Church, on the right, hug the road heading north toward the Green.

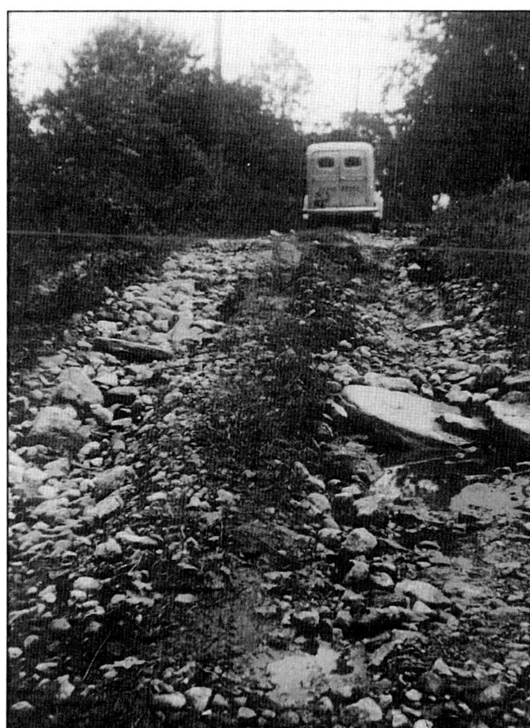

The 1938 hurricane caused such complete devastation on Maiden Lane that T. Raymond Reynolds was forced to abandon his delivery van and find a safe way home.

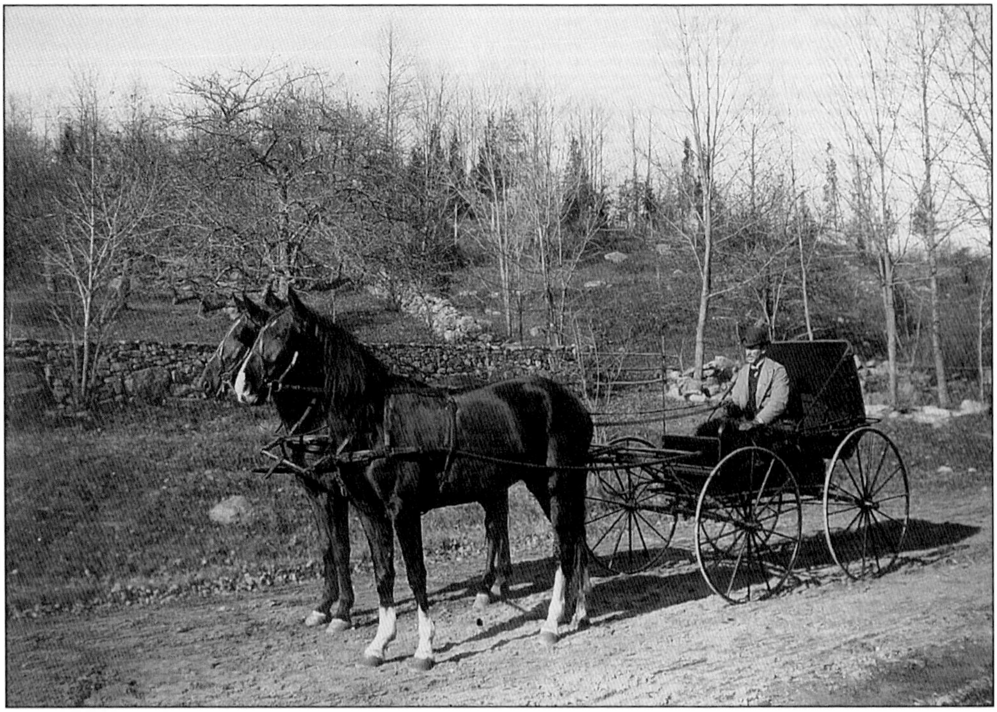

Merwin W. Johnson sets out with his horses on a crisp November day in 1895 to enjoy the pristine beauty of the surrounding countryside. The magnificent stone walls, defining property lines, are a tribute to Yankee ingenuity.

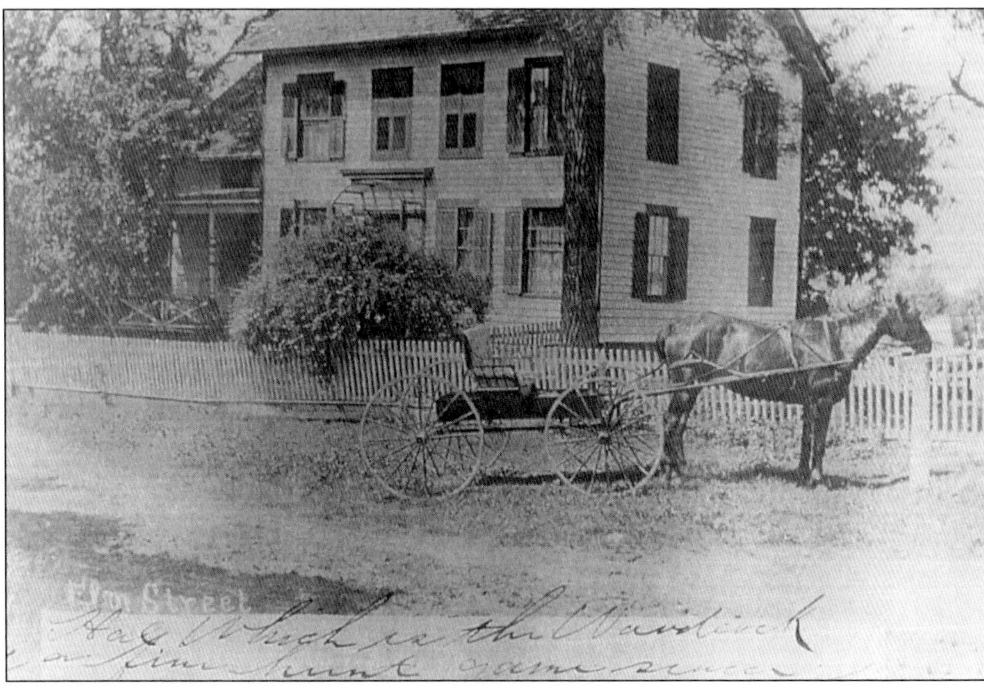

A fine horse and buggy awaits its master in front of the Solon Wales home on Elm Street. Most families had a rig like this as their primary means of transportation.

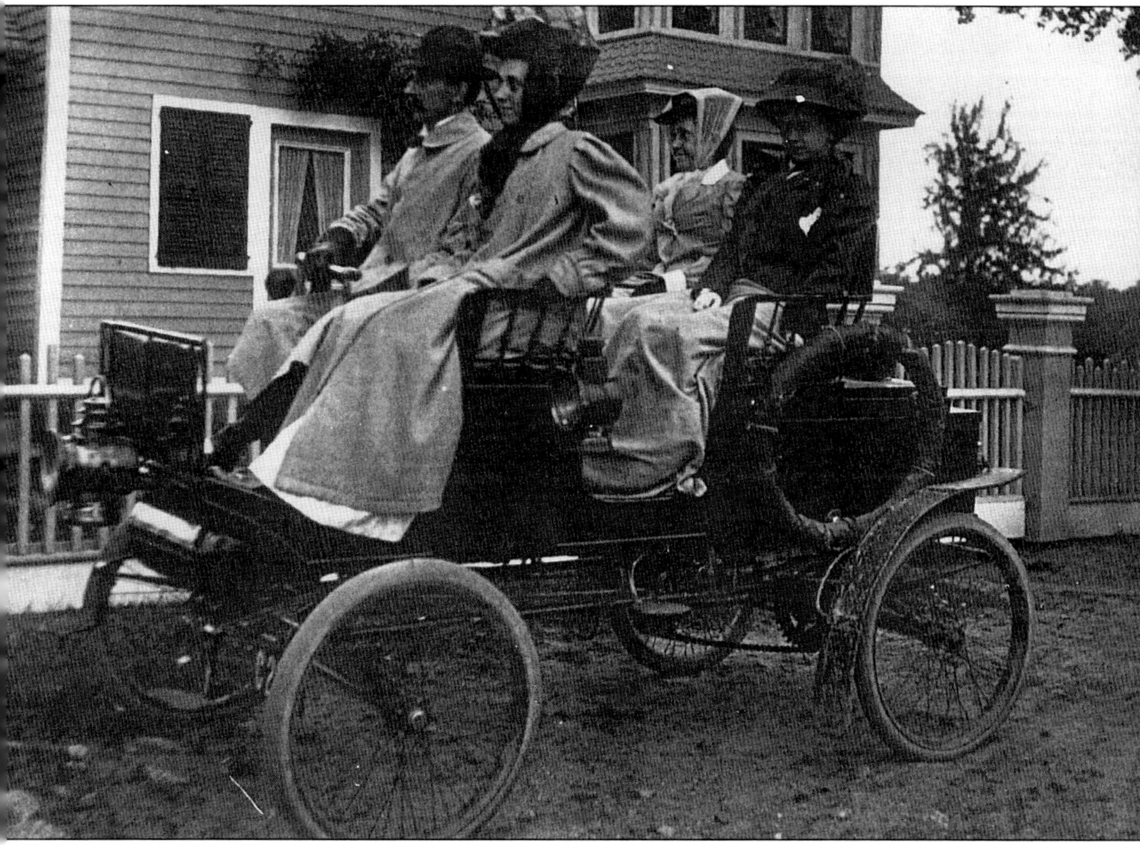

The Slade family of Stepney, properly attired in "dusters," is ready to take a tour around Monroe *c.* 1906. This car had a chain drive and tiller, instead of a steering wheel.

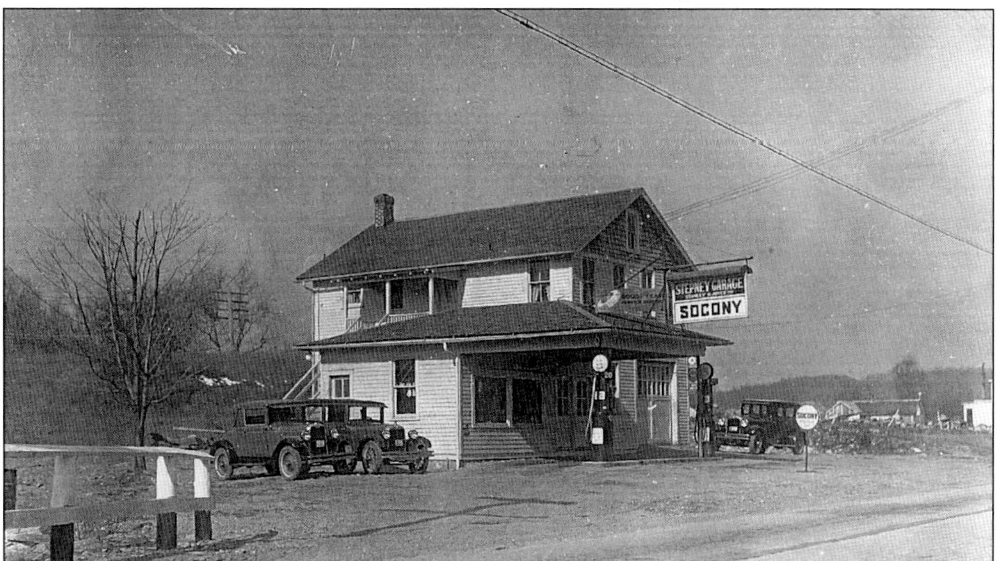

The Stepney Garage on Main Street, owned and operated by Stanley Joyce, was an indication of changing times as automobiles become more and more common.

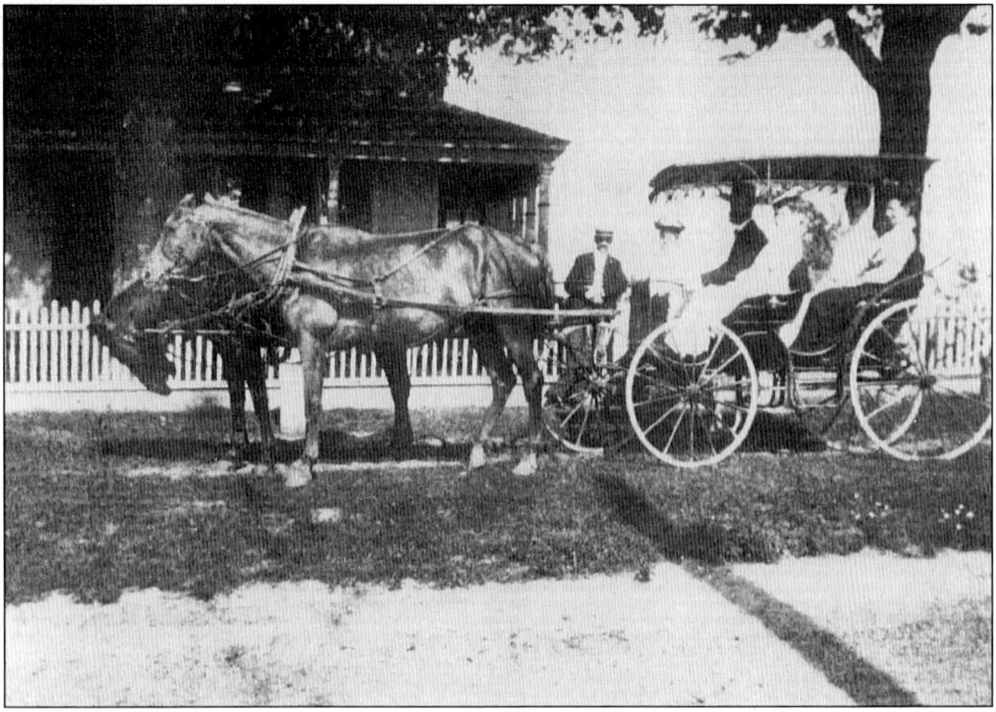

Although there were no seat belts or paved roads, these Monroe folks went visiting in style dressed in their Sunday finery. Could this have been the inspiration for the "Surrey with the Fringe on Top"?

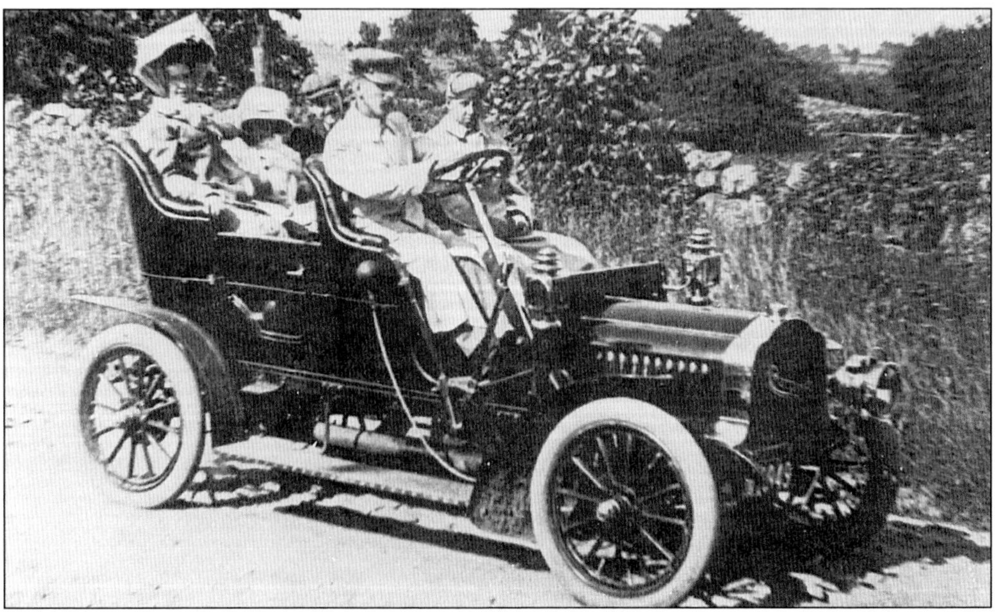

The Merwin Johnson family of Elm Street takes a ride in their brand new Compound car built c. 1906 at a cost of $1,300 in Middletown, Connecticut.

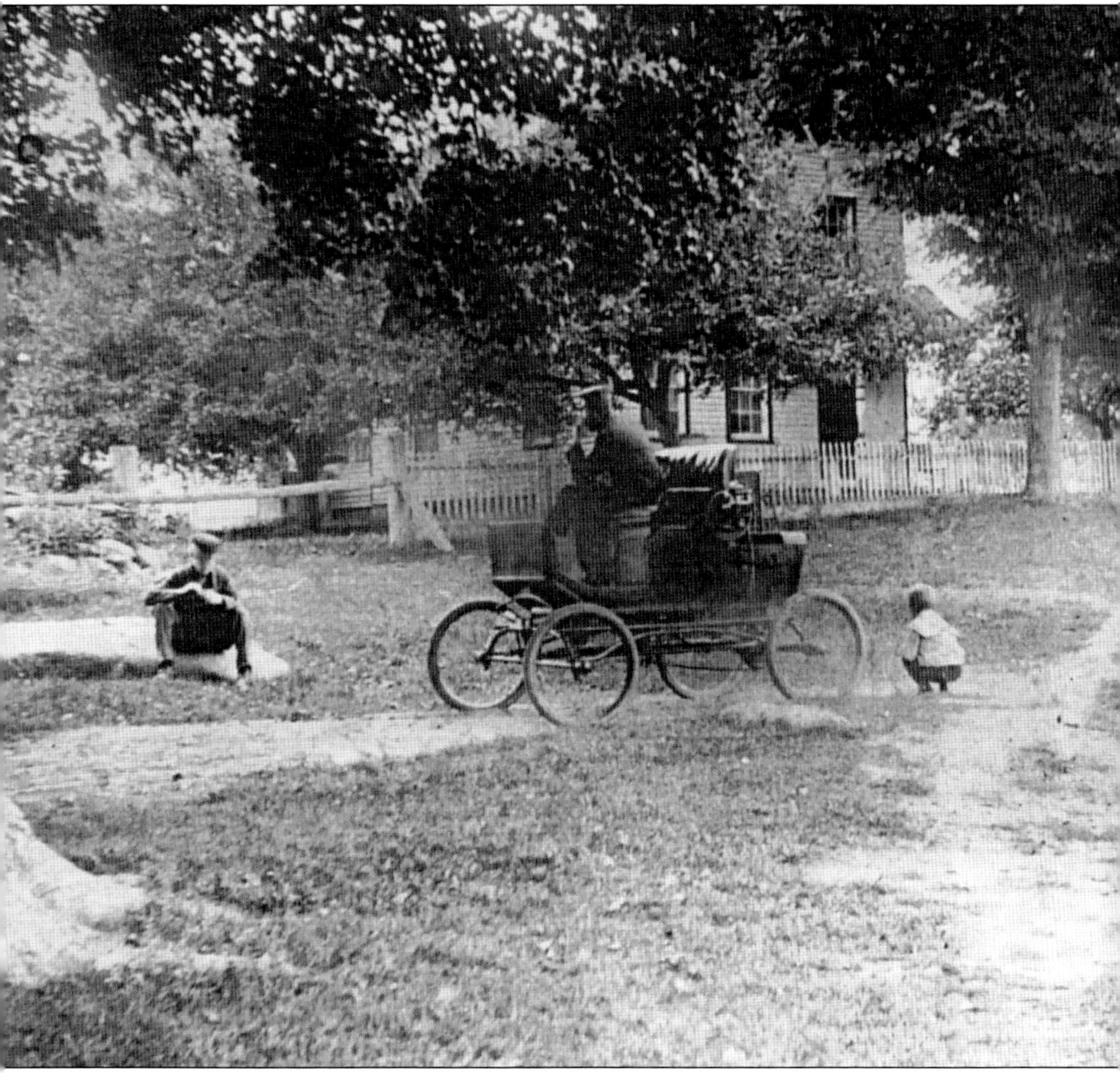

While F.W. Hawley sits on the rock, Alton Hawley peers beneath Smalley's Stanley Steamer. Alton, born in 1904, has recorded a recollection of life in Monroe, available in our public library.

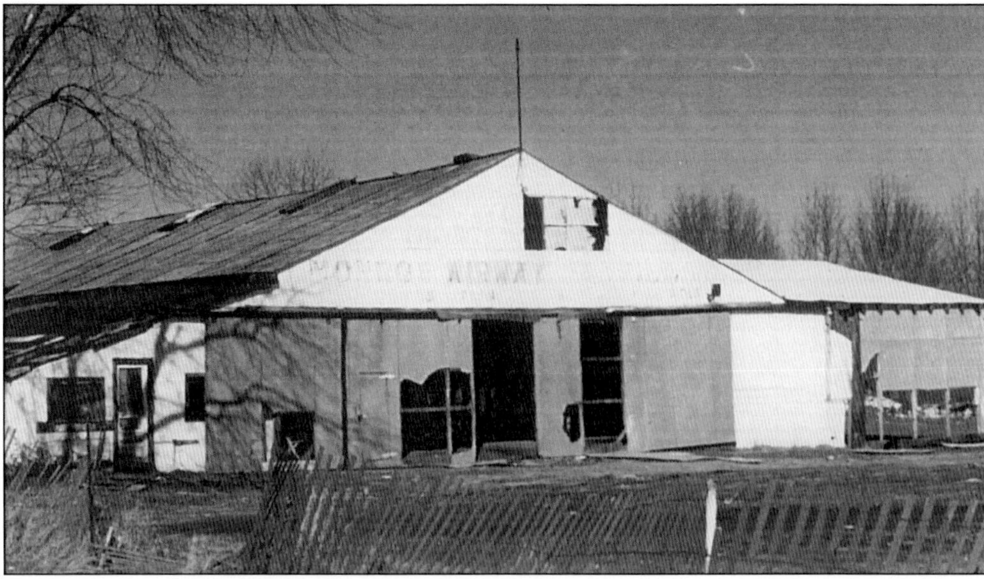

It may come as a surprise to some, but Monroe had its own airport, located at the top of Moose Hill Road. This land was first used as a racetrack in the 1930s. The airport, established by the late Benjamin Hurd, opened in 1940 and continued in operation until 1973. On weekends, parachute jumpers often gathered to go "jumping" in the area. This land is now the site of St. John's Cemetery.

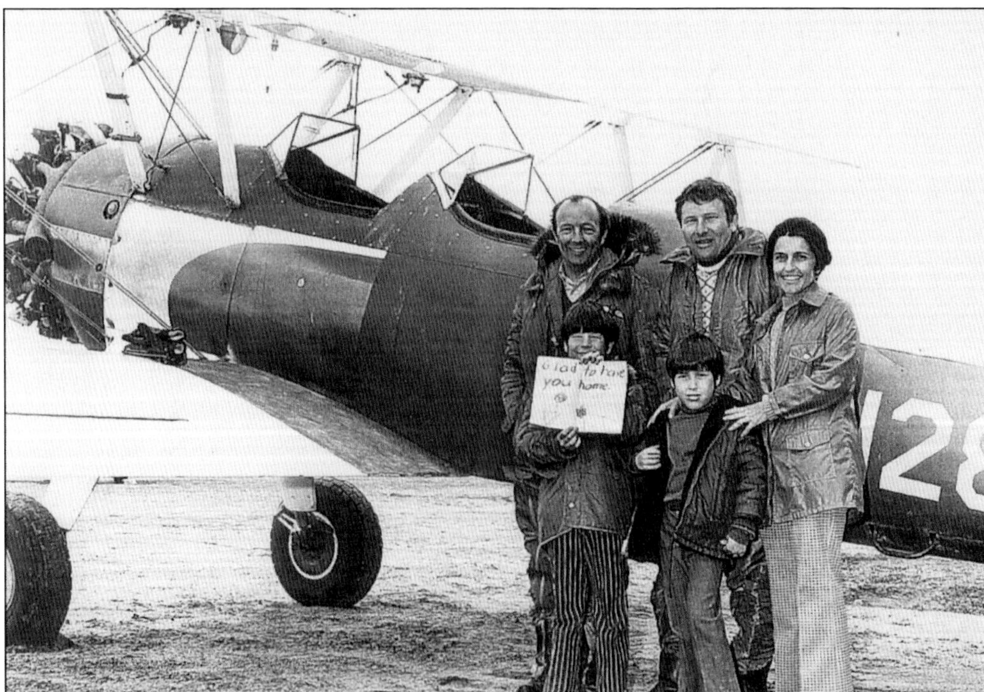

This plane, a Boeing Steerman, was a World War II plane, used by the U.S. Armed Forces as a training plane. It was bought and restored by Chuck Neuchterlein, who is shown here at the Monroe airport with his wife, Judy, in the mid-1970s.

Five

This Land Is Our Land

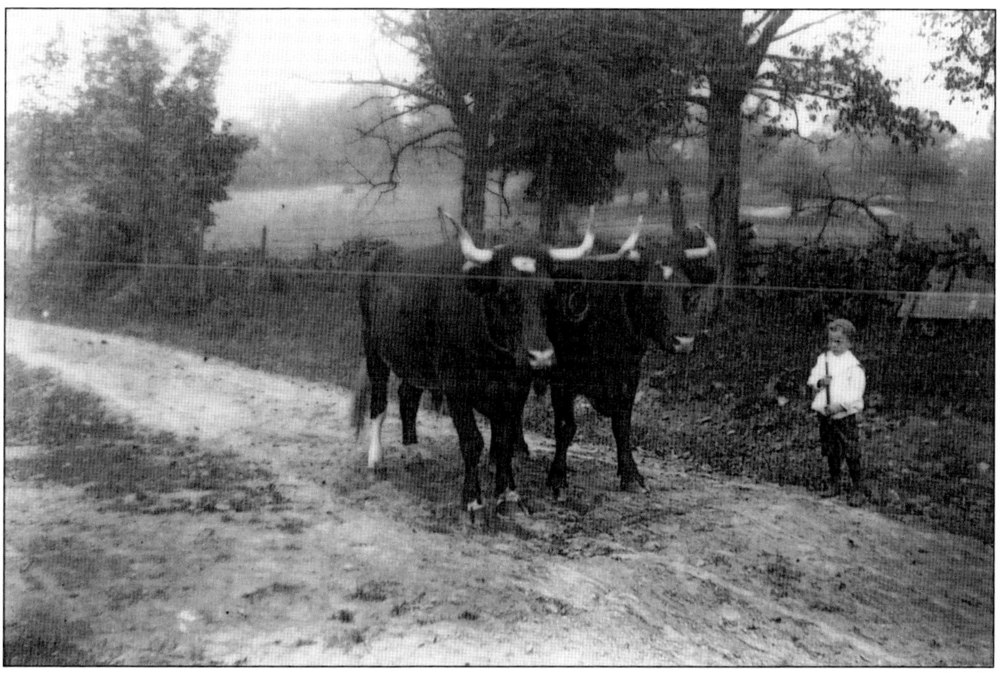

Monroe was primarily an agricultural community, and oxen in pairs were used as draft animals. Oxen also pulled grading equipment to maintain the roads. These animals await their next assignment on Webb Circle. The young boy may have been assigned the task of working the team or watching them while the farmer goes to get the equipment.

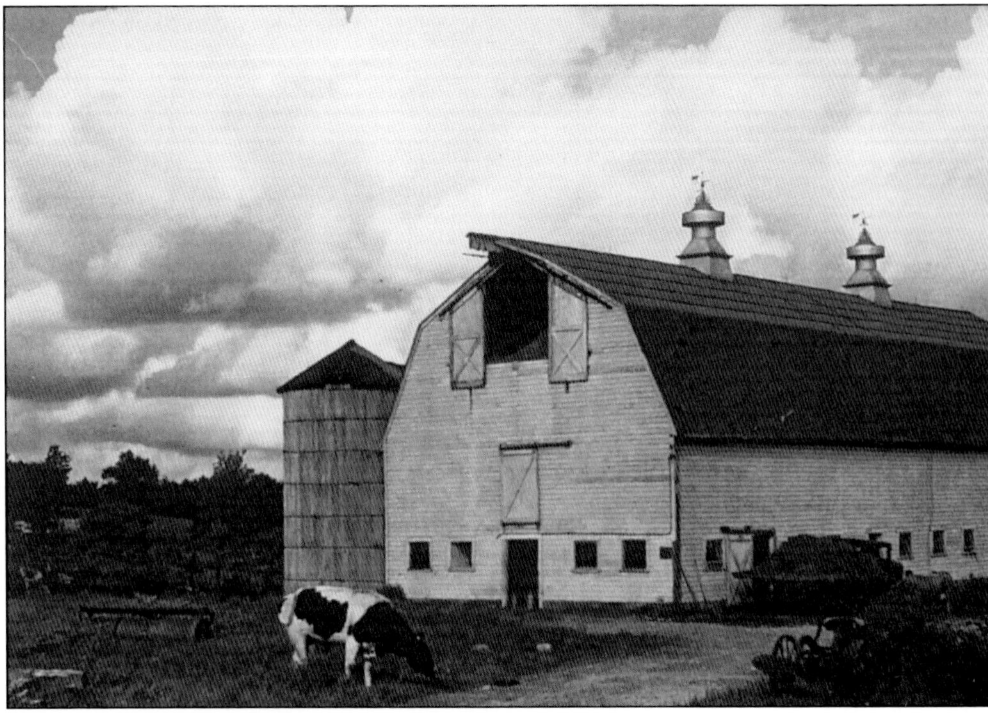

This tranquil view of Whitney Farms shows the distinct barn architecture of the times. The Whitneys purchased the 400-acre Samuel Hurd farm in 1938.

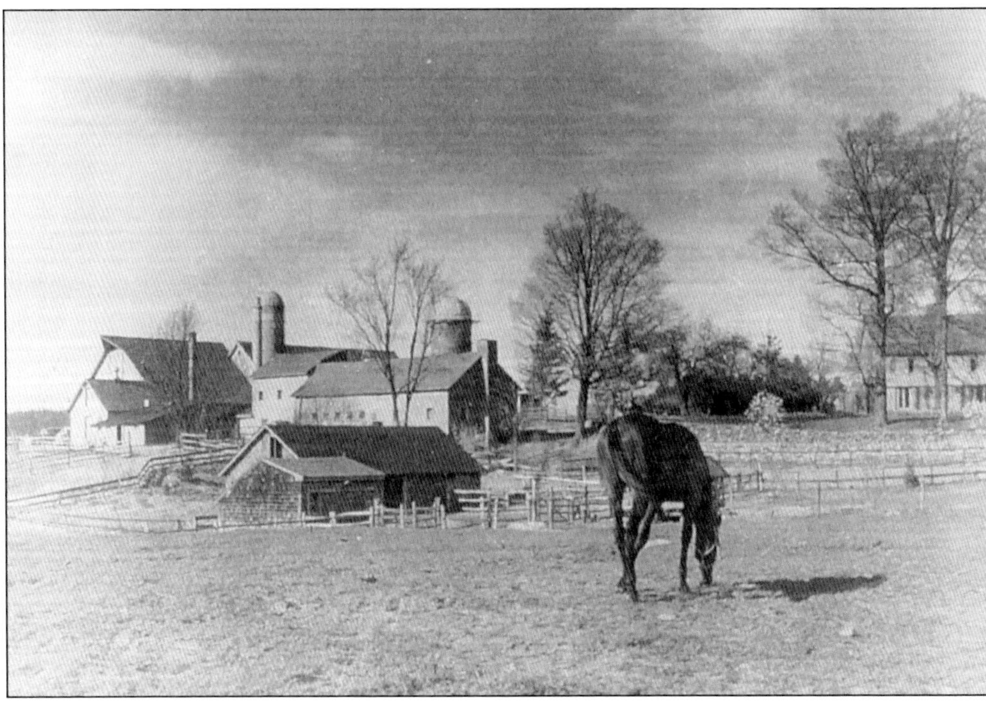

Pastoral scenes like Whitney Farms, which was located opposite what is now the golf course, were common well into the 1950s.

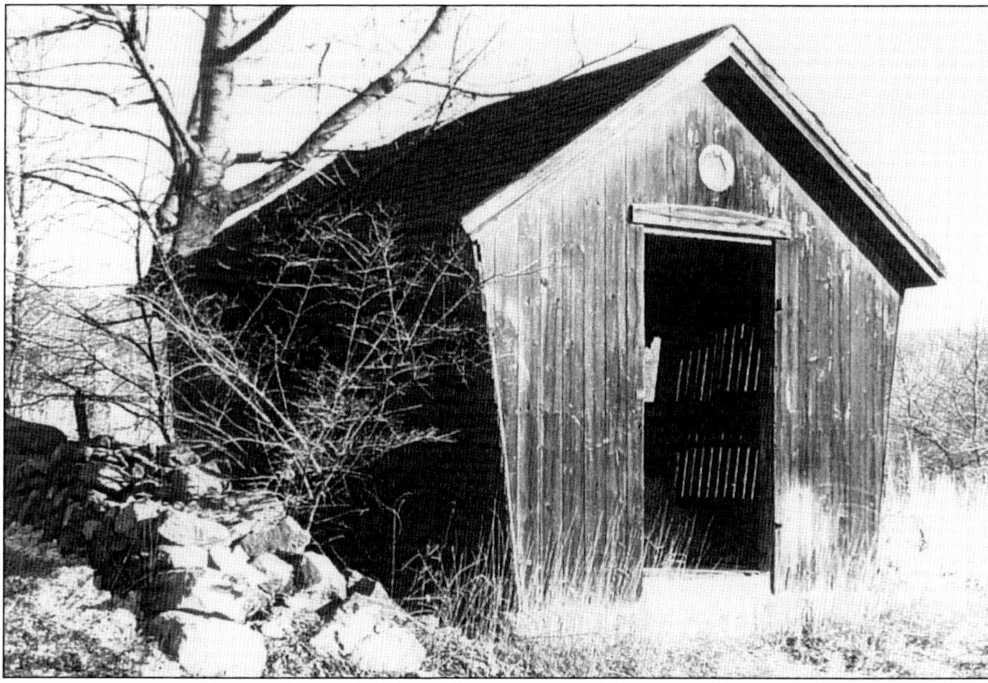

This corn crib on Purdy Hill Road, near Westview Road, is typical of the many that once could be found in Monroe. Look carefully; it's easy to miss.

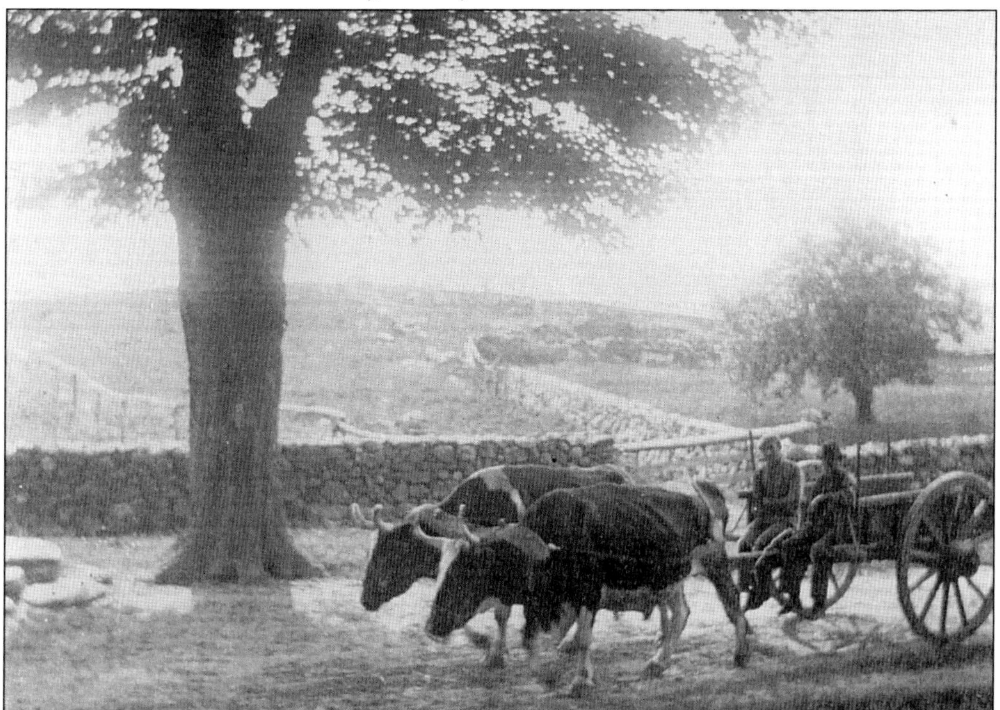

Oxen teams performed many daily functions on the farm. They helped to clear the fields and to move the stone used in building exquisite stone walls like those in the background.

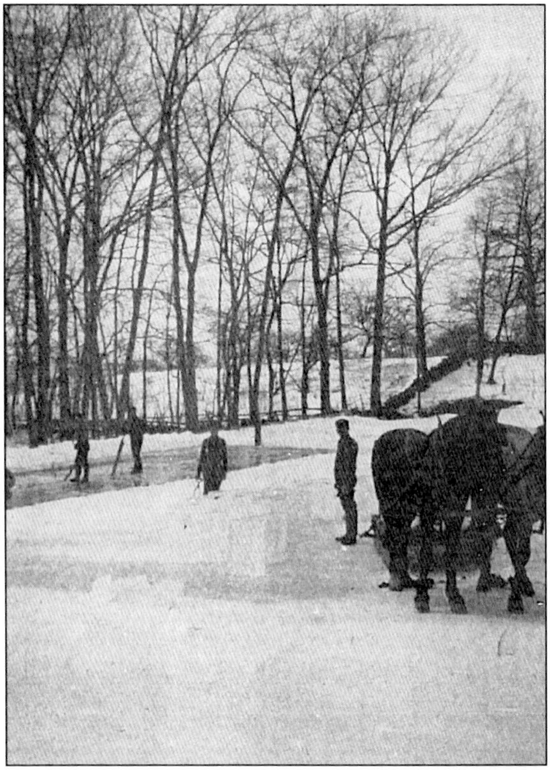

Ice harvesting at Cargill's pond in East Village was an important winter chore before refrigeration.

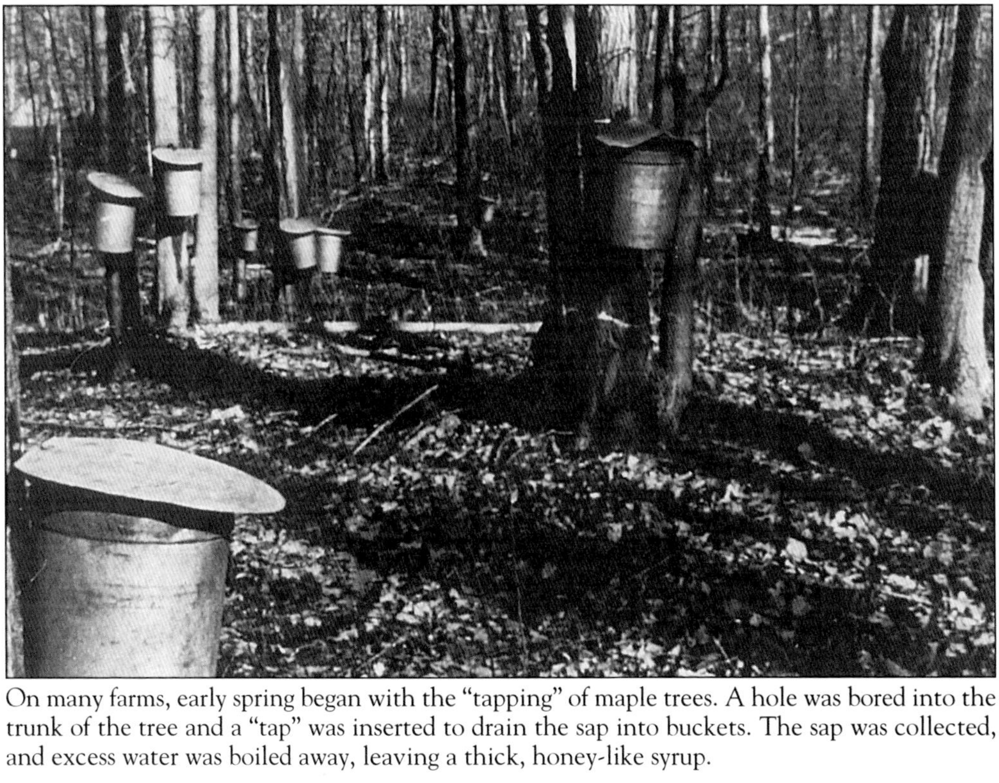

On many farms, early spring began with the "tapping" of maple trees. A hole was bored into the trunk of the tree and a "tap" was inserted to drain the sap into buckets. The sap was collected, and excess water was boiled away, leaving a thick, honey-like syrup.

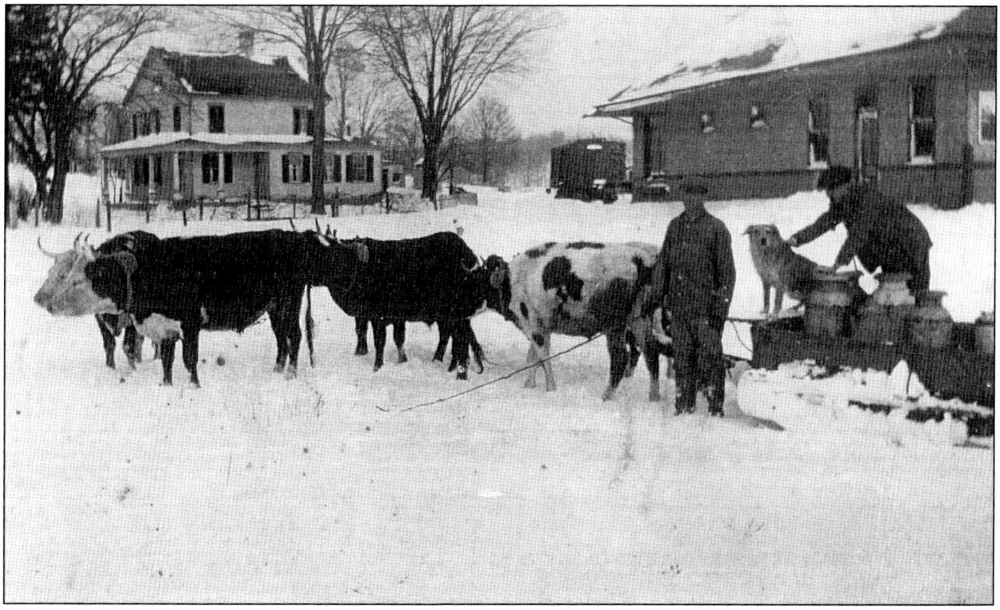

Milk went to market every day of the year. This three-pair team waits for the milk train at the Stepney Railroad Station, c. 1920.

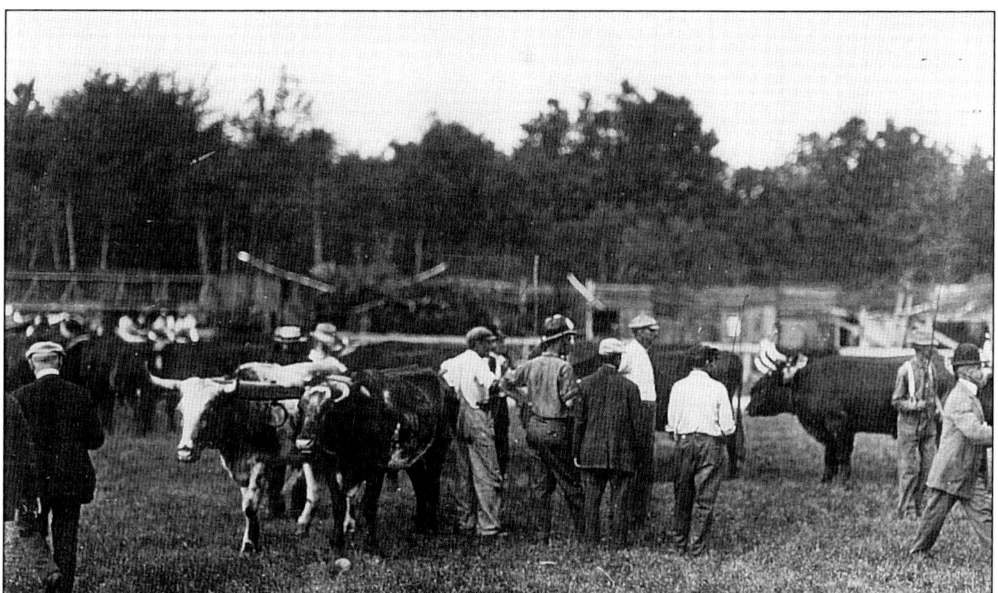

Fred Wheeler checks over his oxen team at the Danbury Fair grounds. This fair offered a great deal of excitement, and many people took the train from the Stepney or Botsford Depot to enjoy the festivities.

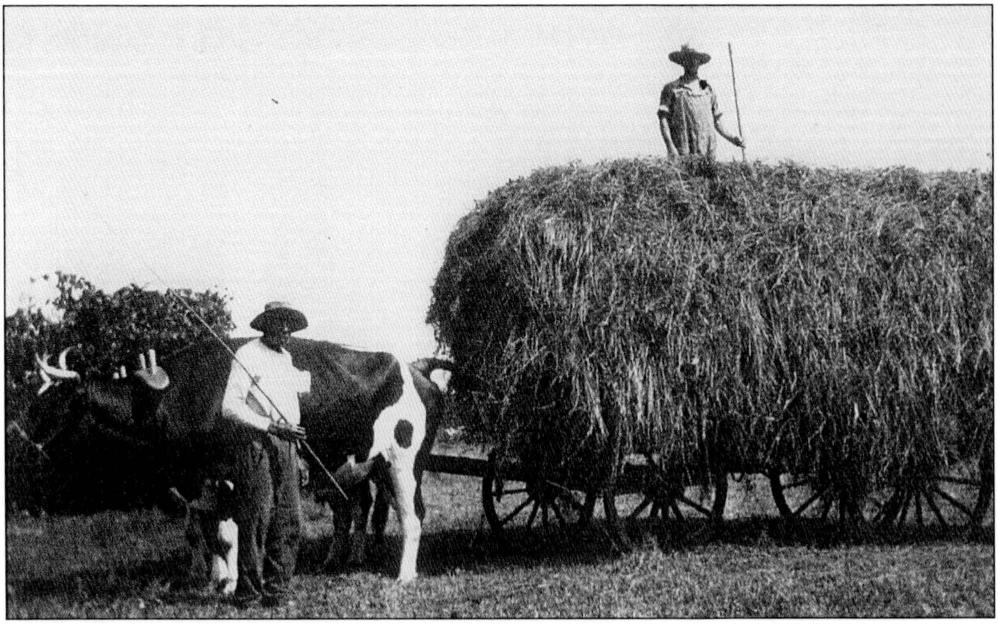

Many helping hands were needed to bring in the hay before it was rained upon and ruined—hence, the saying, "Make hay while the sun shines." These men are bringing in the hay in the 1920s on the Jones Tree Farm. Eventually, mechanical equipment replaced oxen.

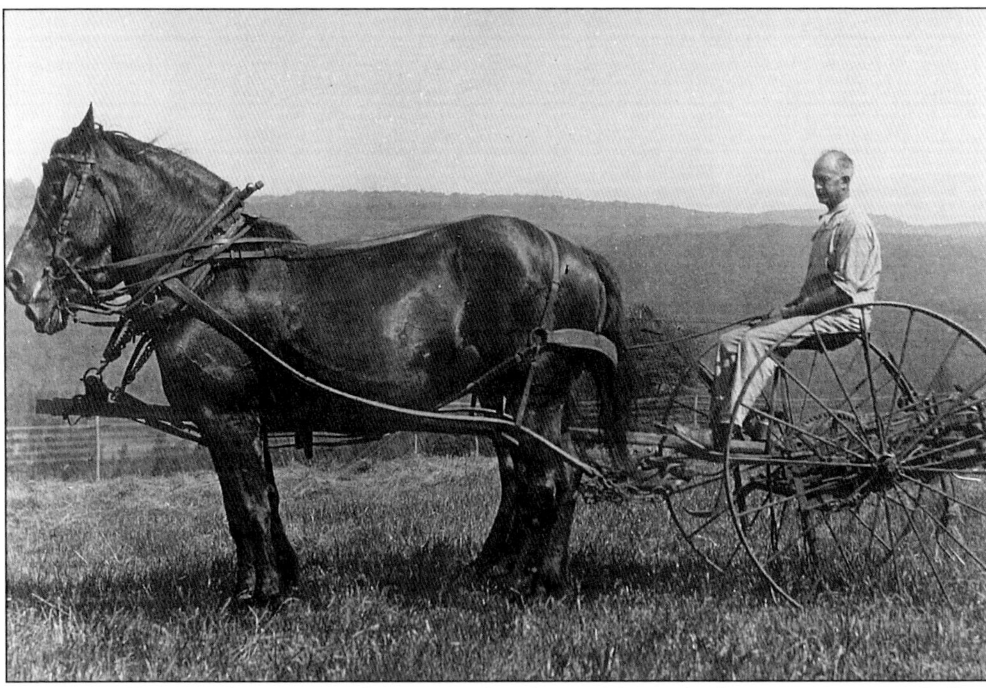

George Webb Burr of Bagburn Hill operates this "hay tedder," which was necessary to fluff, or "kick," the hay for drying. This would have been done several times a day for three days. Then it was raked into "windrows" to be picked up by the hay wagon. After this, it was safe to take the hay to the haymow. Green hay was very combustible and, when not properly dried, caused many a barn to burn down.

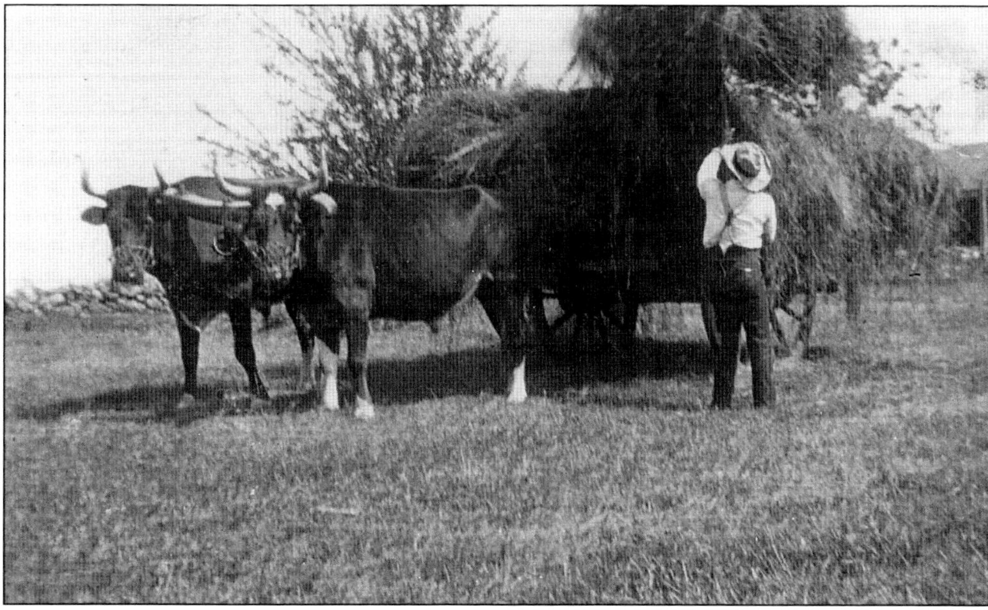

This farmer is "building" a load of hay on a two-wheeled cart drawn by oxen. Building a load of hay was an art that had to be carefully and patiently learned.

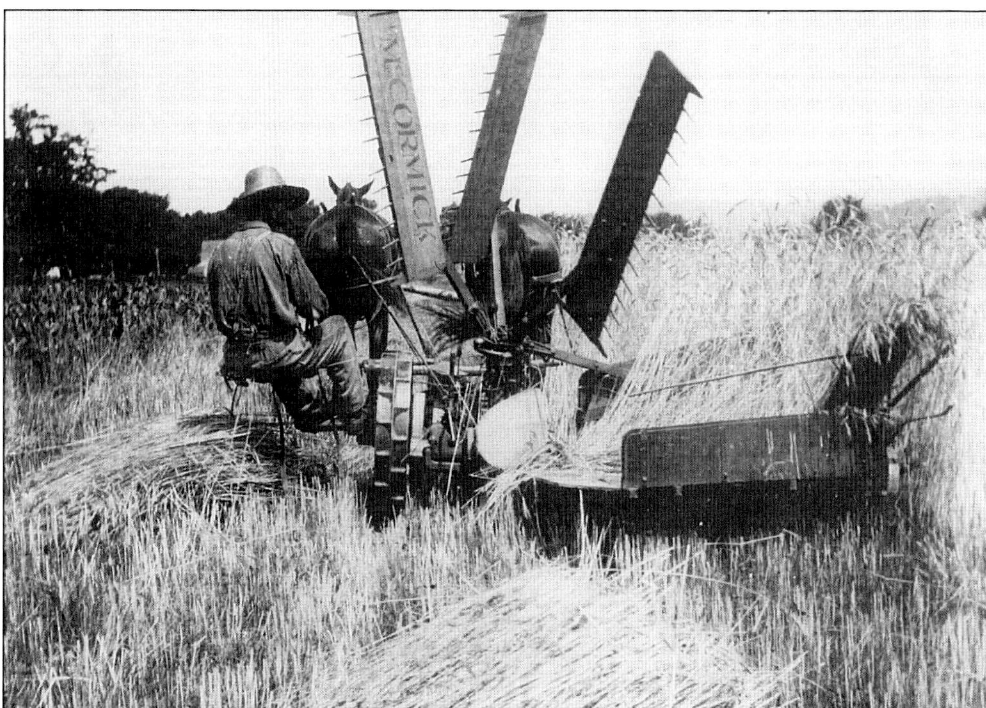

A McCormick threshing machine separated the grain from the stalk and then removed the chaff (pod) that covered it.

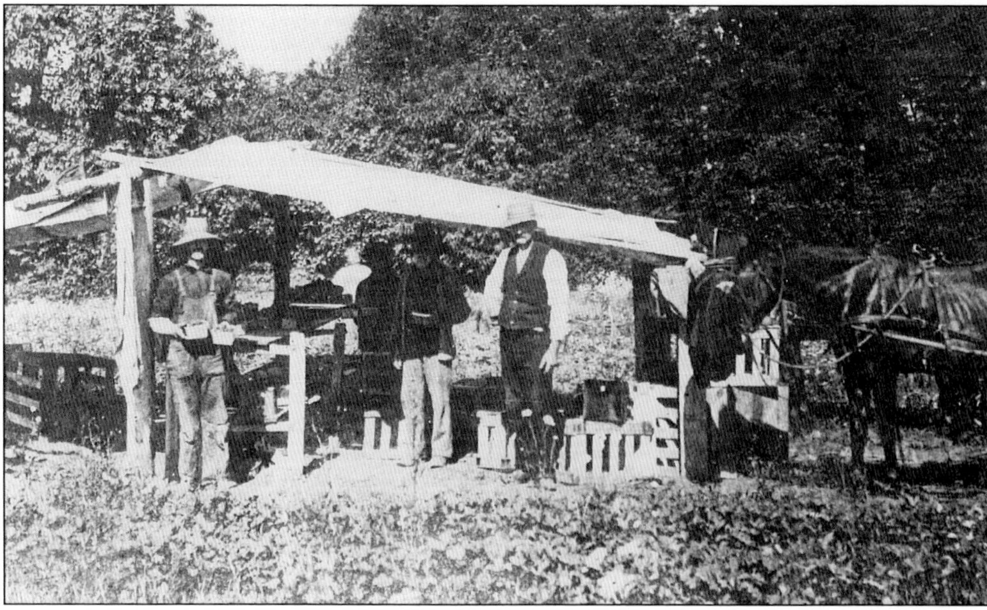

"Strawberry time in Monroe!" This shaded strawberry collection hut was at James Burr's Berry Farm on Elm Street. Thousands of quarts of berries a year supplied most of Fairfield County in the 1890s and early 1900s.

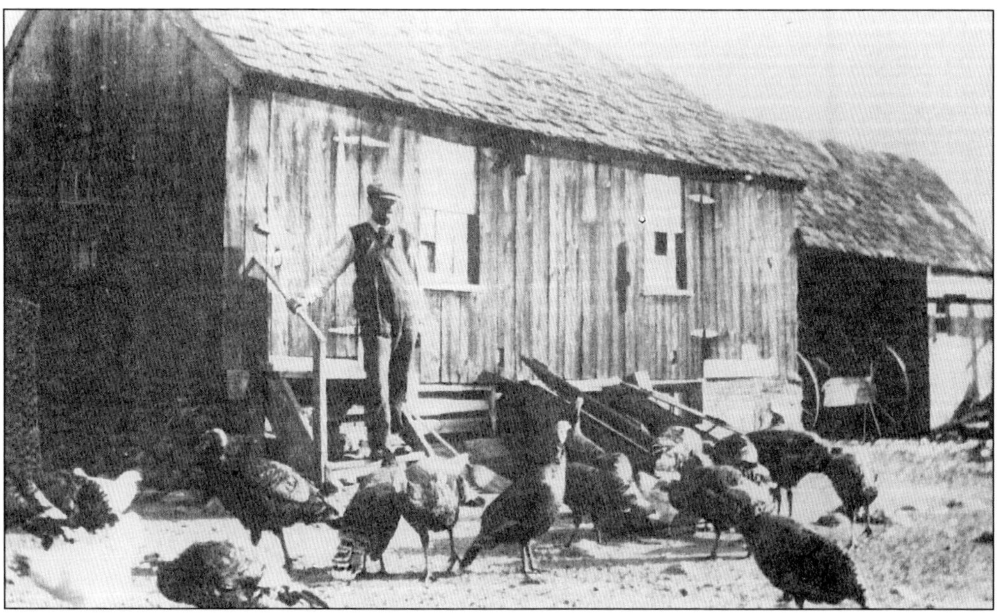

Henry Sherman tends his turkey flock. The Sherman place was on present-day Monroe Turnpike at Five Corners, now the site of the Monroe Post Office complex.

Six

Yesterday's Children

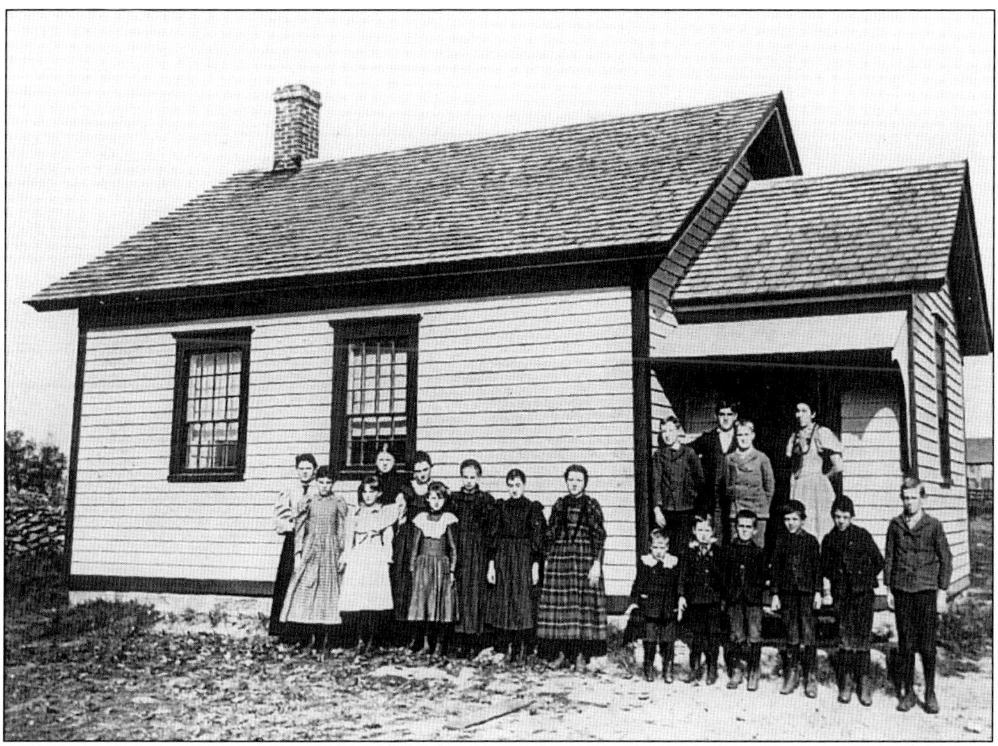

Cutler's Farm School (*c.* 1900) was a one-room schoolhouse where the older children helped the younger, and the faster taught the slower. Ready for the first day of school, the building is freshly painted, and the students and teacher are dressed in their new clothes. This old schoolhouse no longer exists.

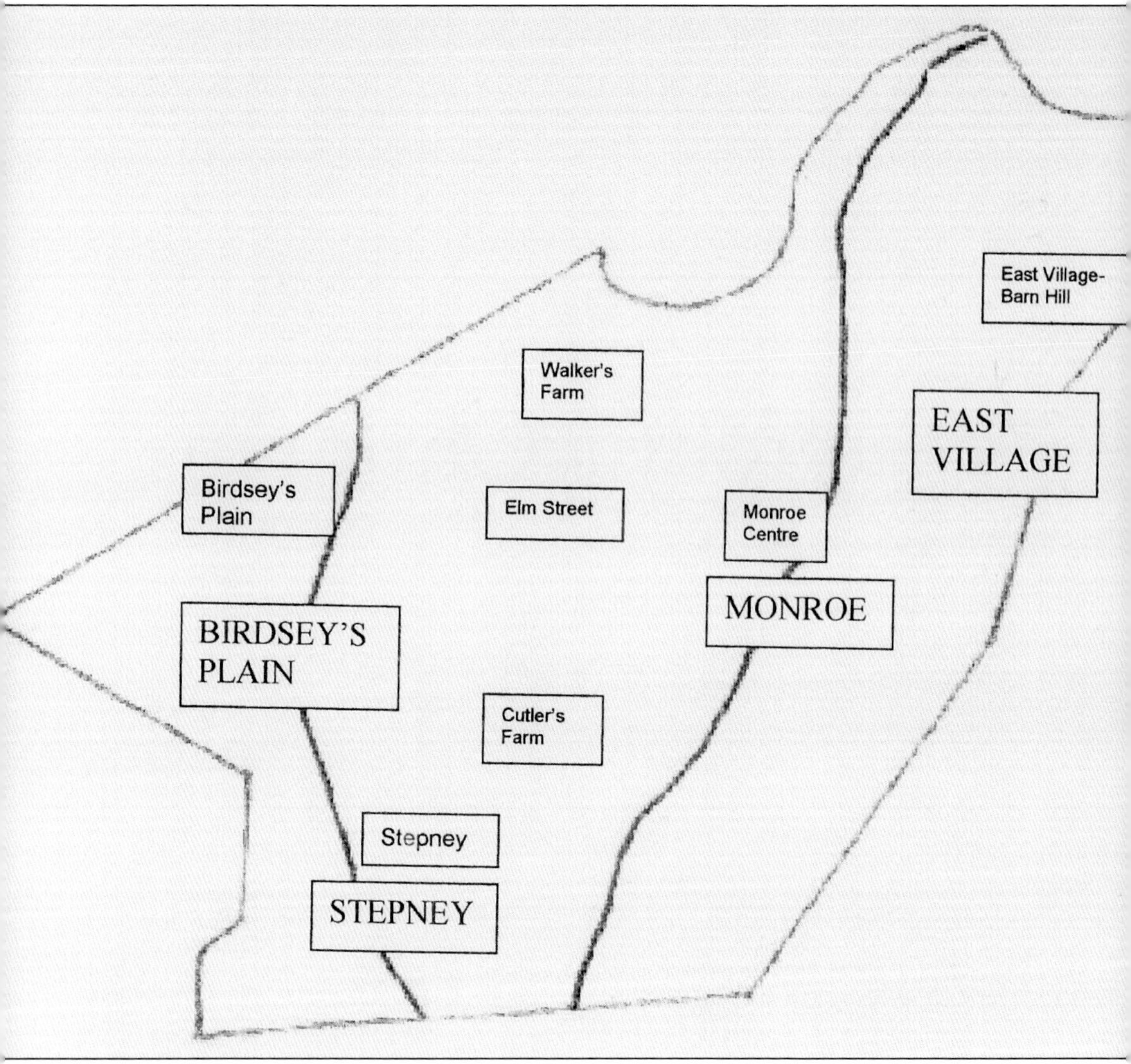

This map defines Monroe's seven school districts and the four principal areas of town.

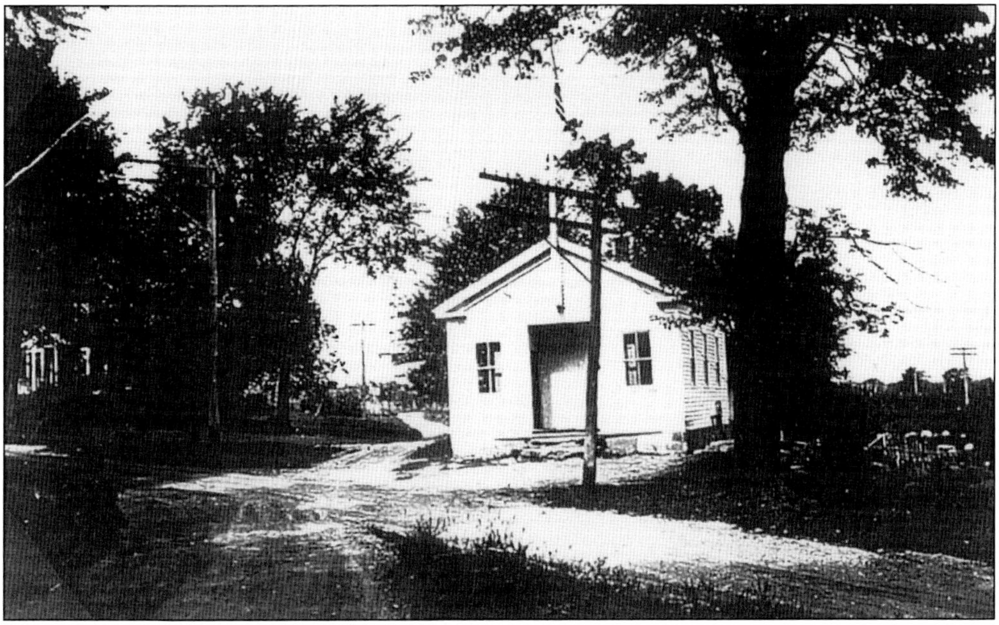

Monroe Centre School (*c.* 1908) was located at the intersection of Old Tannery Road and Wheeler Road. In 1935, when Monroe Consolidated School opened, all seven one- or two-room schoolhouses were sold at auction. This schoolhouse is now a classroom at the Monroe Congregational Church, where it was added on to Beardsley Hall.

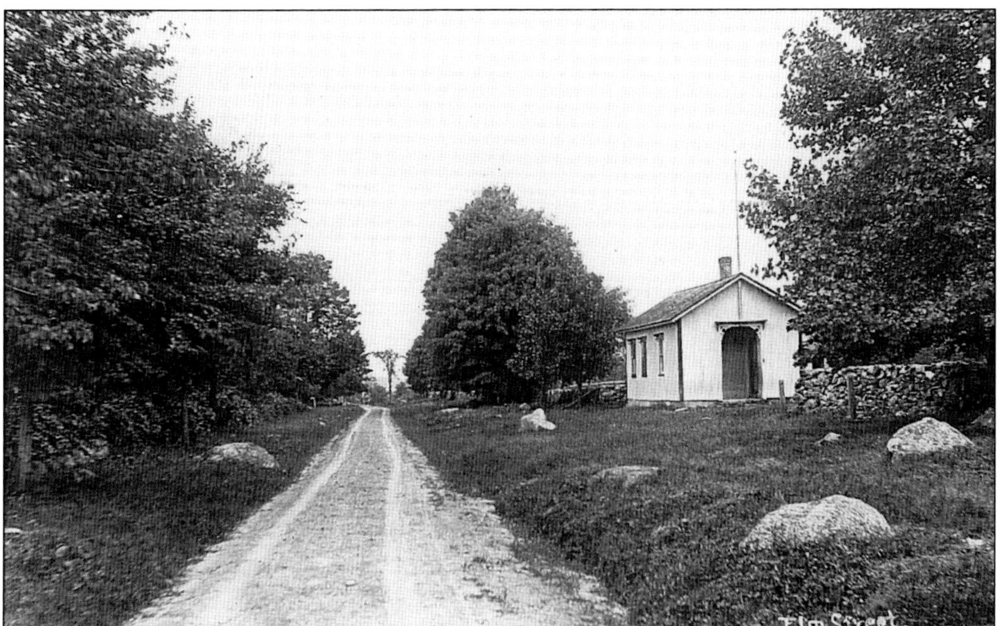

Stones from nearby farms were used to build the stone wall by Elm Street School. This schoolhouse is now part of a private home on the same site.

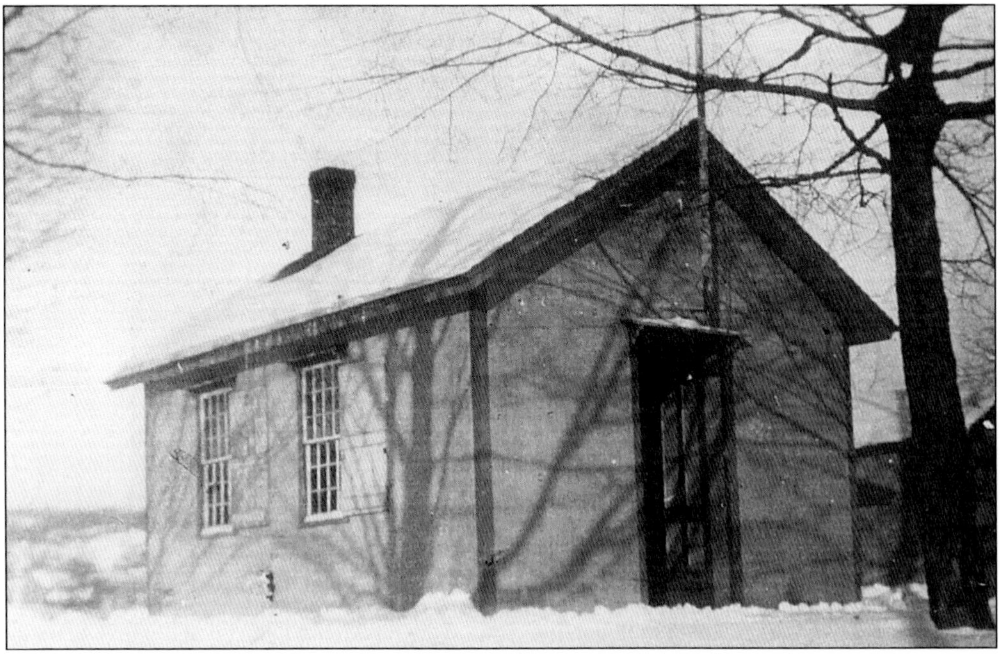

Walkers Farm School, on Hammertown Road near High Rock Road, was a two-room schoolhouse. In 1872, there were 47 students enrolled in this school. While children attended school in the summer and winter, they were needed on the farms in the spring and fall. This building is now part of a residence in the same location.

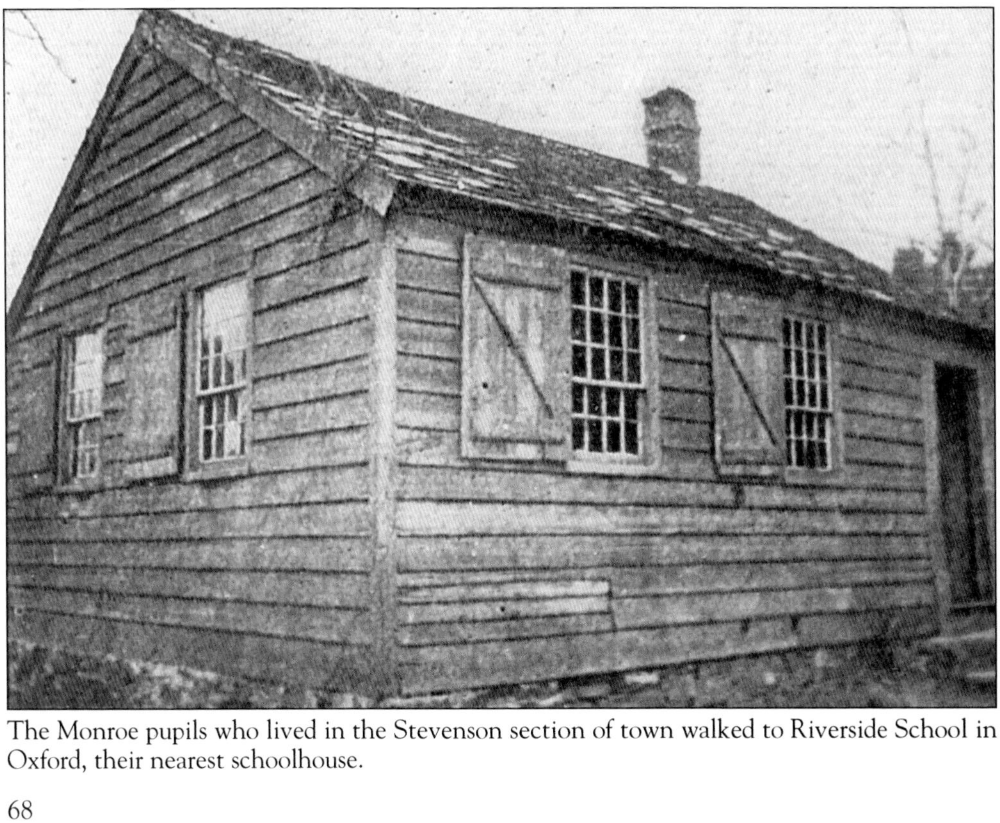

The Monroe pupils who lived in the Stevenson section of town walked to Riverside School in Oxford, their nearest schoolhouse.

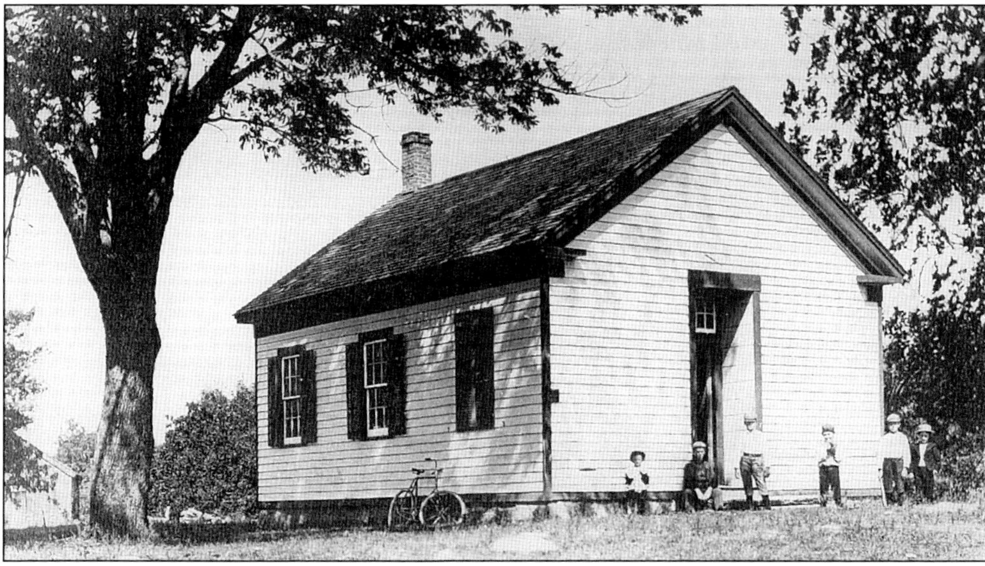

In the early 1900s, children at Stepney School enjoy their recess. Look for this schoolhouse when using the drive-through window at the Dutchess Restaurant in Stepney.

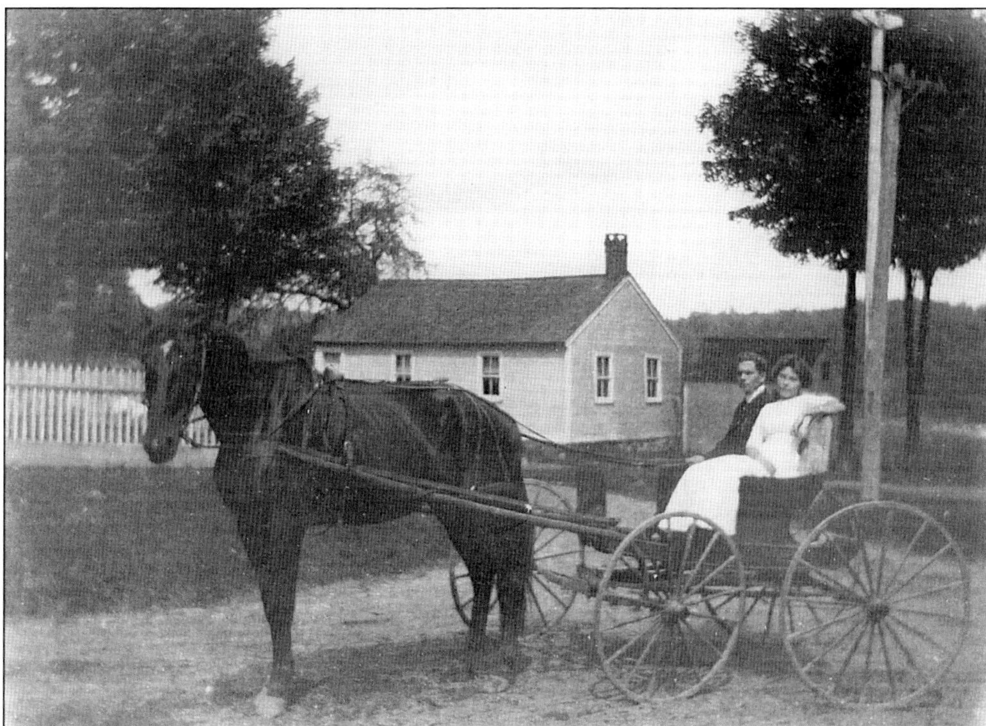

Teacher Vera Hubbell (Blakeman) and Herman Jacot share a quiet moment in the early 1900s at the East Village-Barn Hill Schoolhouse (c. 1790). In 1935, the East Village Methodist Church bought the school for $25 and moved it to the church grounds. It was used for Sunday school as well as church suppers. Later, it was donated to the Monroe Historical Society with the condition that the building be moved.

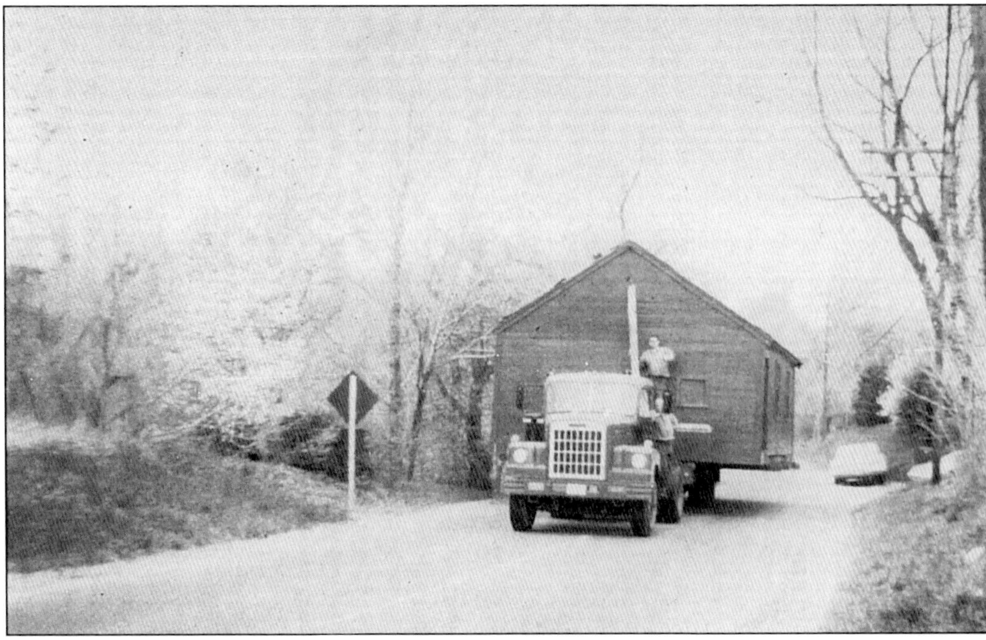

In 1969, the East Village Schoolhouse was moved from its original site to its present location on Wheeler Road and restored by the Monroe Historical Society. This shows the schoolhouse being moved to its current location.

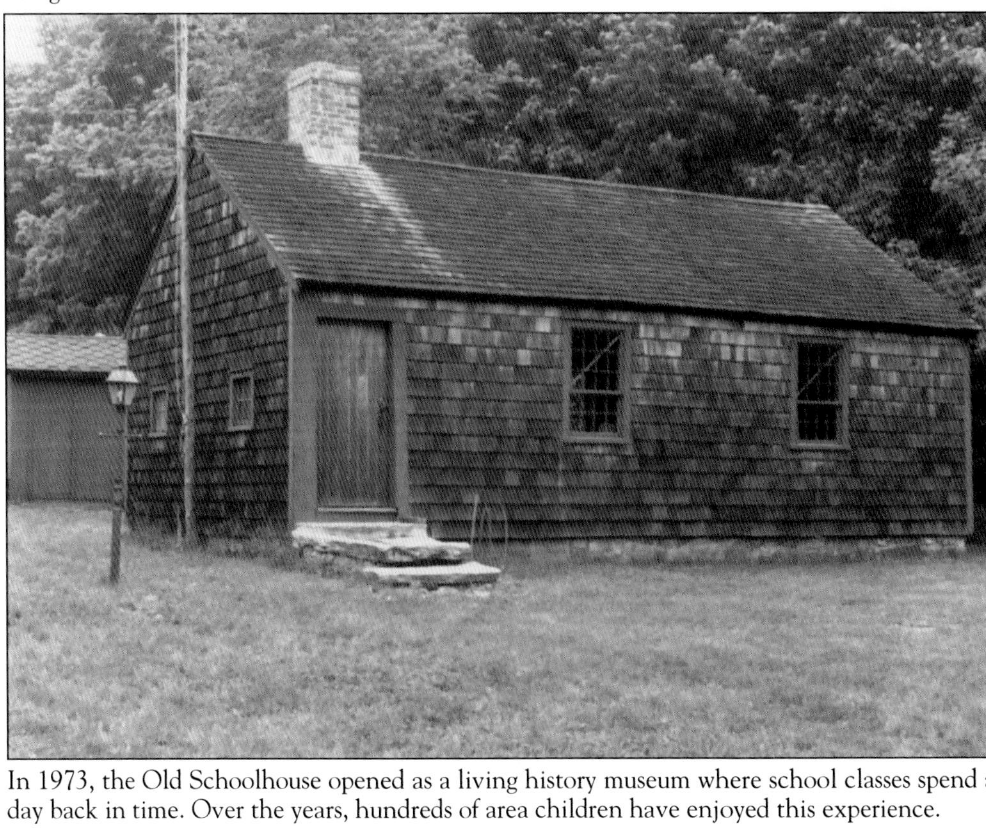

In 1973, the Old Schoolhouse opened as a living history museum where school classes spend a day back in time. Over the years, hundreds of area children have enjoyed this experience.

Elm Street residents Fannie (top image) and Jennie Burr (bottom image), daughters of James Burr, gained considerable recognition as artists. At a time when few educational opportunities were offered to women, Jennie attended Mount Holyoke College for two years. Both Fannie and Jennie studied at the Yale School of Art and the Art Students League in New York City.

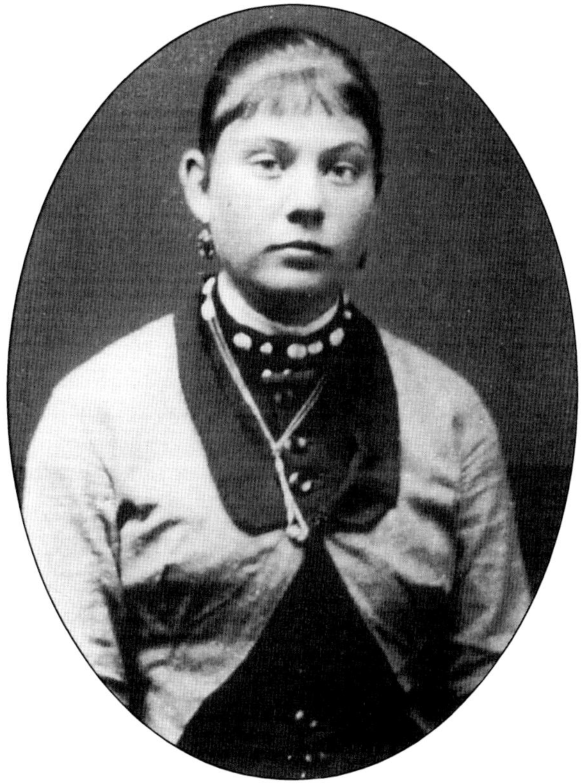

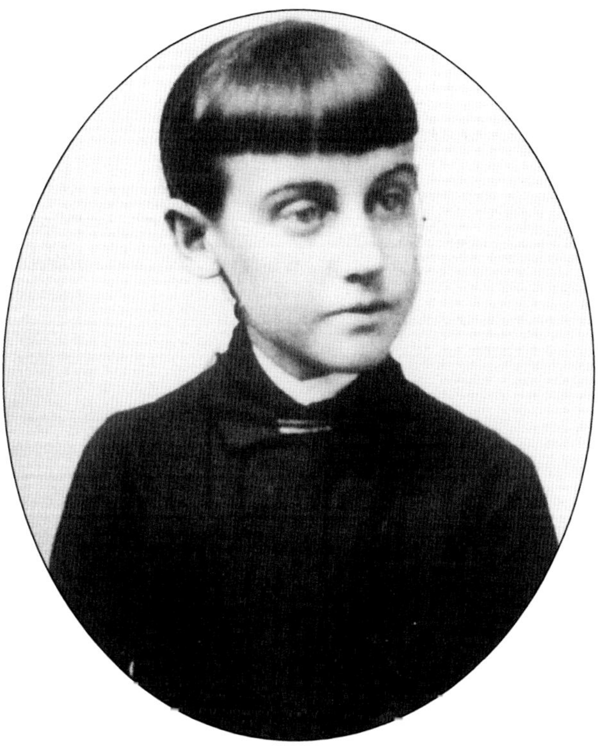

Extensive correspondence between the two sisters during their early years presents a clear picture of the role of women in that time period. In 1990, a major exhibit of their paintings was held at the New Britain Museum of American Art, winning wide recognition for their work.

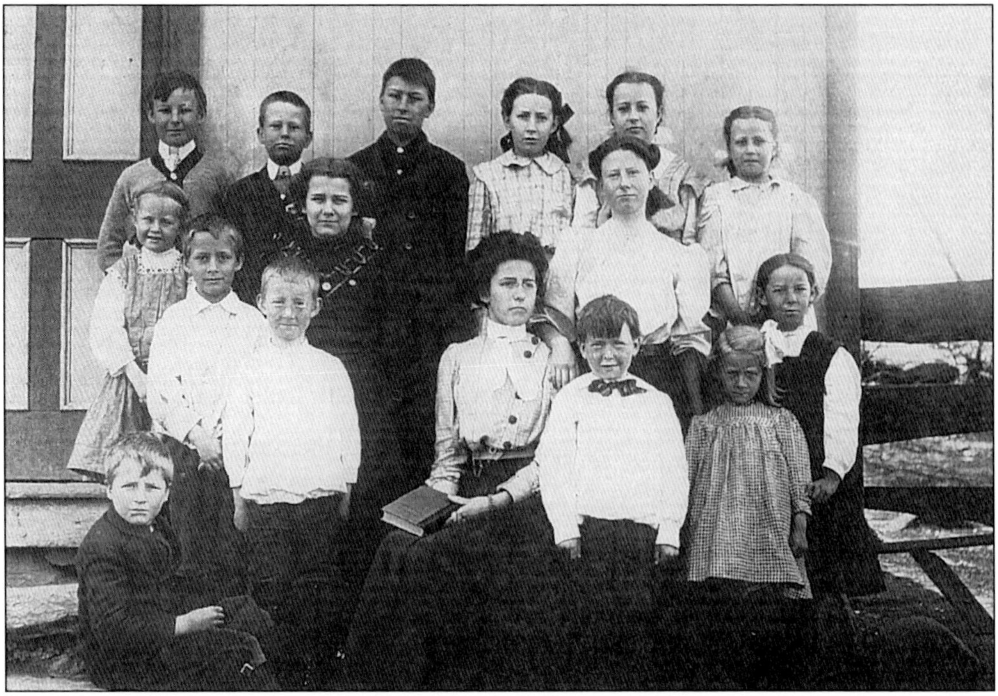

This turn-of-the-century teacher poses with her pupils at Halfway River School. Often the schoolteacher boarded with families in the district as a part of his/her salary. Monroe students and also those in neighboring Oxford and Newtown attended this school.

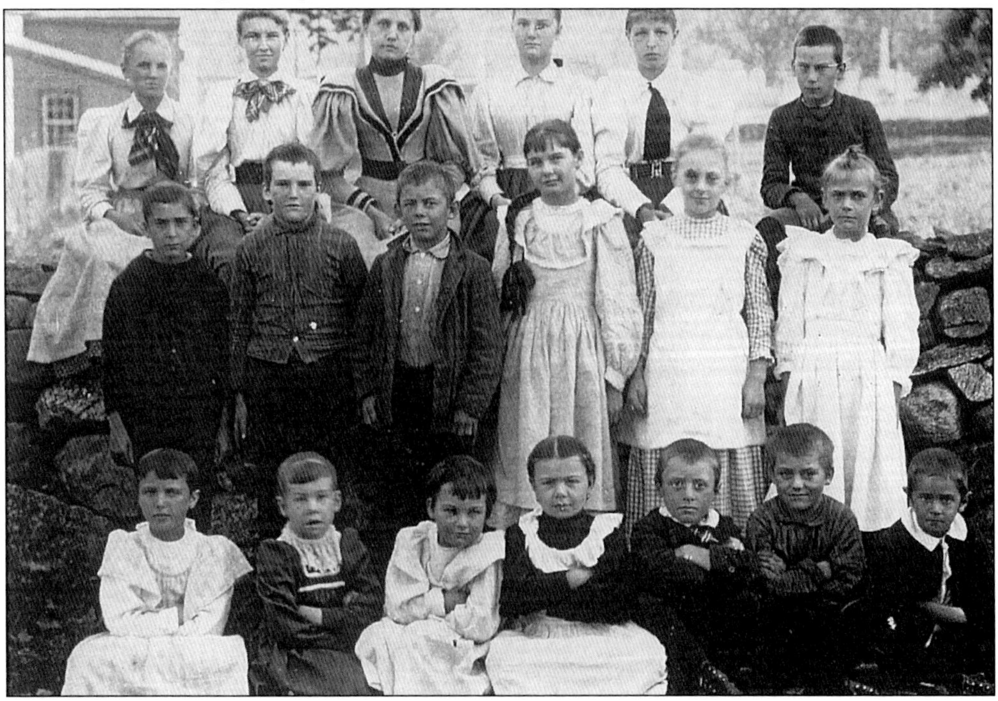

Families in East Village sent their children to East Village School, where Alice Pope was teacher in 1895.

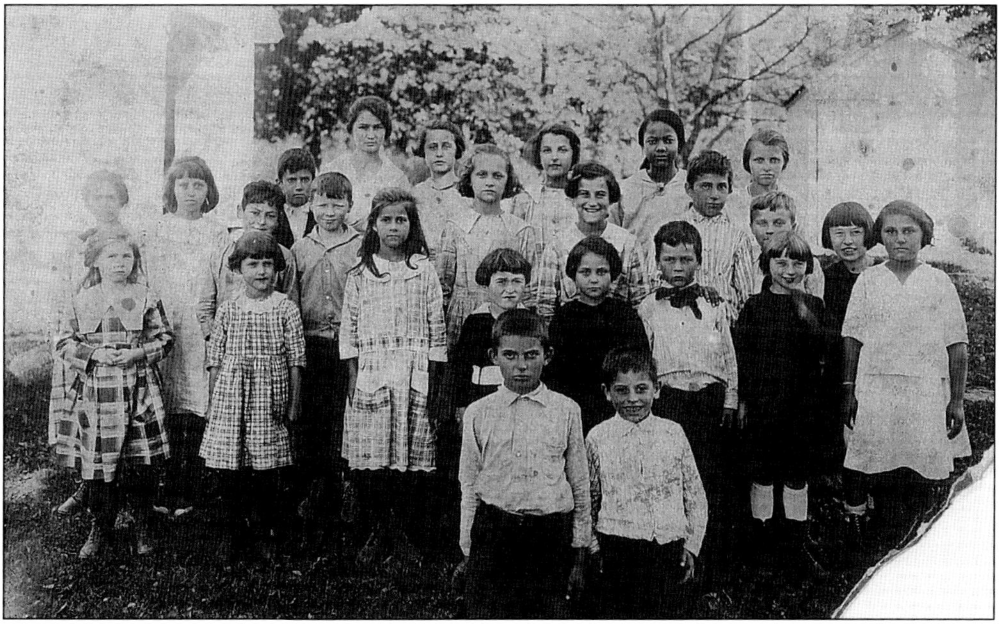

Longtime residents of Monroe remember Bessie Smick as their teacher at Monroe Elementary School. Here she is pictured (second from the far right in the second row) at Cutler's Farm School (*c.* 1915). She later became principal at Stepney Elementary School.

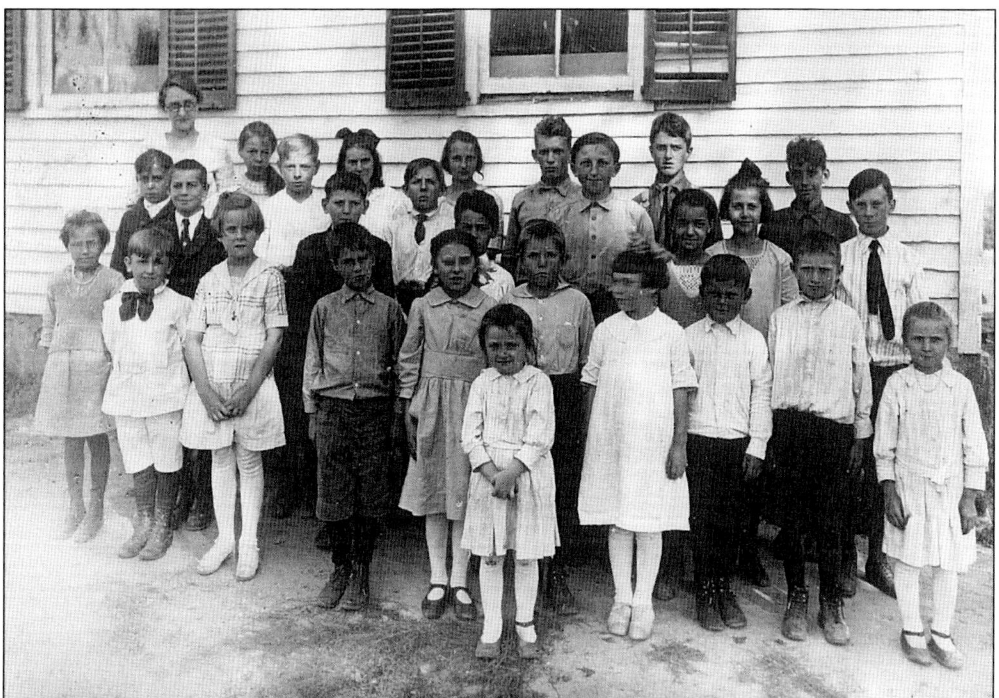

Teacher Alice Beardsley poses with her students of varying ages at Monroe Centre School (*c.* 1920).

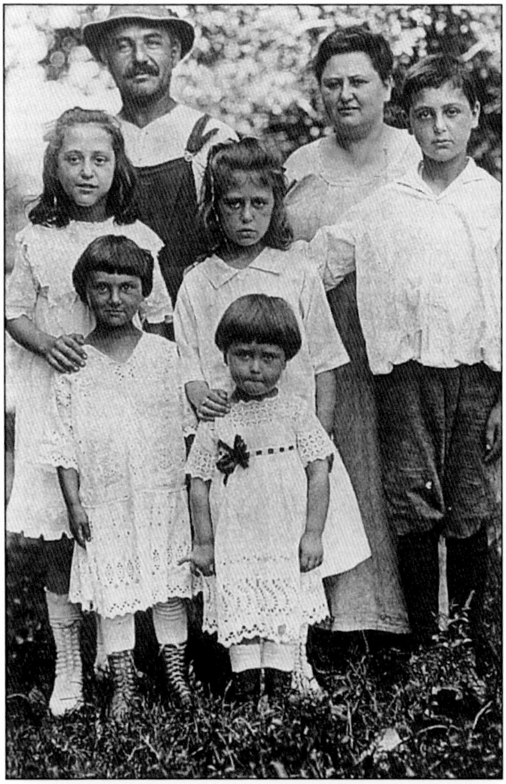

The Loss family emigrated from Russia in the early 1900s. Max and Ida Loss are pictured here with their children, Rose, Lillian, Bertha, Bessie, and Irving. Max and Ida were the owners of the Stepney Elm House, a popular summer vacation retreat.

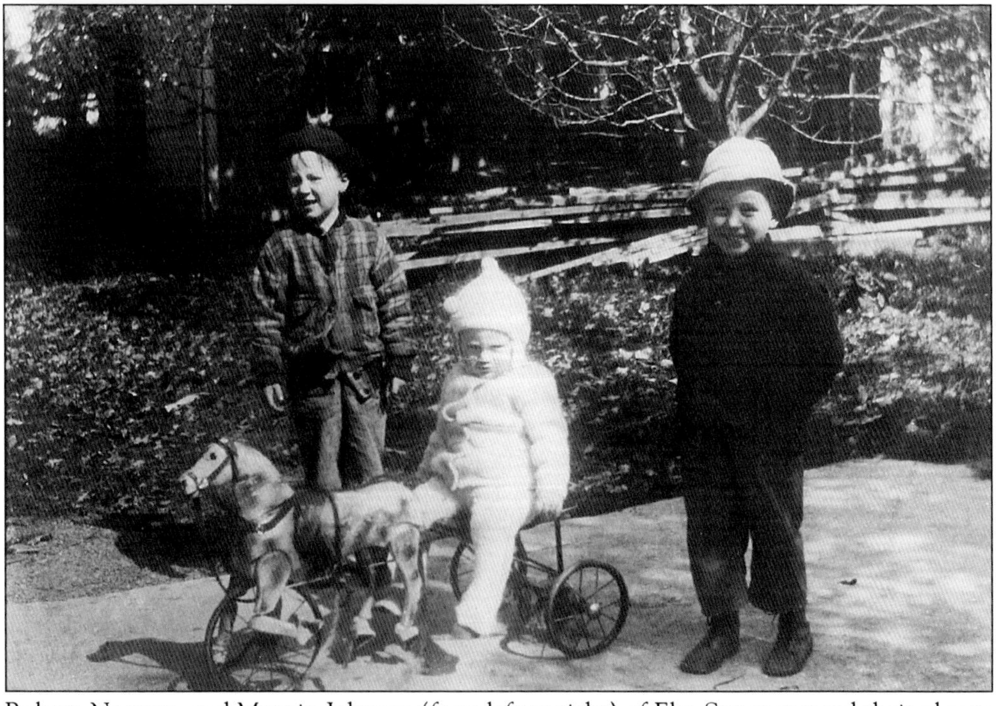

Robert, Norman, and Merwin Johnson (from left to right) of Elm Street stopped their play to have this picture taken (*c.* 1929).

Grace Smith (Stevens) and Herbert Hurd Johnson pose in their "best" clothes. These formal photographs were treasured by their families. Grace was the daughter of Arthur W. Smith and Eliza Jane Sherwood.

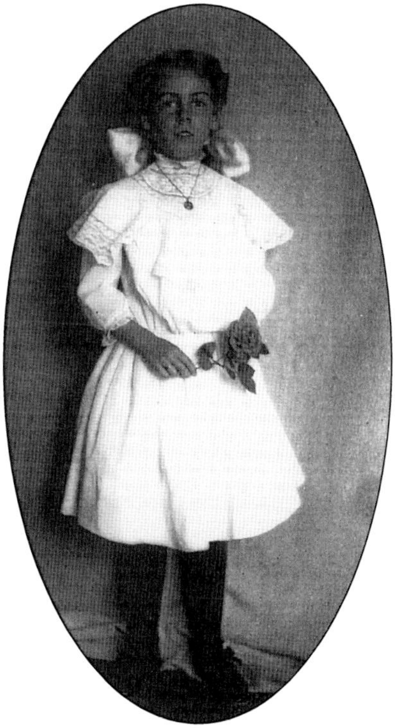

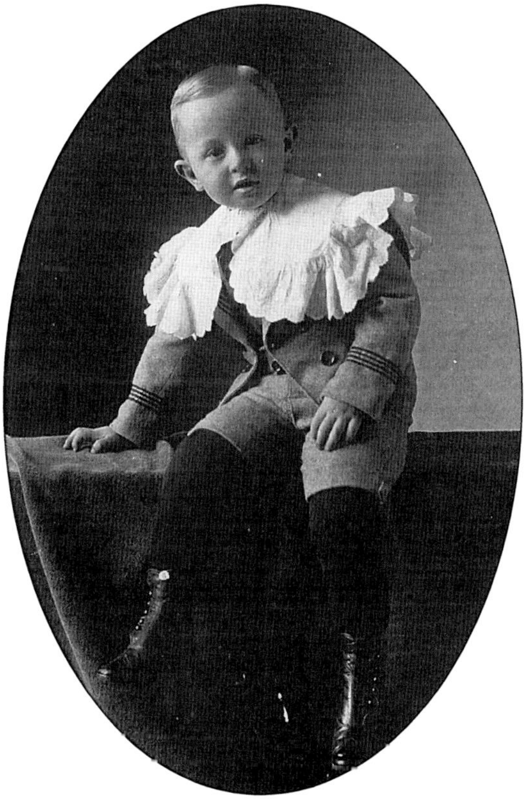

Herbert Hurd Johnson was the son of Merwin and Martha Hurd Johnson. Both the Johnson and the Stevens families are longtime Monroe residents.

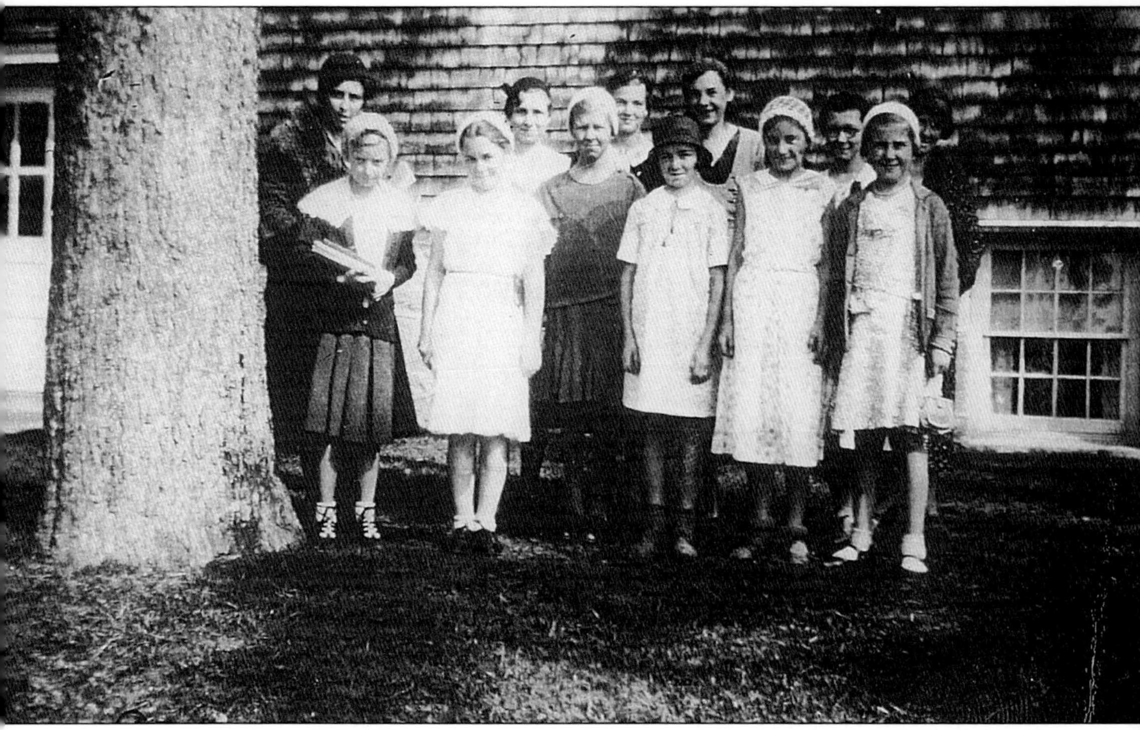

Education took place in other settings besides the public school. This Sunday school class is at St. Peter's-on-the-Green in the late 1920s. Those pictured are Mrs. Earl Lewis, Myra Eastwood, Beatrice Hawley, Lillian Nichols, Margery Swendsen, Beverly Mix, Barbara Jones, Miss Norton, Alice Habersham, Faye Hawley, Marie Swendsen, and Mrs. Philip Jones.

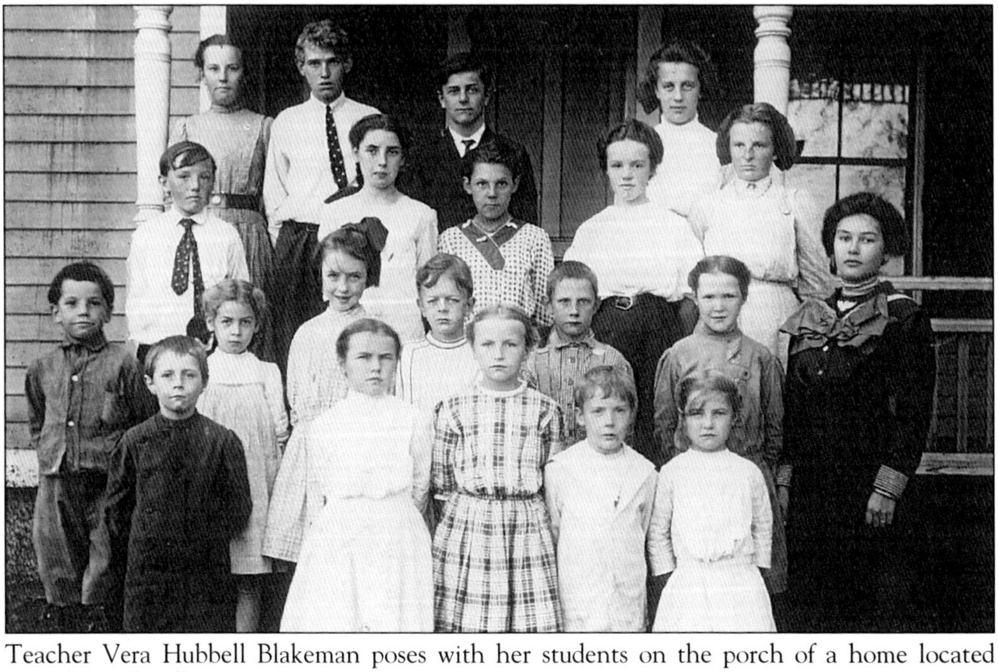

Teacher Vera Hubbell Blakeman poses with her students on the porch of a home located near their schoolhouse.

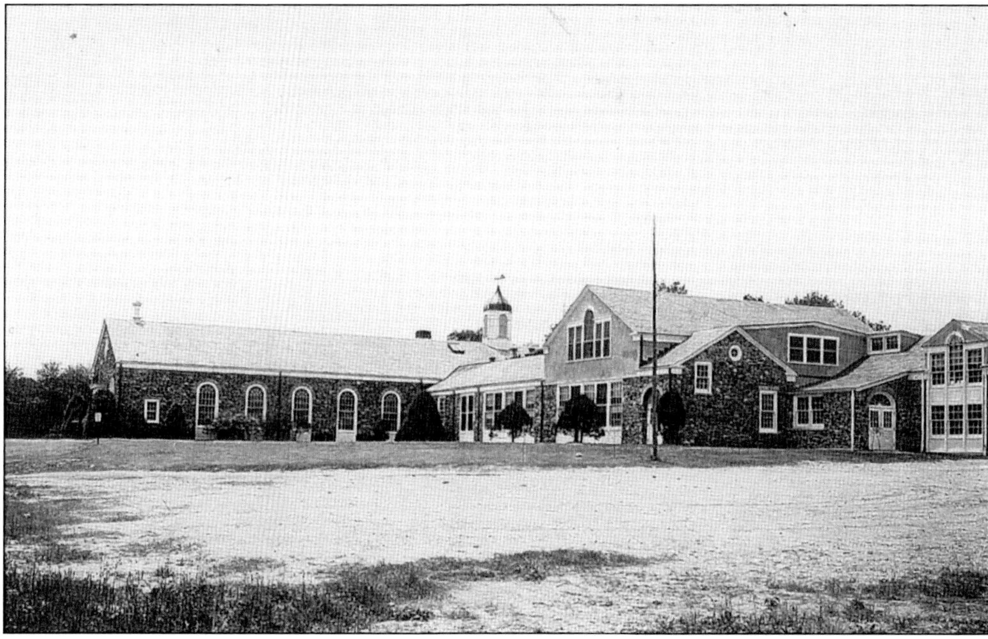

Monroe Consolidated School, built out of local fieldstone, was opened in 1935. The funding for this was provided through a government program, the WPA (Works Projects Administration). The seven district one- and two-room schools and their contents were auctioned to raise funds for classroom materials for the new school. This photograph was taken after additions were built.

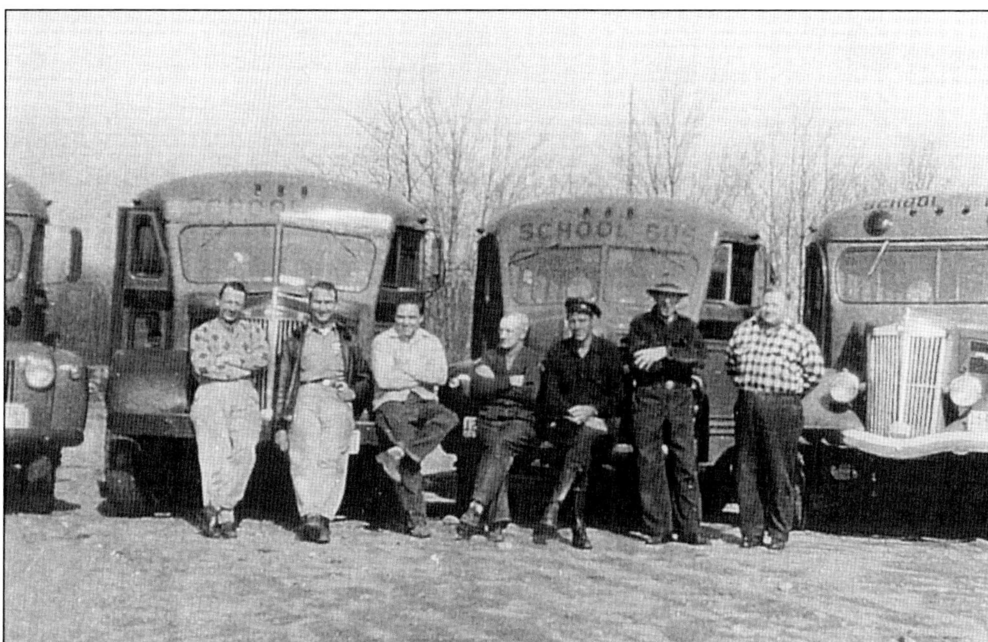

It was wonderful no longer having to walk to school! School bus drivers drove the students to Monroe Consolidated School as well as to high school in Bridgeport. In 1935, teachers earned $85 a month, and the bus drivers were paid about twice that amount.

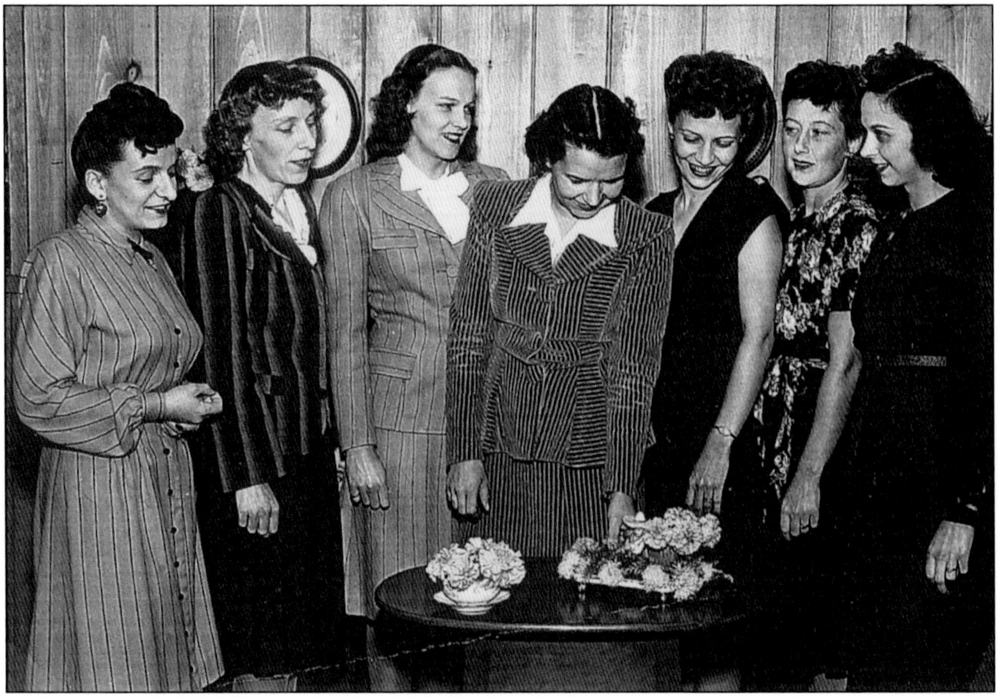

The Monroe Mothers' Club (first called the "Busy Mothers' Club") was instrumental in the establishment of kindergarten instruction for our children. From left to right are Helen Nelson, Ann Hancox, Eleanor Lewis, Allie Tramposch, Eileen DeLong, Grace Renz, and Patty Schultz, pictured in the 1940s.

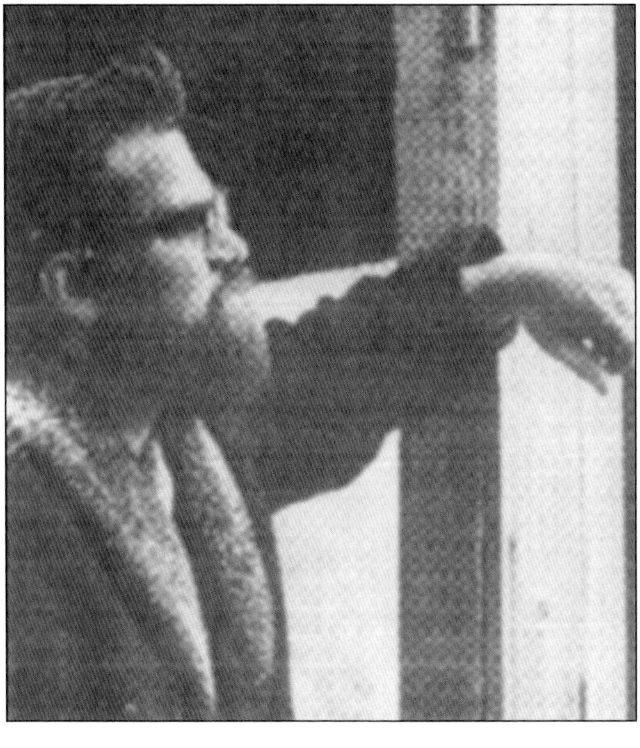

David Merrill, who spent his childhood in Monroe, has gained recognition for his landscapes. His paintings capture the essence of rural New England.

Seven

Around Our Greens

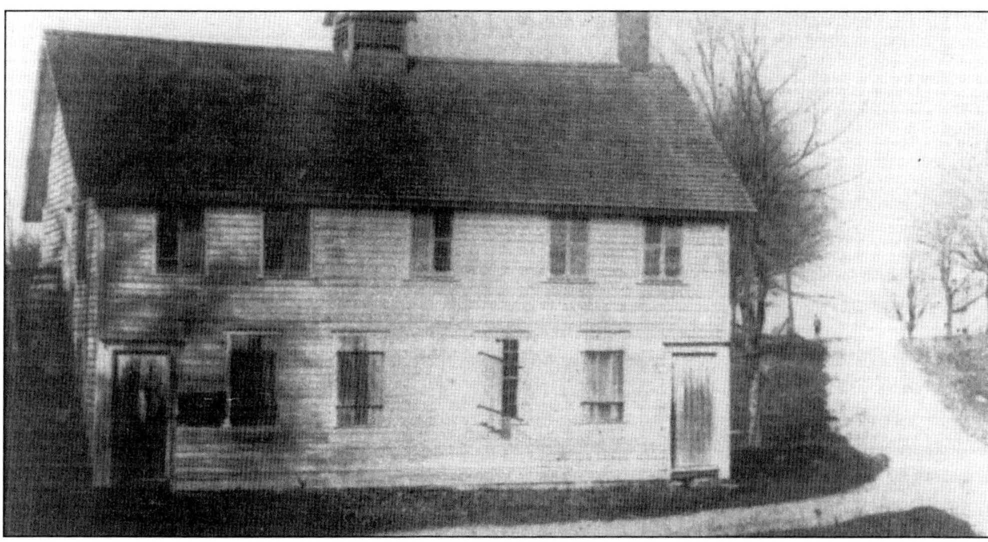

This building, constructed in 1799–1800 as a Masonic Temple, was Monroe's first town house. On the second floor were Masonic meeting rooms. The first floor was rented to Dr. Beardsley's Academy and to Hazel Hall, a well-known nineteenth-century Monroe private school. After 1823, the building served as Monroe's first town house until the "new town hall" was erected in 1896–97. The structure was taken down in 1977 after being used as a garage at another site for many years.

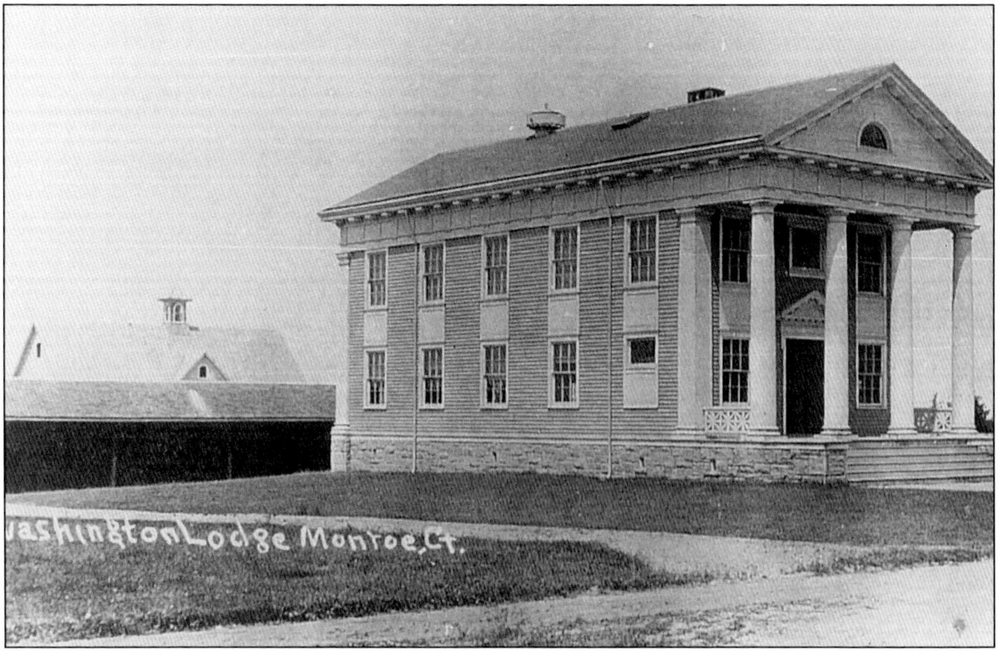

Washington Lodge #19, Monroe's oldest fraternal organization, was formed in 1791 with nine members. This second Masonic Temple, dedicated in 1904, is said to have been designed after the center section of the White House.

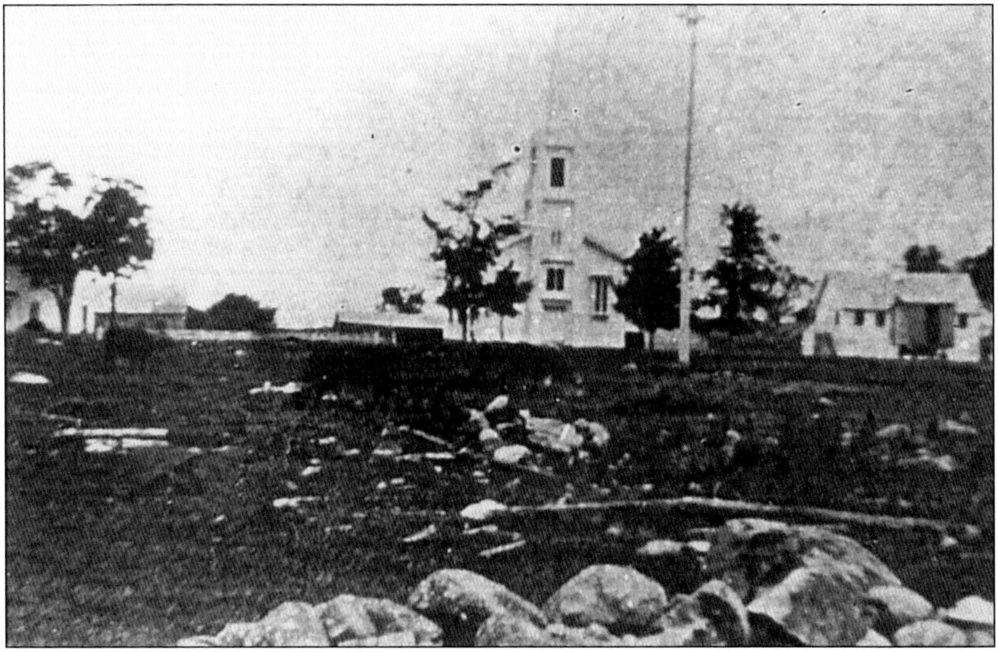

Earliest records show that Monroe Centre Green was known as "Brushy Ring." The militia used it for mustering, and it was the site of the Monroe Centre Town Pound kept by Nehemiah deForest. In 1870, the two churches on the Green formed an association and purchased more land from neighbors to expand the Green. The purchase was financed by early strawberry festivals.

Looking very dapper, Frederick W. Wheeler, first selectman, waits with his horses and shay in front of St. Peter's Episcopal Church. The shay was a widely used form of transportation, whether going to church, going visiting, or going wherever one needed.

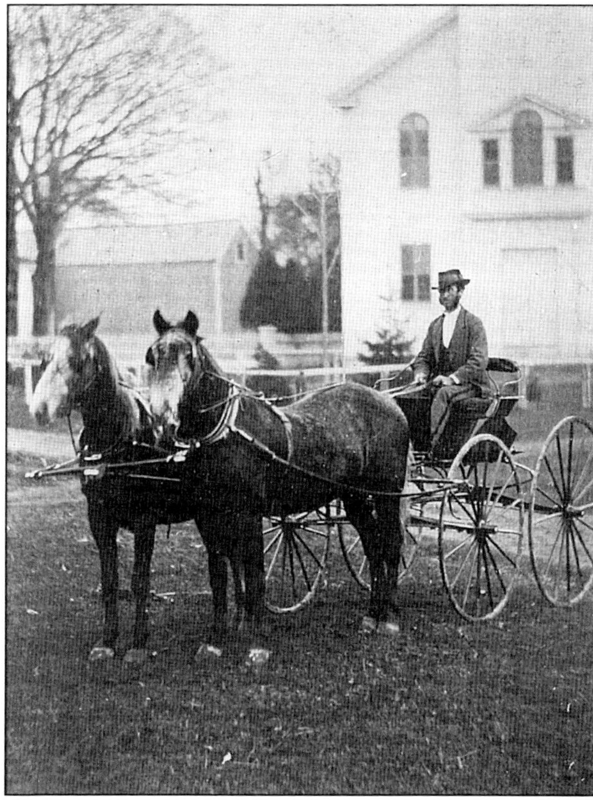

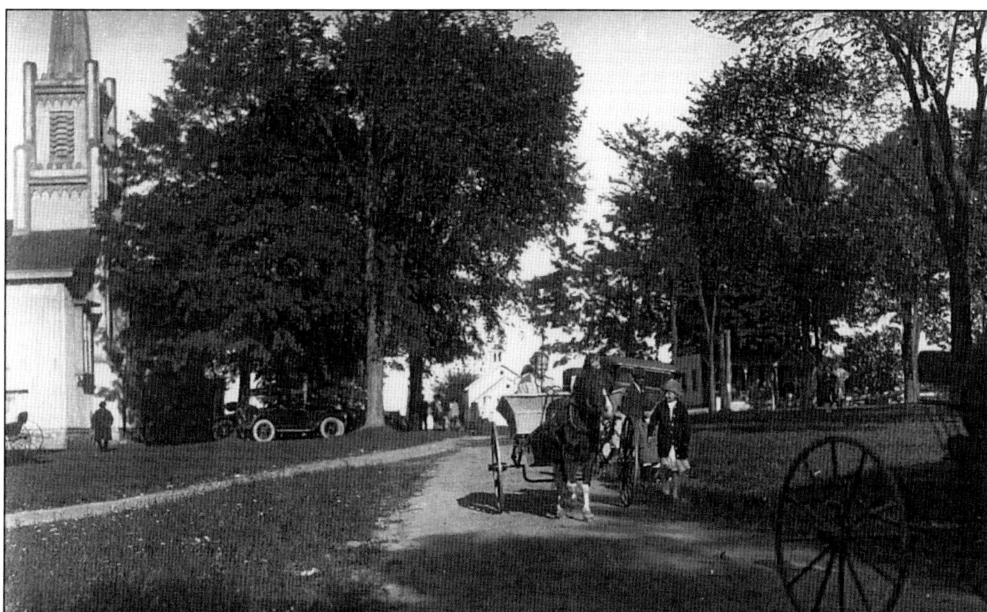

Perhaps this pony cart at the Monroe Green was going to Sunday services. The early automobile on the left was an indication of changing times.

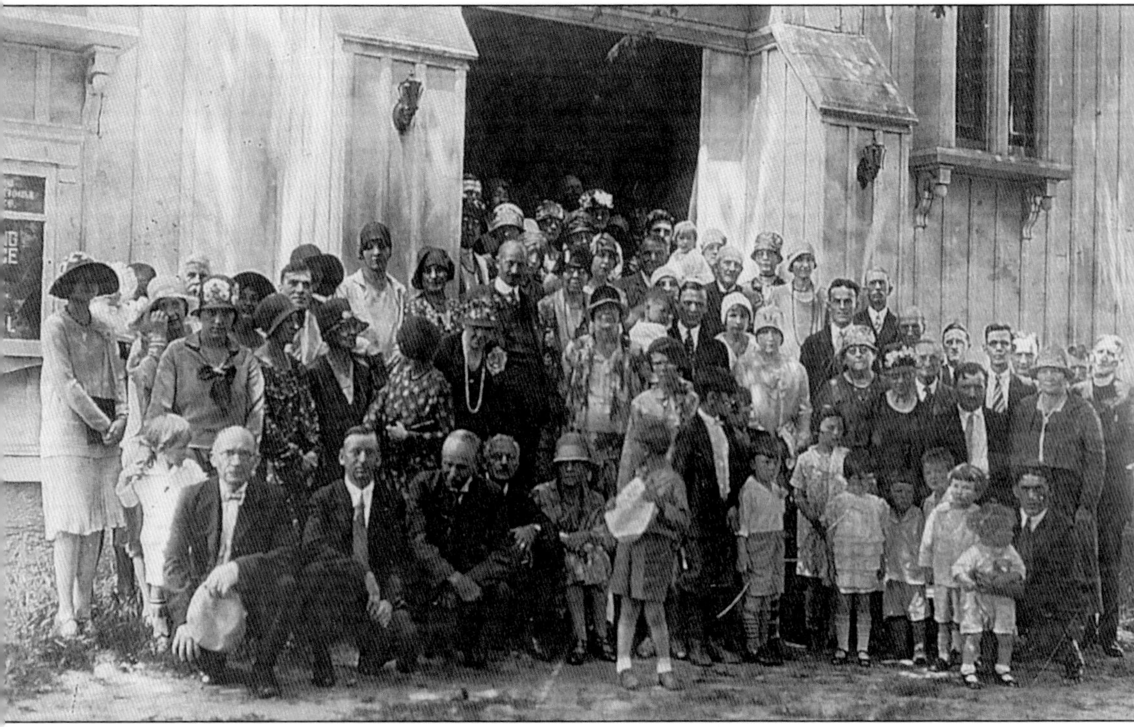

The members of the Monroe Congregational Church gather for an annual photograph. Parishioners of all ages spill out of the doorway to be included in the picture. Note the variety of ladies' hats.

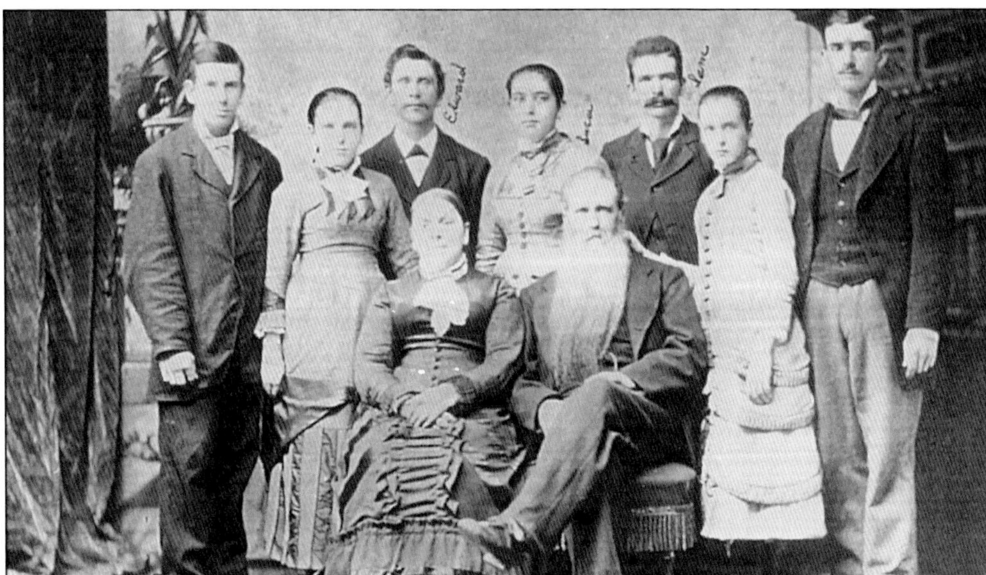

This family portrait shows the Dr. Edward M. Beardsley family. The original section of Beardsley Hall was erected in 1886 when Mrs. Elizabeth Beardsley contributed the financial help and leadership to have the church building erected in memory of her husband, the late Dr. Edward McEwen Beardsley, who was the town's physician.

The New Stratford Church (Monroe Congregational), founded in 1764, was the first church established in Monroe. That same year, the Reverend Elisha Rexford was called to be its first pastor, a position he served at for 44 years until his death in 1808, the longest pastorate in Monroe to date. A learned man, the Reverend Mr. Rexford was an educator, a Revolutionary War chaplain, and a highly respected friend to all.

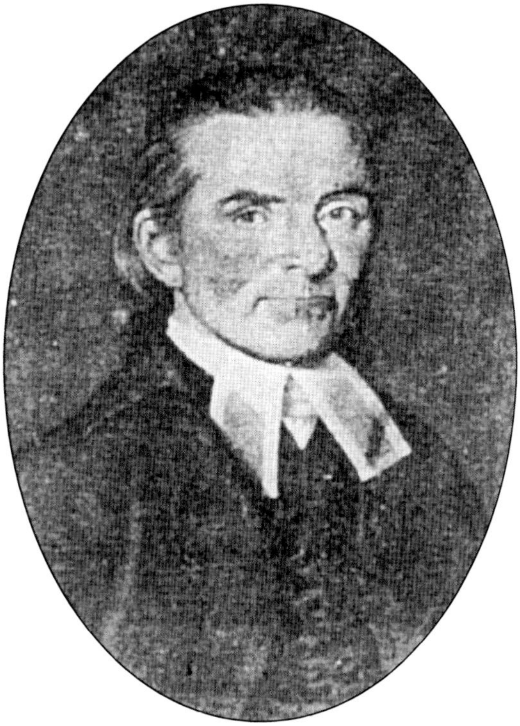

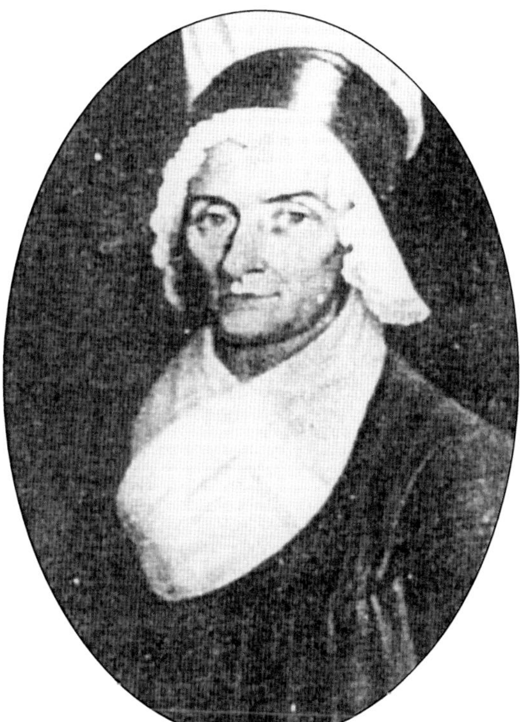

Rexford House, on the Congregational church grounds, is a tribute to the Reverend Rexford's many years of service both to the church and to the community. He and his wife, Sarah (Lewis) Rexford, are depicted here in portraits painted in 1799.

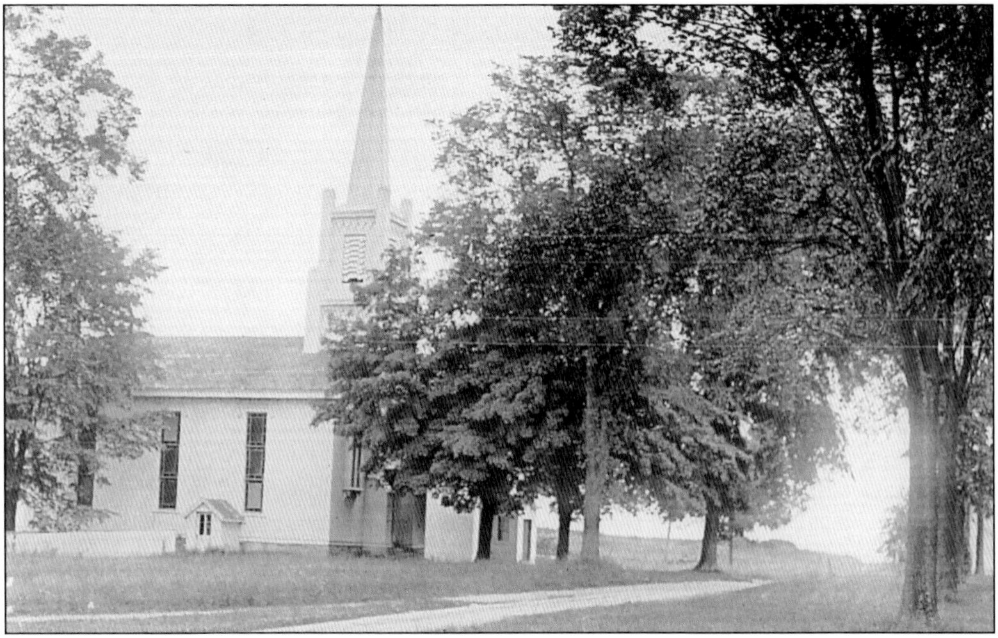

The "second" Monroe Congregational Church is pictured in an early photograph. Gothic in design, its steeple reaches toward heaven. Since there were no bells, at first members were called by the roll of a drum.

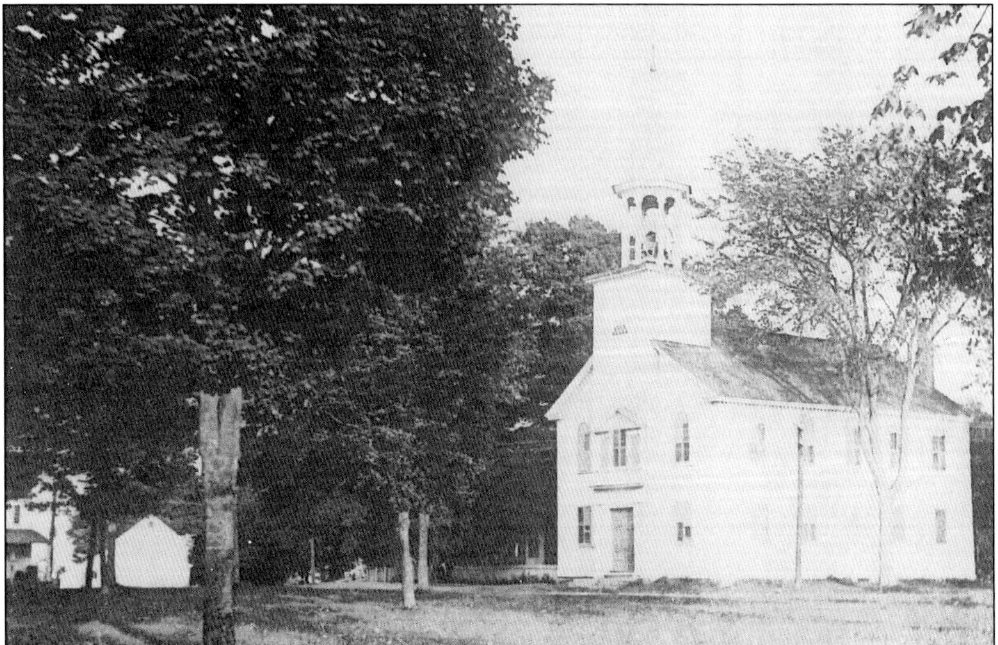

Construction was begun on St. Peter's Episcopal Church-on-the-Green in 1801. Today it is Monroe's oldest standing house of worship, the second oldest in Fairfield County. This 1910 view shows the church before it was raised, and social rooms were added to the basement.

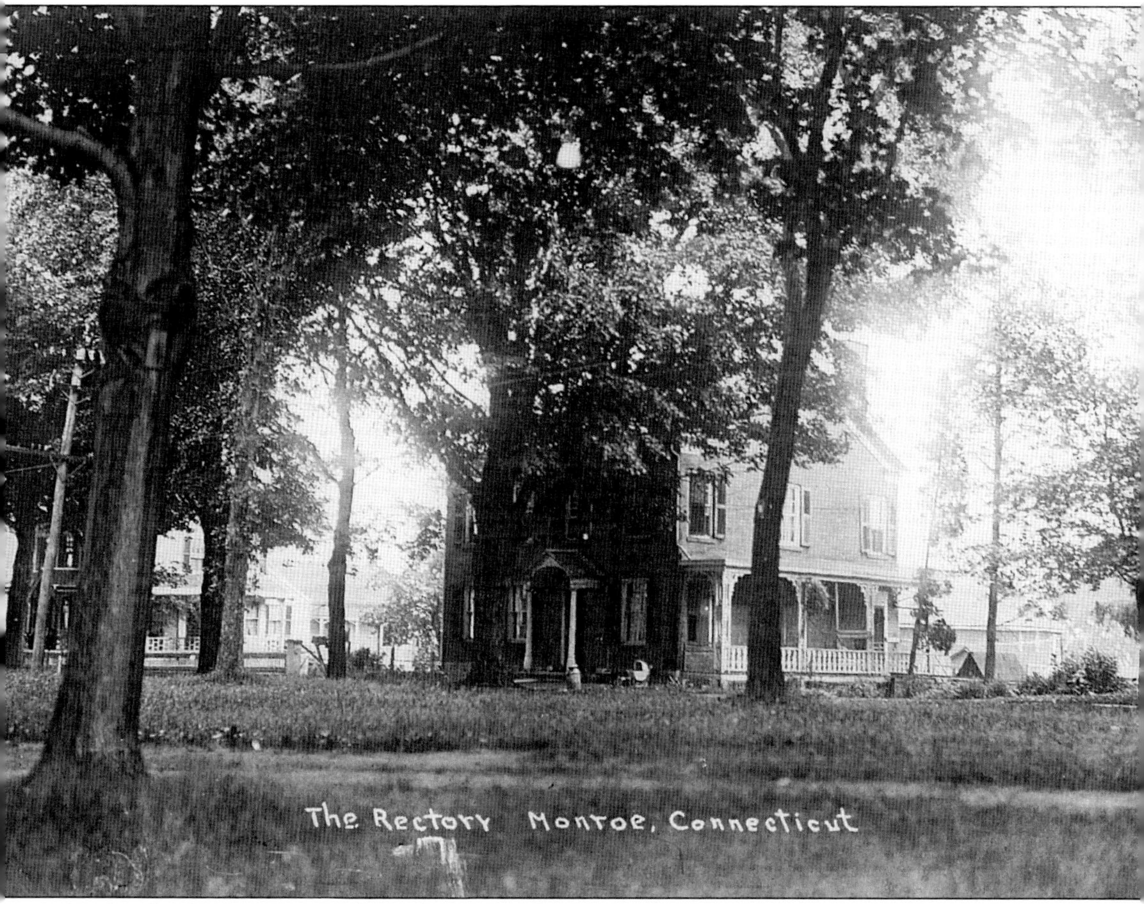

This fine brick Georgian residence bordering the town green has experienced numerous lives, both ecclesiastical and secular. Built in the 1820s, the house has been an early school of the classical tradition known as Gray's Academy, the St. Peter's Episcopal Rectory, an attorney's office, and, presently, the rectory for St. Jude's Catholic Church. In a 1970s renovation, a wall was removed in the living room, exposing a massive fireplace and bringing the total fireplaces to nine. Finely carved woodwork and mantles have been carefully preserved. In the basement great ovens were used to bake for the academy students.

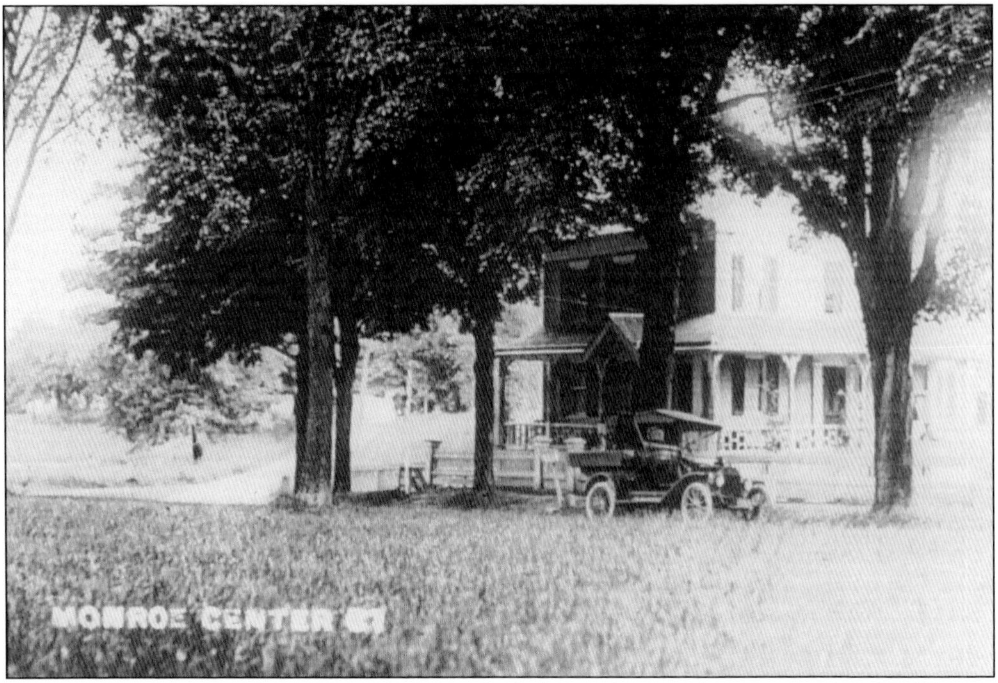

This early photograph shows the Clarke-Nichols house (*c.* 1827), an example of half-house architecture, built by John Clarke. The eighteenth-century store of Captain Joseph Moss stood on this site at the corner of Church Street and Monroe Turnpike.

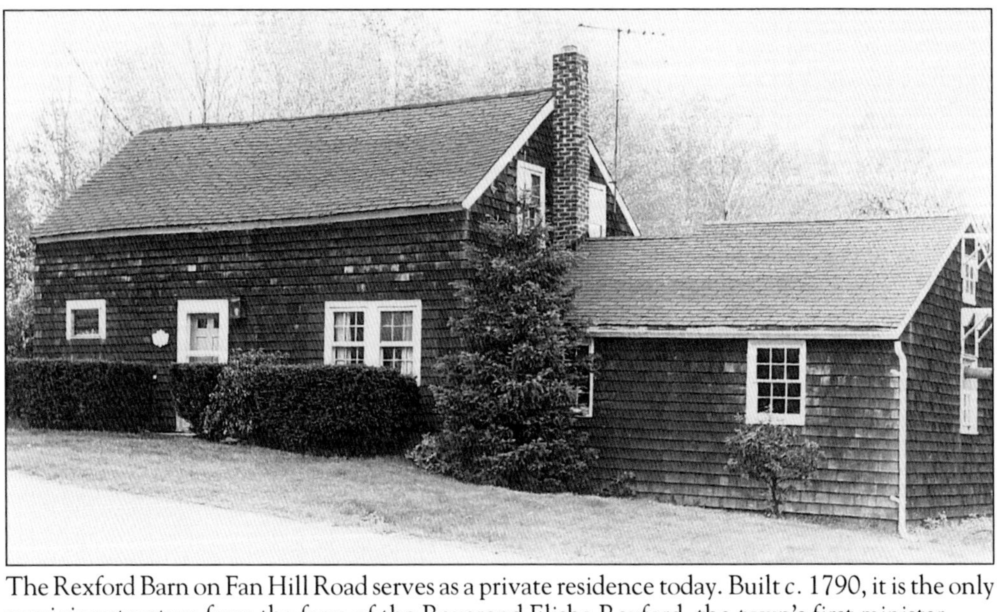

The Rexford Barn on Fan Hill Road serves as a private residence today. Built *c.* 1790, it is the only surviving structure from the farm of the Reverend Elisha Rexford, the town's first minister.

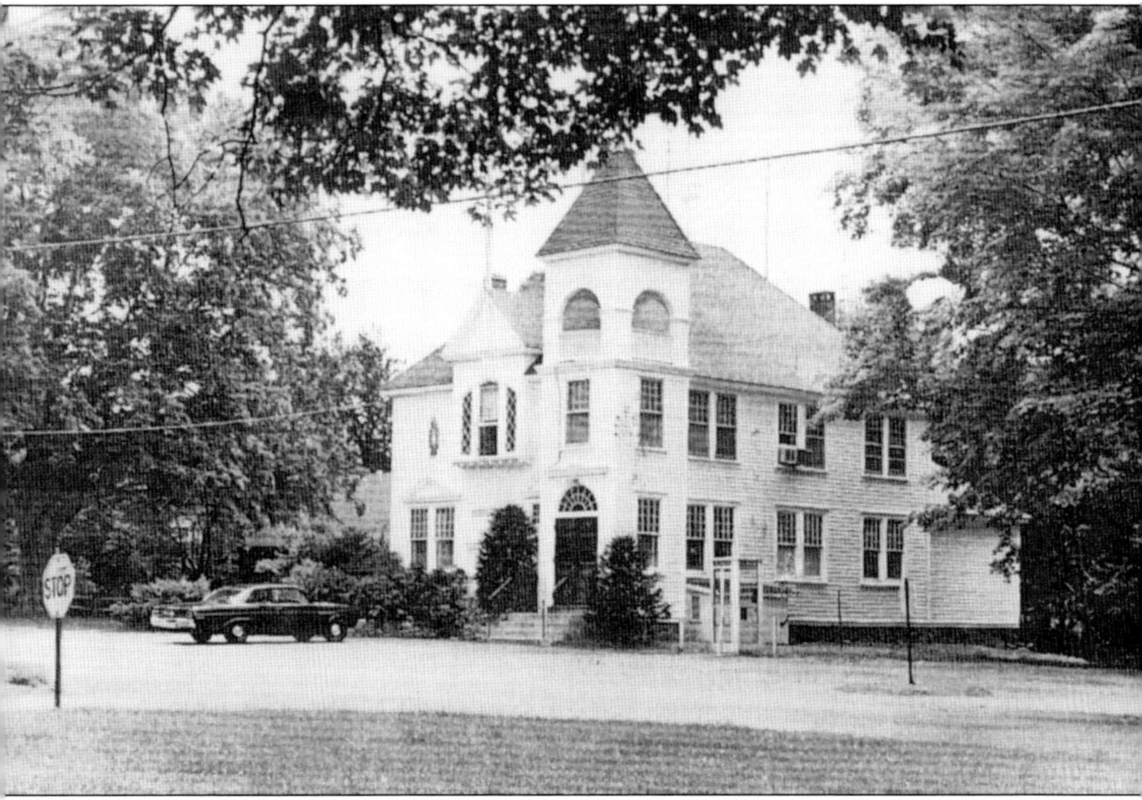

Our second town hall was erected in 1897—at a cost "not to exceed $2,500." Taxes increased eleven mills on a dollar in order to construct the building. This town hall was demolished in 1972 to make way for the expansion of municipal services.

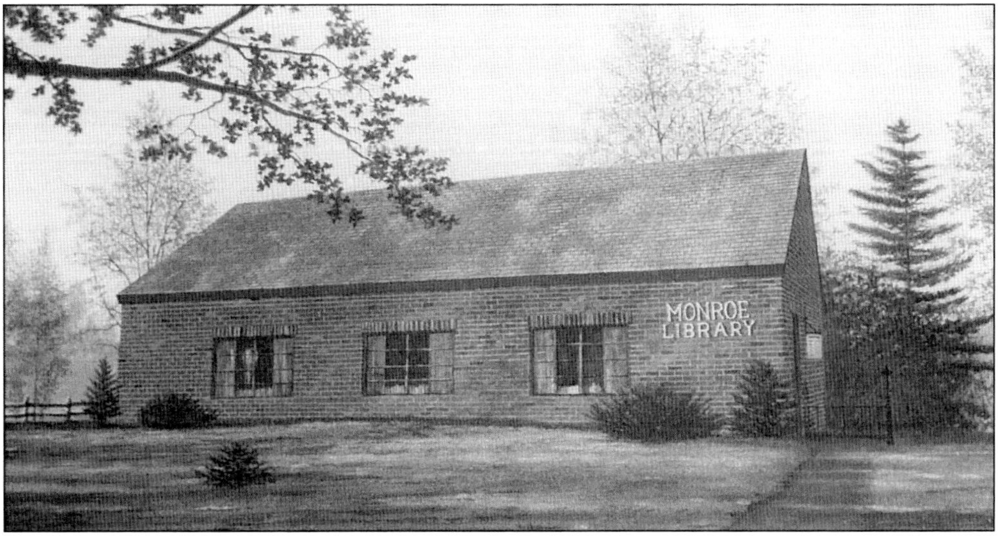

Monroe's first library building was constucted in the 1950s and was funded with private donations of money and labor. The building is depicted here in a painting by David Merrill. One big bulldozer demolished the library in twenty minutes in the early 1970s to make way for the present town hall–library complex.

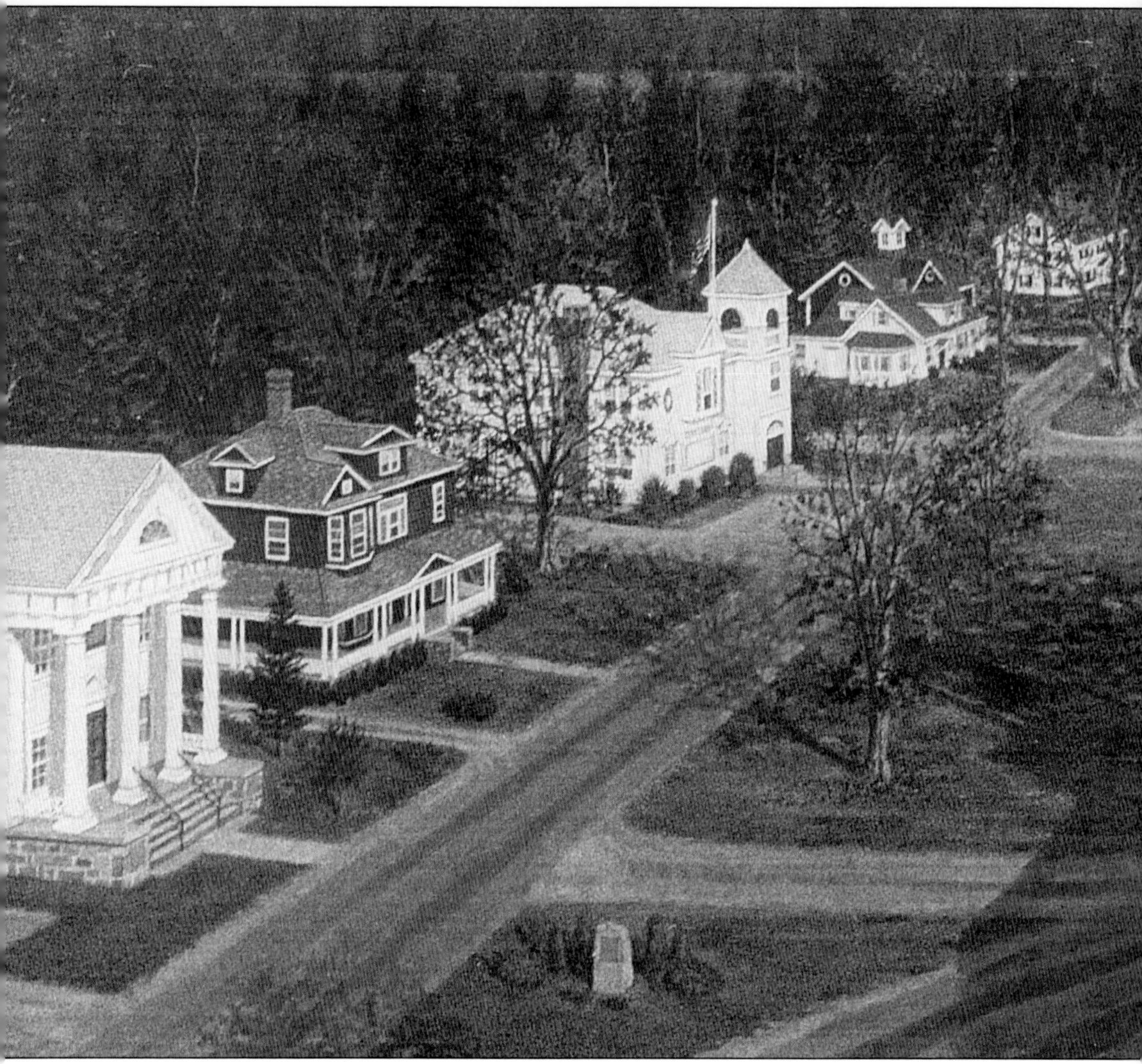

A panoramic view of the Monroe Centre Green in the late 1940s is depicted in a painting by David Merrill. The Lord House (also known as the Vernik mansion) was situated next to the town hall and was the scene of many social events. Later it became the town hall annex, only

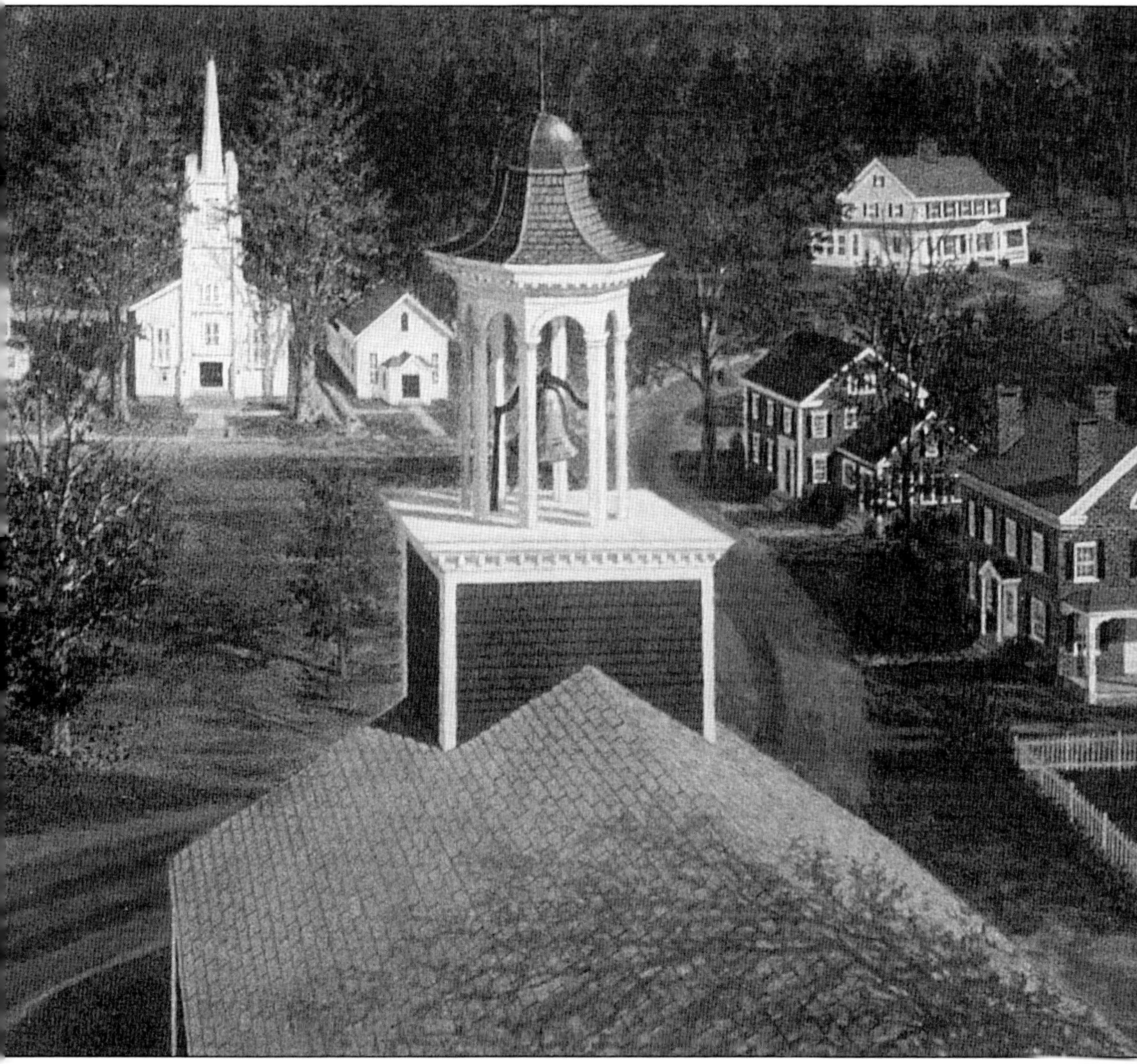

to be demolished to make way for the present town hall. The painting preserves the spirit of the typical unhurried and peaceful New England green.

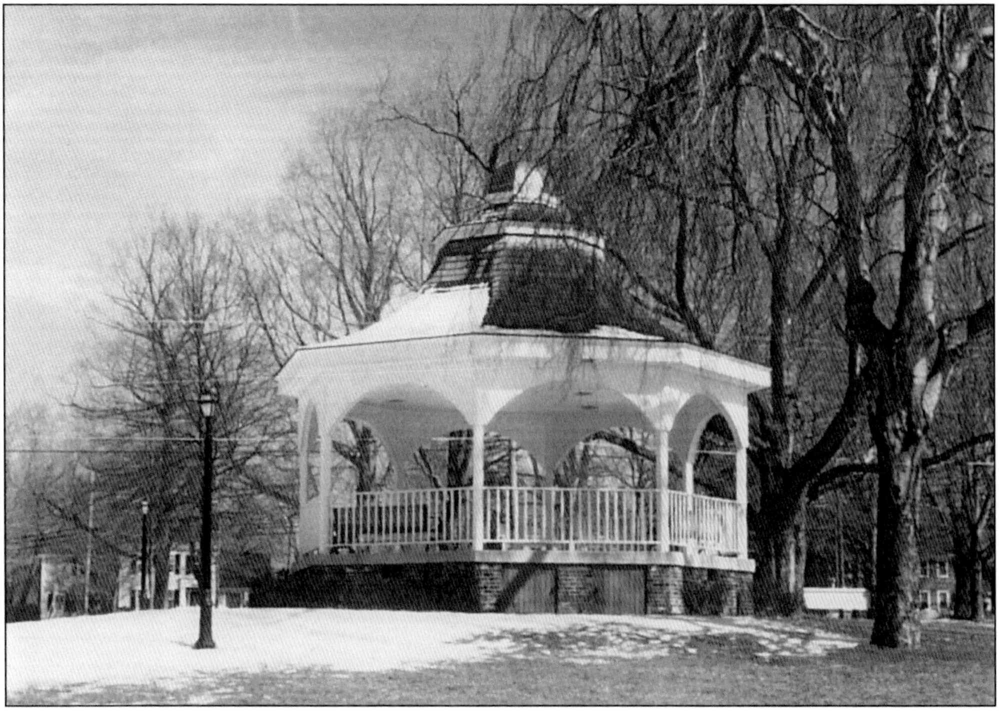

The Gazebo, situated on the Town Hall Green facing the Monroe Centre Green, was built in 1990 with a generous donation from the Barton Weller Fund. It is used for special town events such as concerts and serves as a popular place for taking photographs.

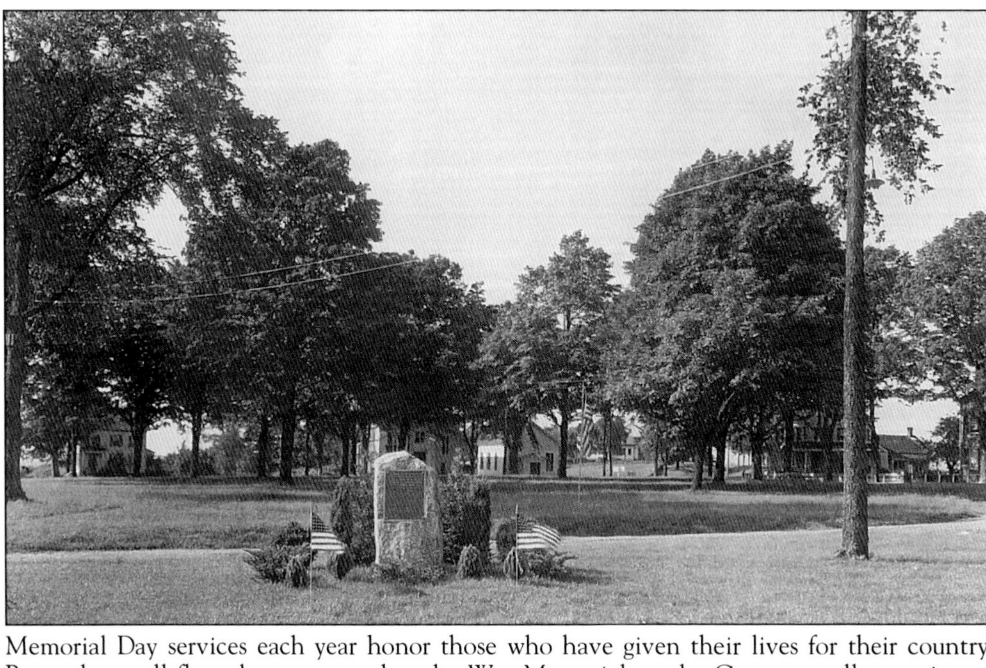

Memorial Day services each year honor those who have given their lives for their country. Recently, a tall flagpole was erected at the War Memorial on the Green to call attention to this important place.

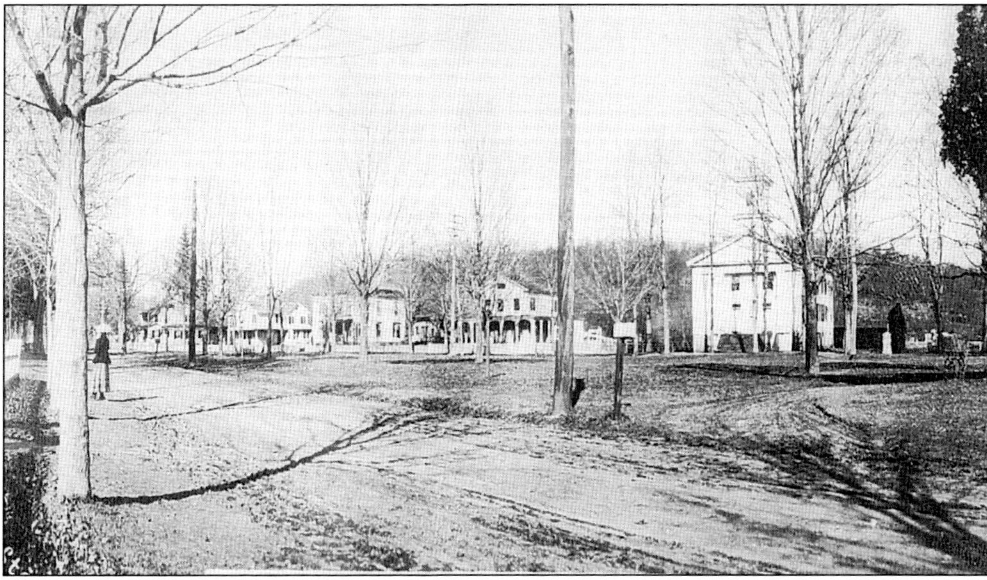

This rare photograph shows the Birdsey's Plain Green (now the Stepney Green) area (*c.* 1900). The Burial Ground, two churches, and fine homes surrounded the Green at that time.

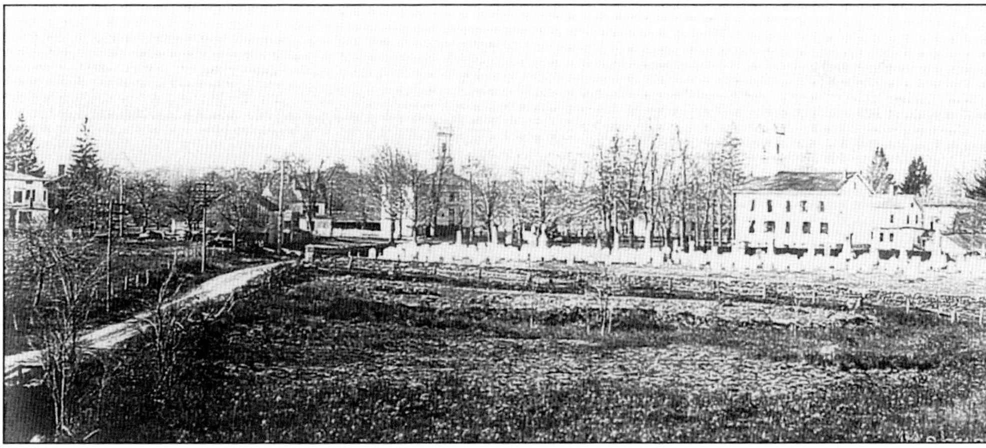

This unusual photograph of an earlier time shows the Stepney Green area as one approaches from Pepper Street. Looking west, one can see the Birdsey's Plain Burial Ground of the nineteenth century, the former Stepney Methodist Church, and several vintage homes at the right. In the center is the Stepney Baptist Church, and to the left, several more venerable old homes can be seen.

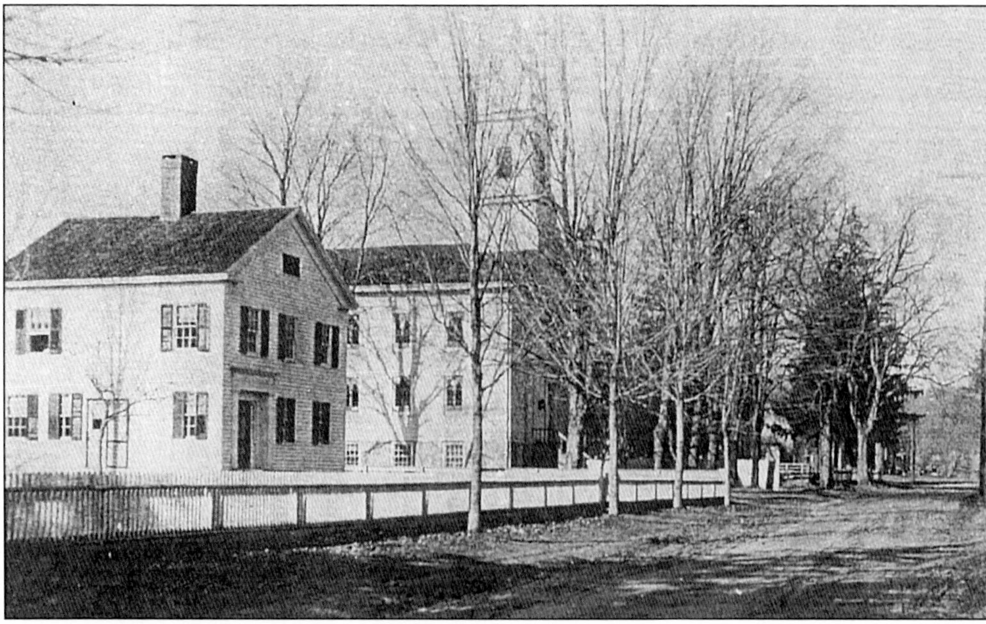

This view of the Stepney Baptist Church on the Stepney Green was taken when Main Street was a narrow, unimproved road. In the foreground is the Baptist parsonage.

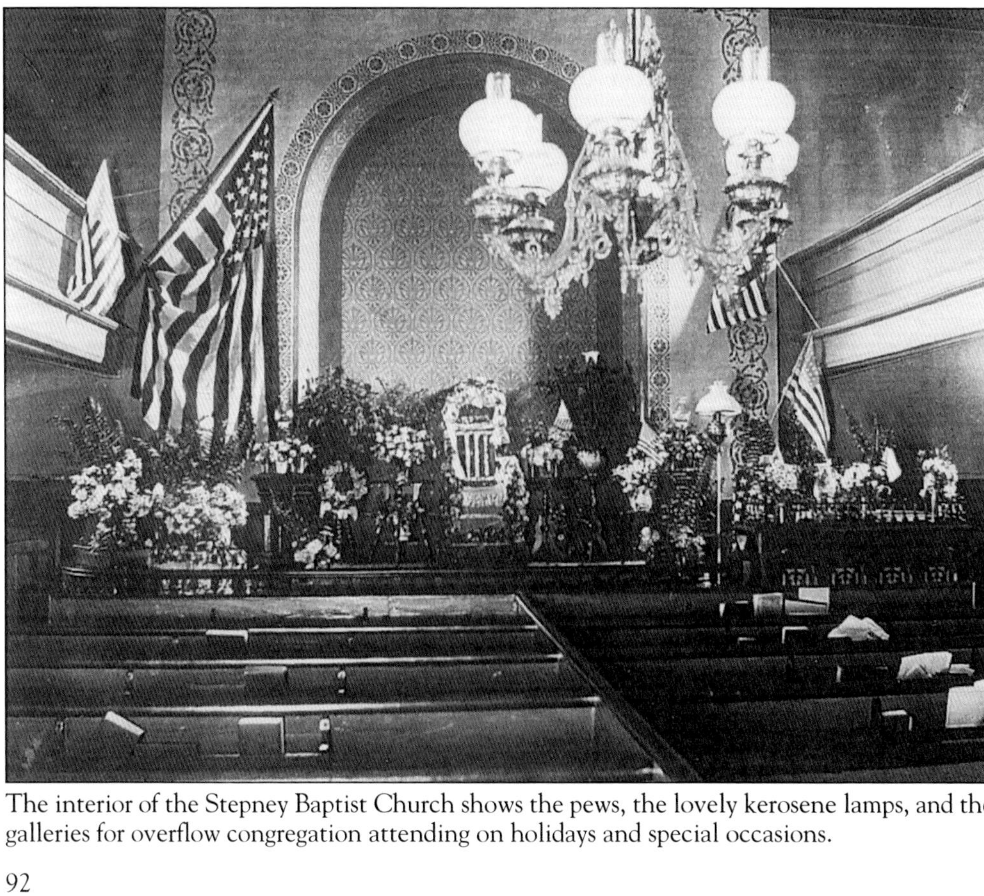

The interior of the Stepney Baptist Church shows the pews, the lovely kerosene lamps, and the galleries for overflow congregation attending on holidays and special occasions.

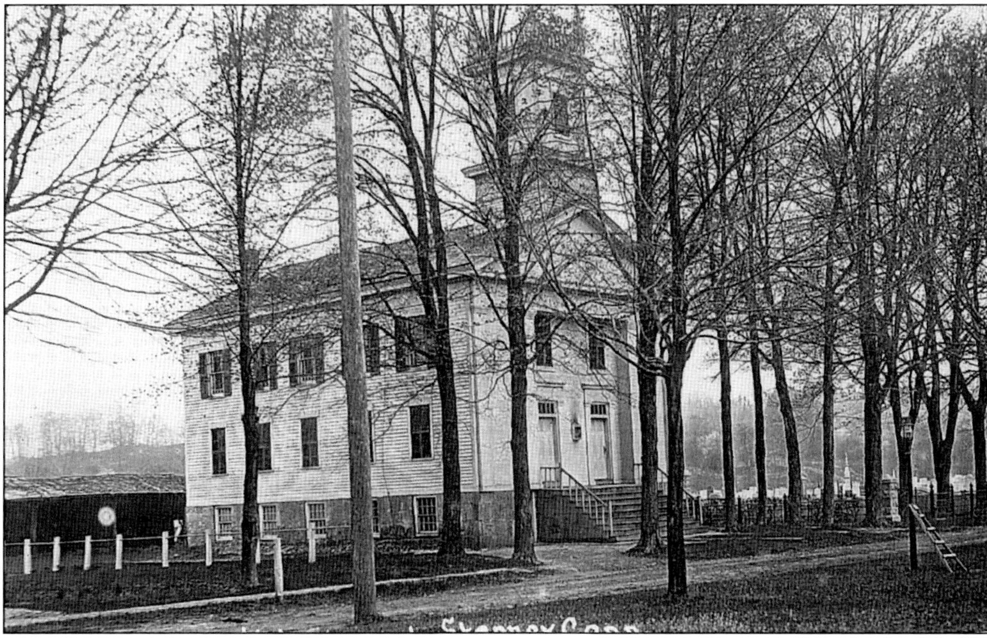

The Stepney Methodist Church was completed in Greek Revival style and dedicated in 1839. One of the "twin" churches on the Green, the church was closed in 1972 and sold. It is now Our Lady of the Rosary Chapel, where the traditional Latin Mass is celebrated. Parishioners come from surrounding towns and states to participate.

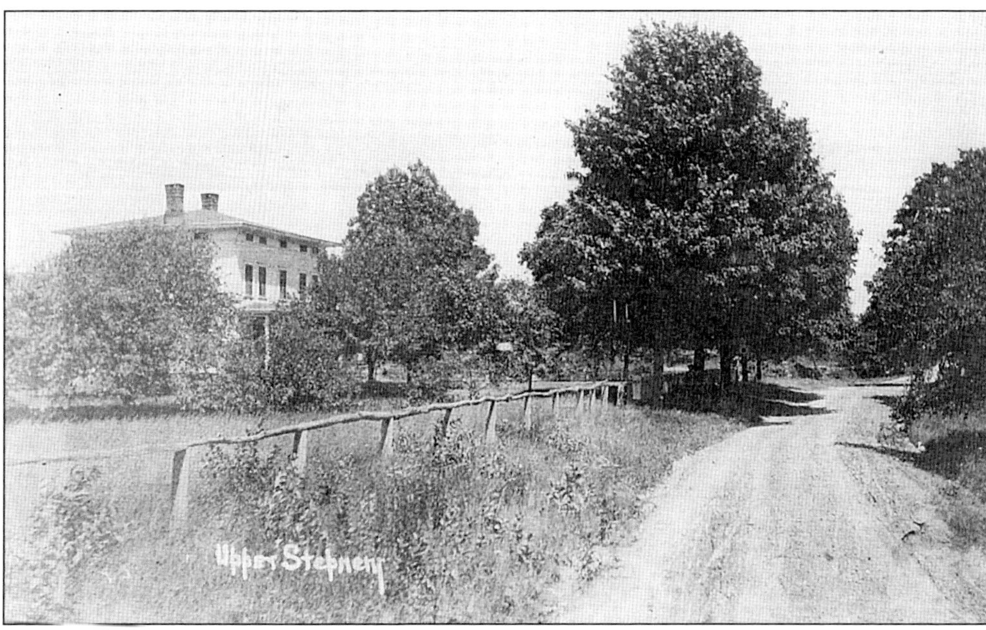

This photograph shows a home built by Hanford Hull in the Victorian/Italianate style. The house is very close to Main Street and is next to Brown's Monument Works.

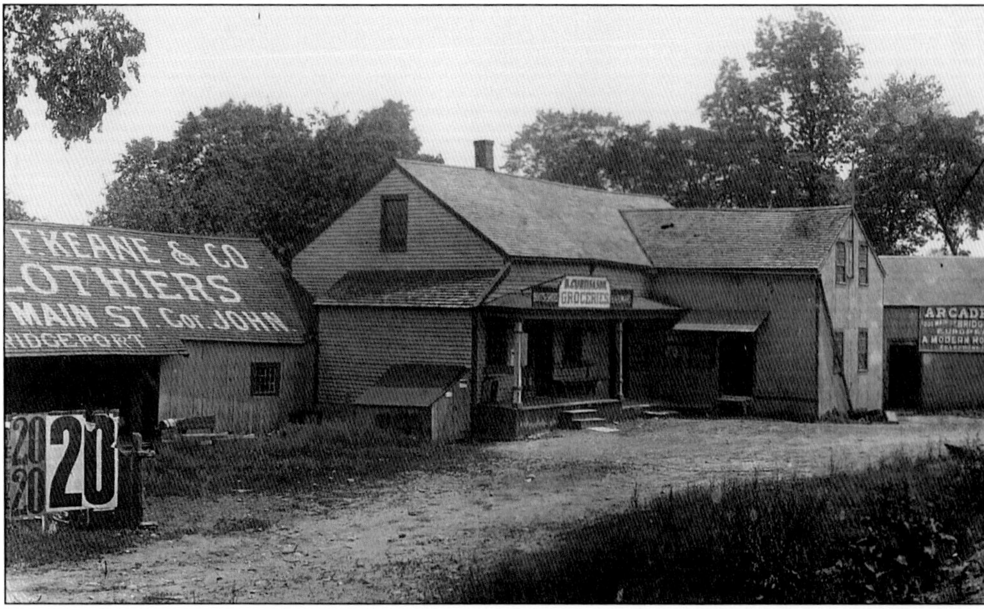

This building near the old Stepney Railroad Station served as B. Curtis and Son's store, a post office, and a livery stable. The train brought the mail to Stepney Depot to be distributed to several post offices in Monroe.

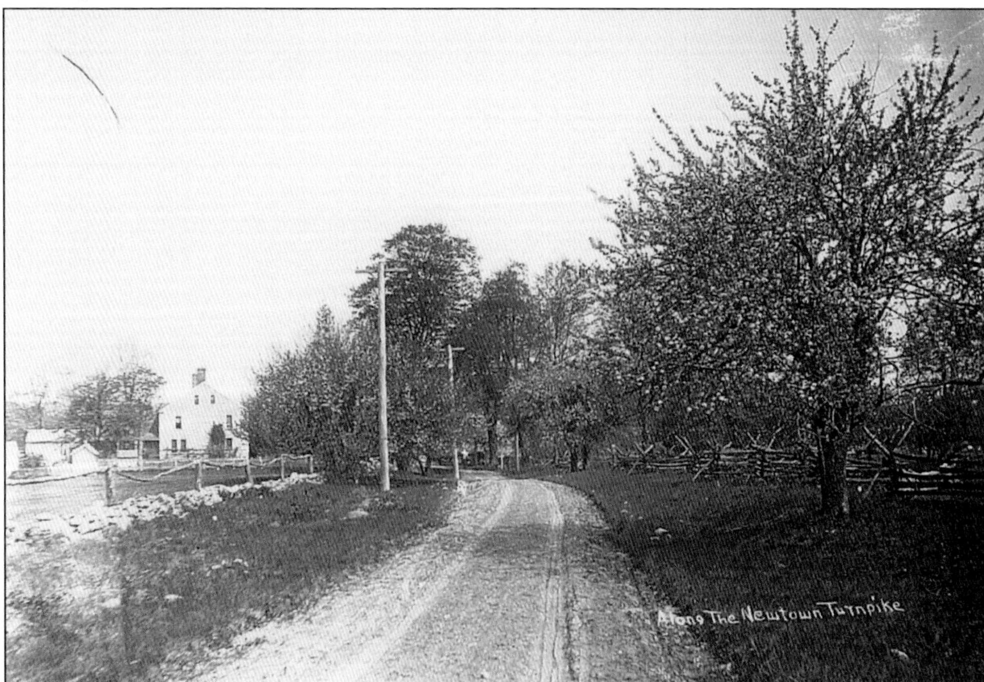

The Burr Nichols house, built *c.* 1780, stood at the intersection of Main Street and Pepper Street. Note the zigzag fence on the right, which was typical of the period; it kept animals in and kept out drifting snow. L. Graham Patmore purchased the house in the 1930s and restored it, making it into a show place for weekend guests. It was torn down in the 1980s to make way for a commercial enterprise.

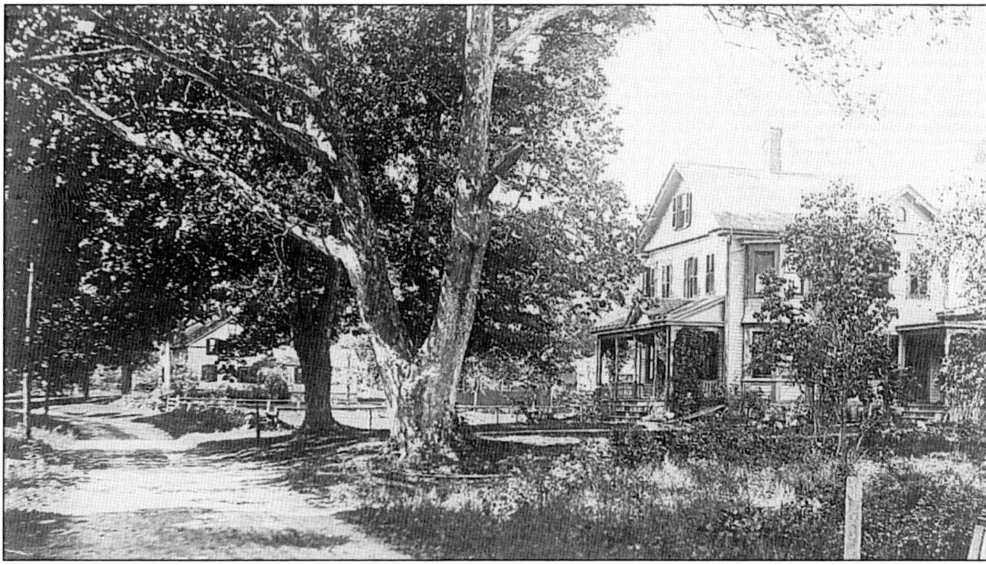

The Charles F. Nichols's house, located on Main Street, was moved from Judd Road in Easton. Today the house is gone, and a feed store and mini-mall are located on the property.

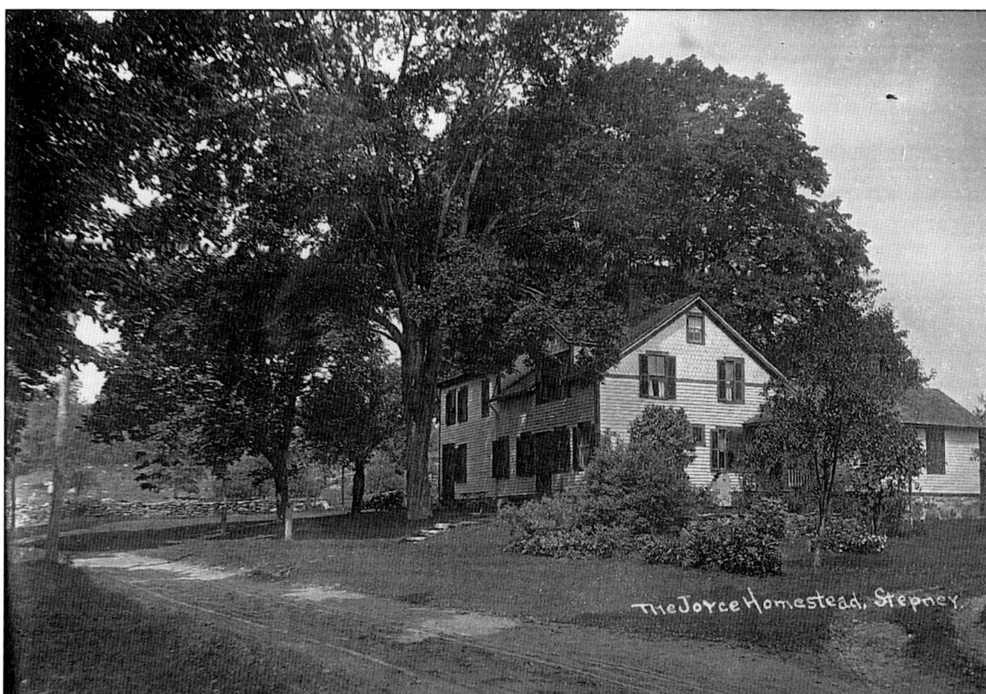

Located on Judd Road, this was the homestead of Stanley Joyce, who married Ruth Beardsley in the 1920s. The homestead was torn down by the Bridgeport Hydraulic Company in the 1930s.

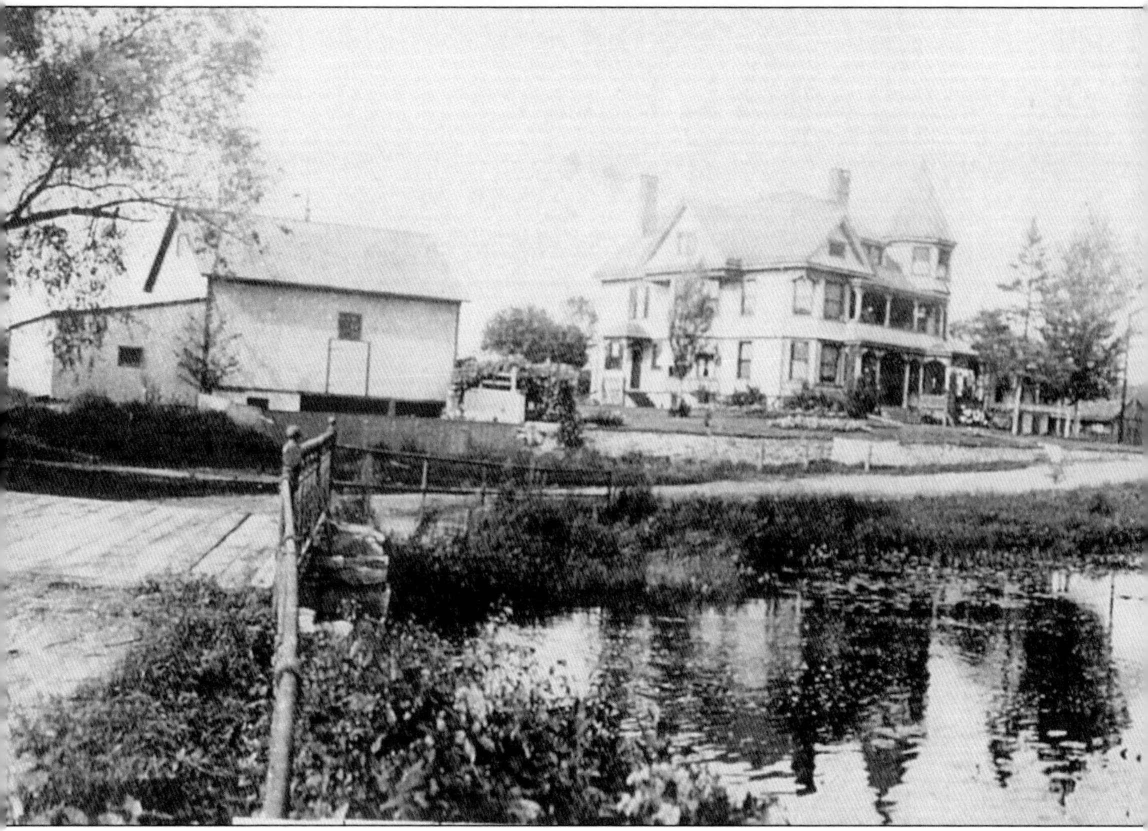

The Barnum Curtis mansion, a 6,000-square-foot Sears American Renaissance catalog model, was considered one of the finest houses in either Trumbull or Monroe. This residence was similar to the Johnson and Blakeman houses in town. Curtis, a businessman, dubbed his home "Times Square," as he used to take the train from New York to the nearby Stepney Depot on weekends.

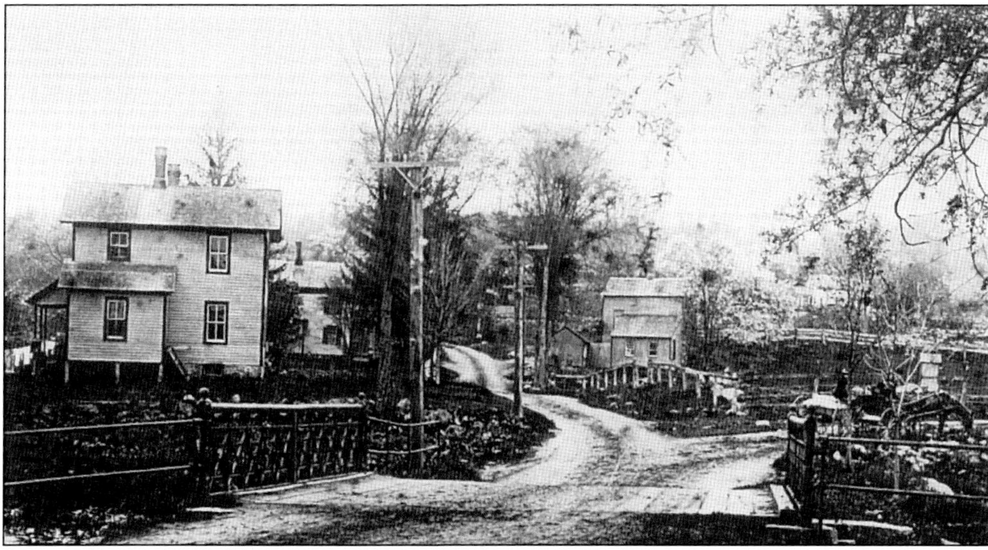

The E.L. Smalley homestead was located in close proximity to Smalley's Blacksmith Shop in Lower Stepney on Main Street.

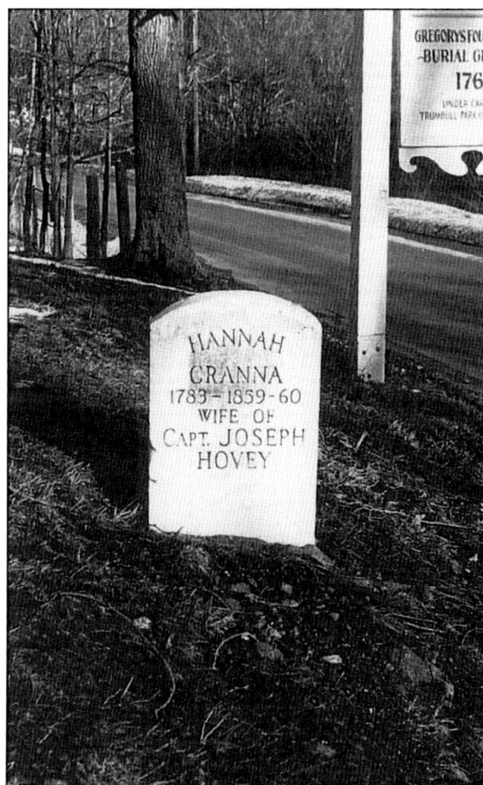

The grave marker for Hannah Cranna, Monroe's "witch," is just over the town line in Trumbull in Gregory's Four Corners Burial Ground. According to one legend, Hannah said she would take herself to her grave. As her coffin was being carried over the ice, the coffin slid down the hill and into the grave by itself.

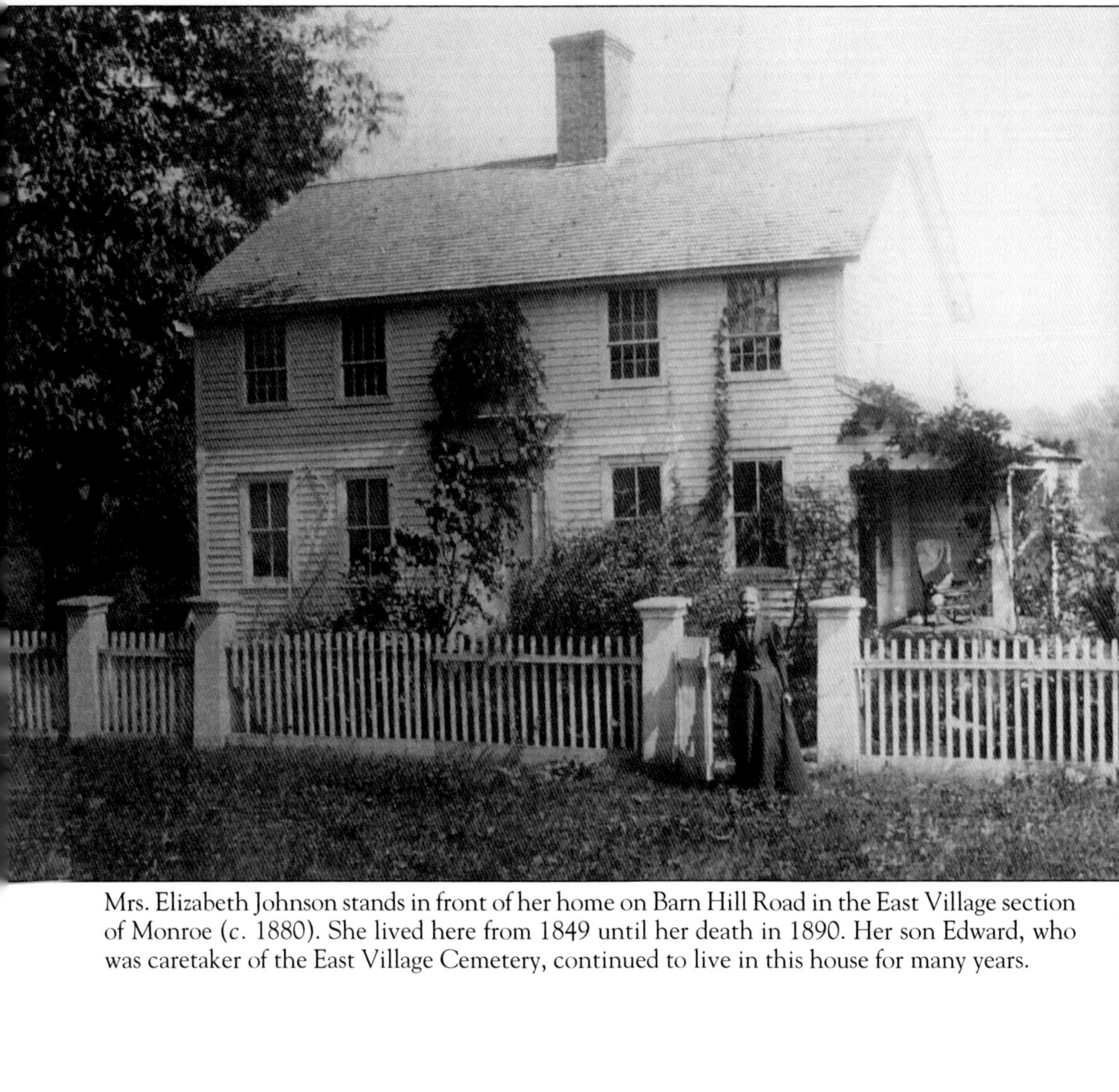

Mrs. Elizabeth Johnson stands in front of her home on Barn Hill Road in the East Village section of Monroe (*c.* 1880). She lived here from 1849 until her death in 1890. Her son Edward, who was caretaker of the East Village Cemetery, continued to live in this house for many years.

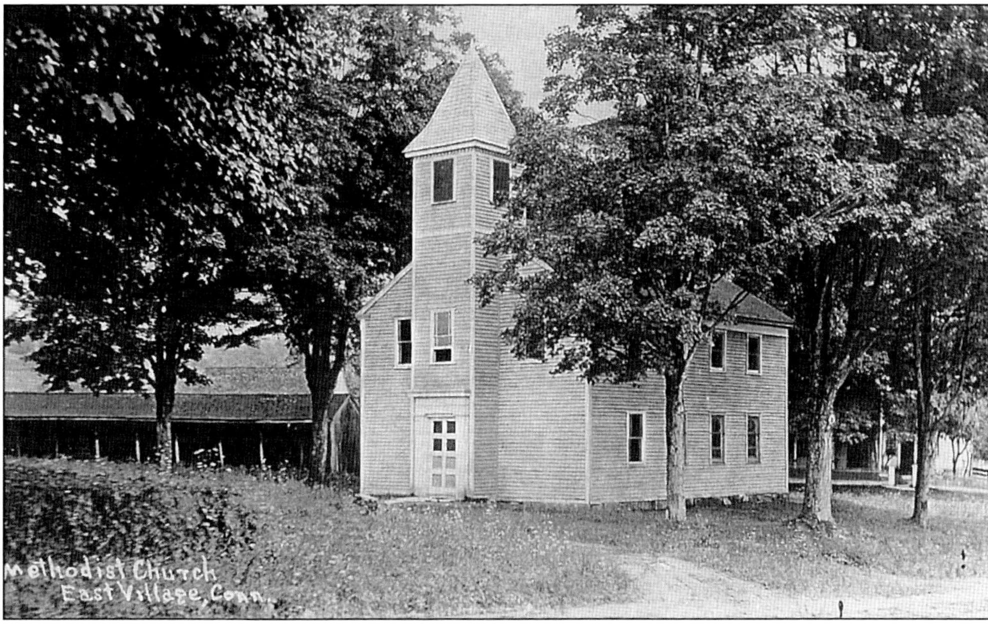

The East Village Church is located at the intersection of Barn Hill and East Village Roads. Carriage sheds provided shelter for horses and buggies during inclement weather.

Built in 1811, the East Village Meetinghouse (its original name) is the second oldest religious edifice in Monroe. This 1916 photograph shows a steeple, which has since been taken down. The building is now owned and maintained by the Monroe Historical Society.

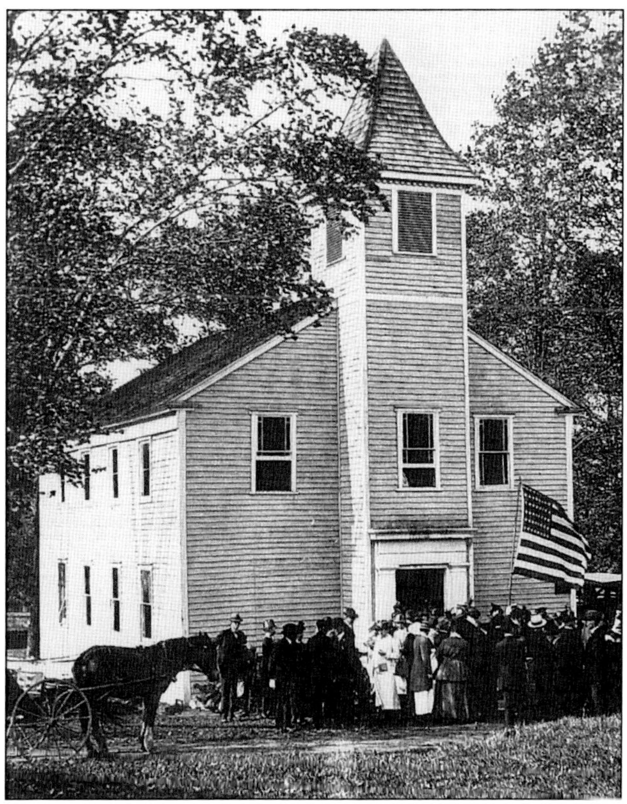

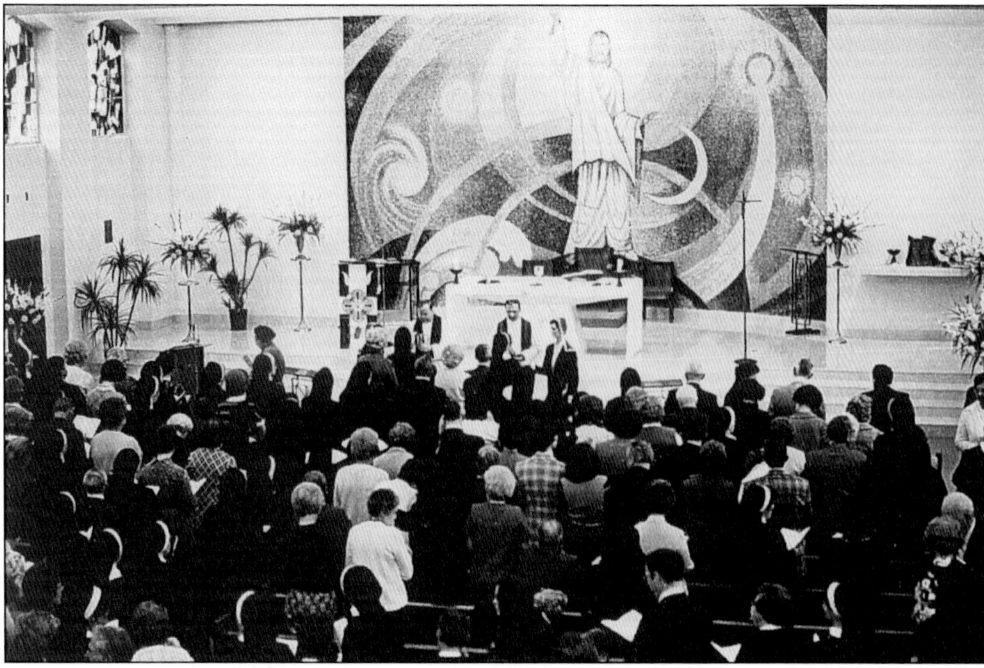

The beautiful mosaic behind the altar at the Marian Heights (Sisters of the Holy Family of Nazareth) Chapel is admired by those gathered for the dedication. Marian Heights was at one time a private girls academy. Now its a retirement home for the Sisters of Nazareth.

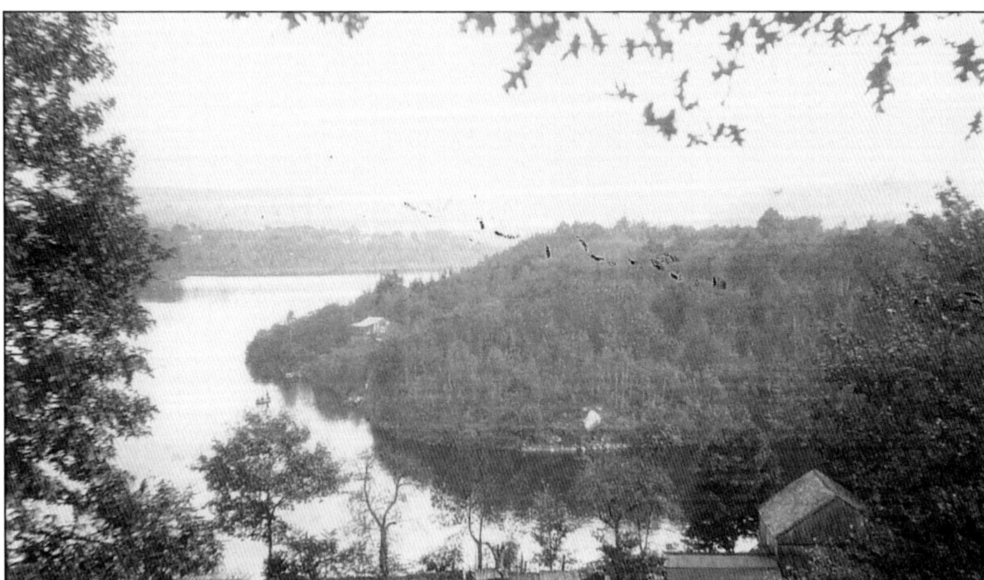

A small marina is located at Point Lookout, a cove in Stevenson. On the right, Halfway River enters into the lake at this cove.

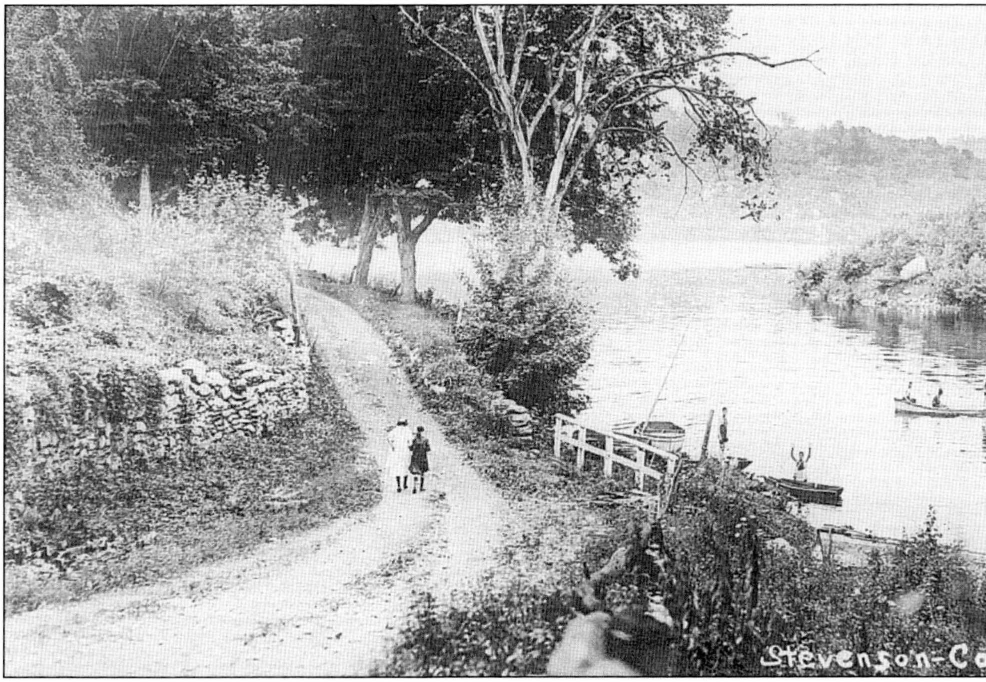

Before the building of the Stevenson Dam, the Housatonic River flowed peacefully along. These residents, out for a leisurely stroll, can enjoy the tranquility of a summer's day along the river.

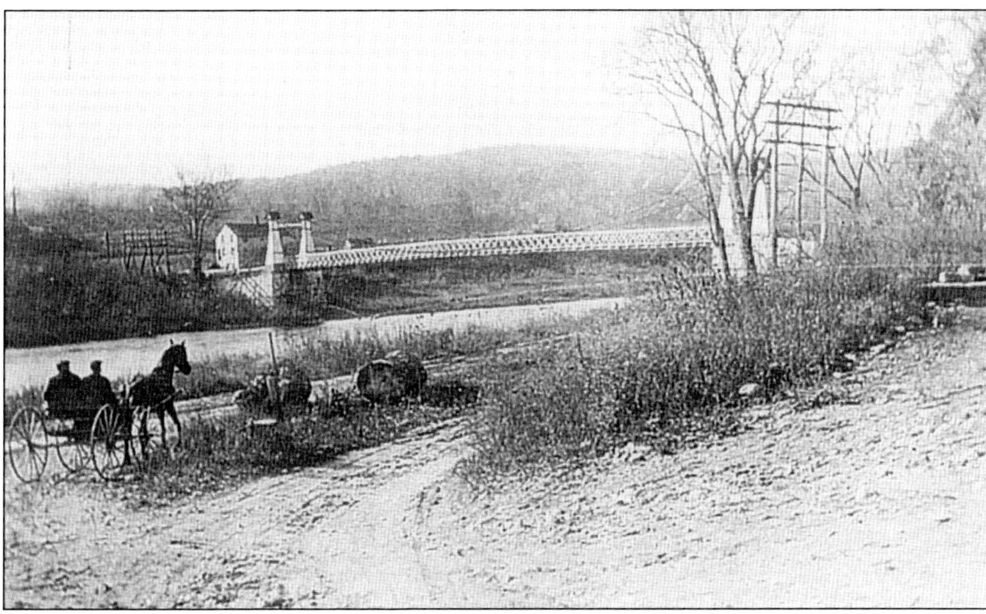

"Over the river and through the woods." This suspension bridge at Zoar was built in 1876 and blown up in 1919 when Lake Zoar was completed and Stevenson Dam was opened for traffic. It was the only way to cross the Housatonic between the covered bridge at Derby/Shelton and Bennett's Bridge in Newtown.

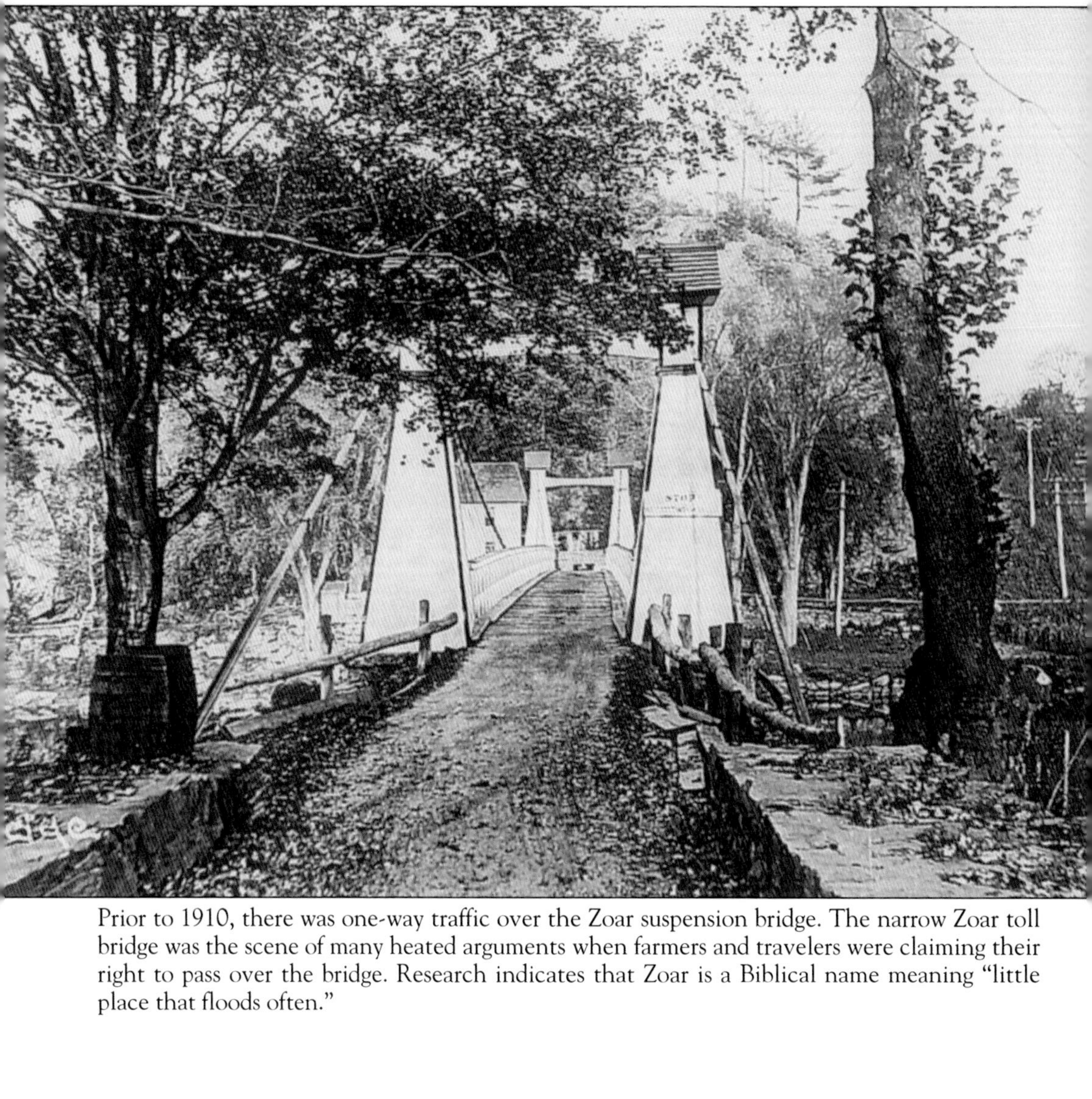

Prior to 1910, there was one-way traffic over the Zoar suspension bridge. The narrow Zoar toll bridge was the scene of many heated arguments when farmers and travelers were claiming their right to pass over the bridge. Research indicates that Zoar is a Biblical name meaning "little place that floods often."

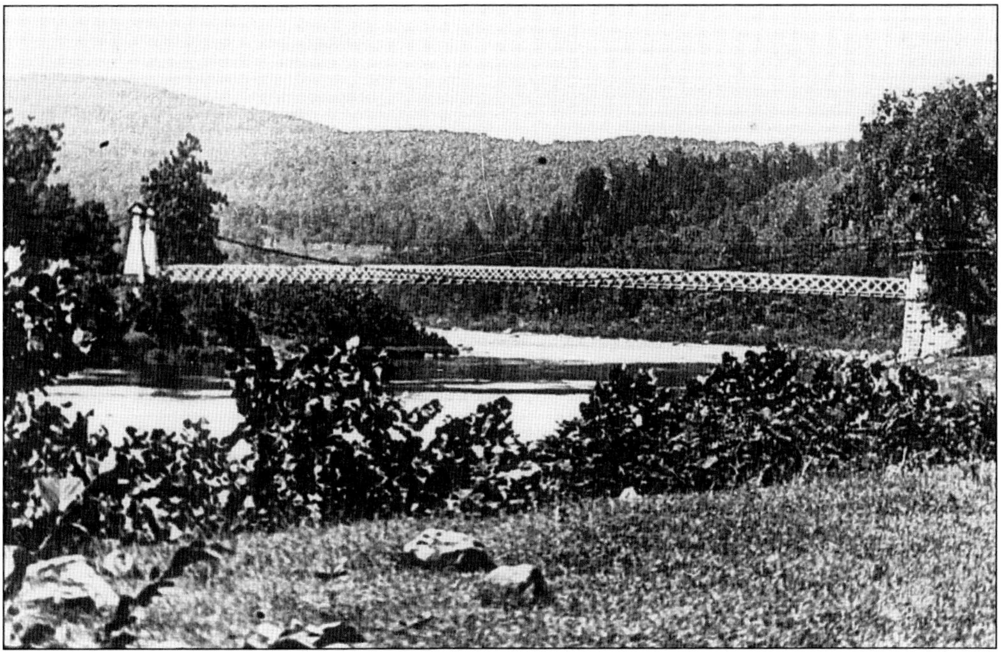

The old Zoar bridge was destroyed to make way for the Stevenson Dam. Pine tar was spread across the wood and set afire. Then the cable on the Monroe side was cut, and that side went down. Lastly, the cable at the other end was cut.

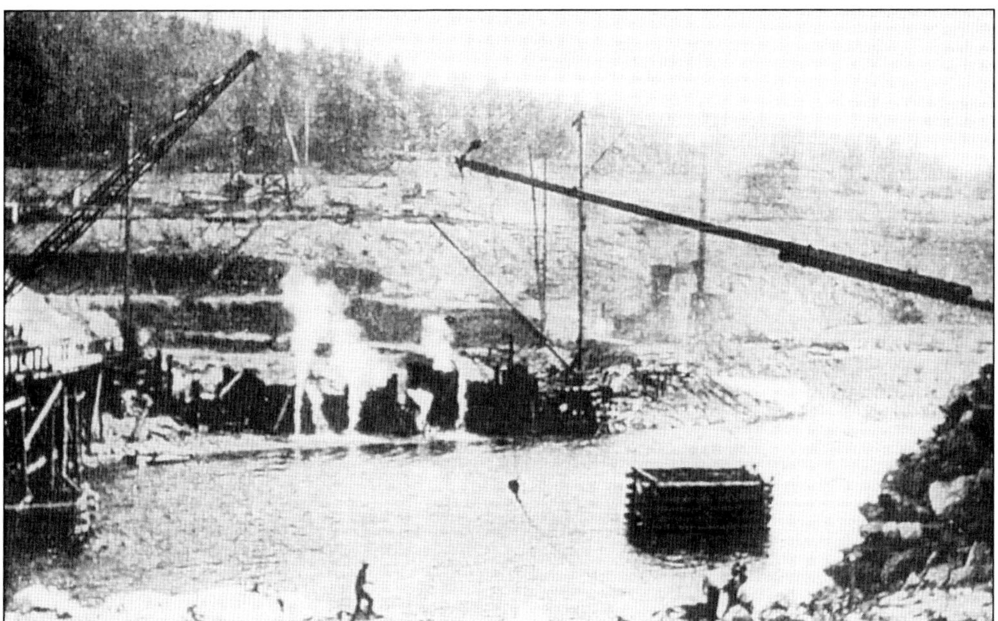

Cranes and other construction equipment were brought up to the construction site on flatbed railroad cars—so were the workers, who stayed at a nearby barracks specifically built to house them.

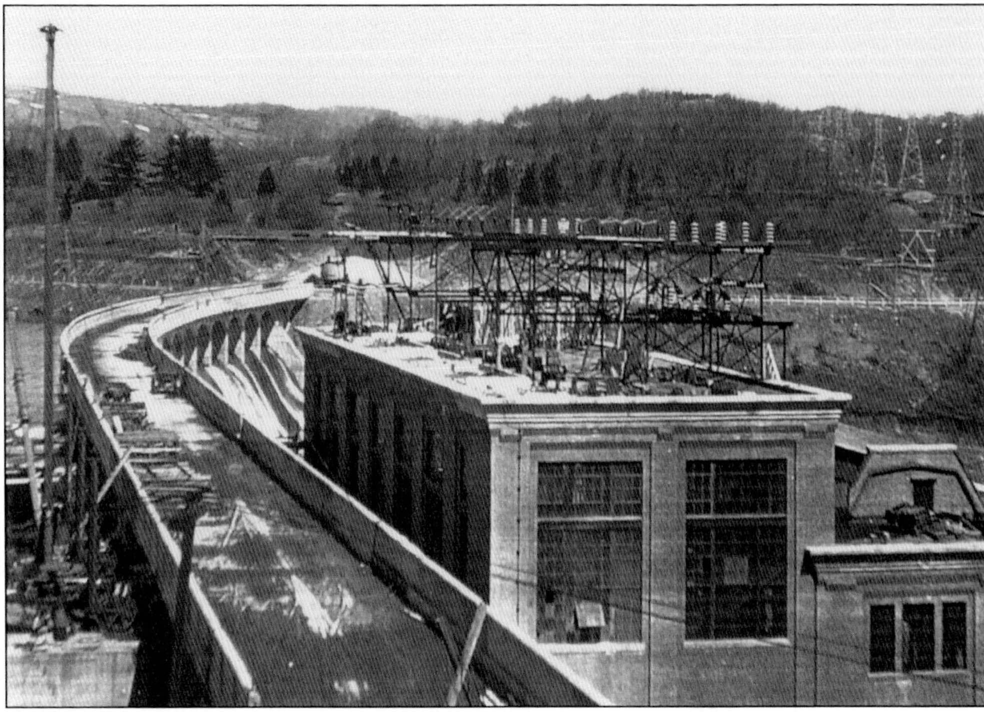

The construction of the Stevenson Dam by Connecticut Light and Power (1917–19) changed the natural terrain of Monroe, providing both an important power source and a means of crossing the Housatonic.

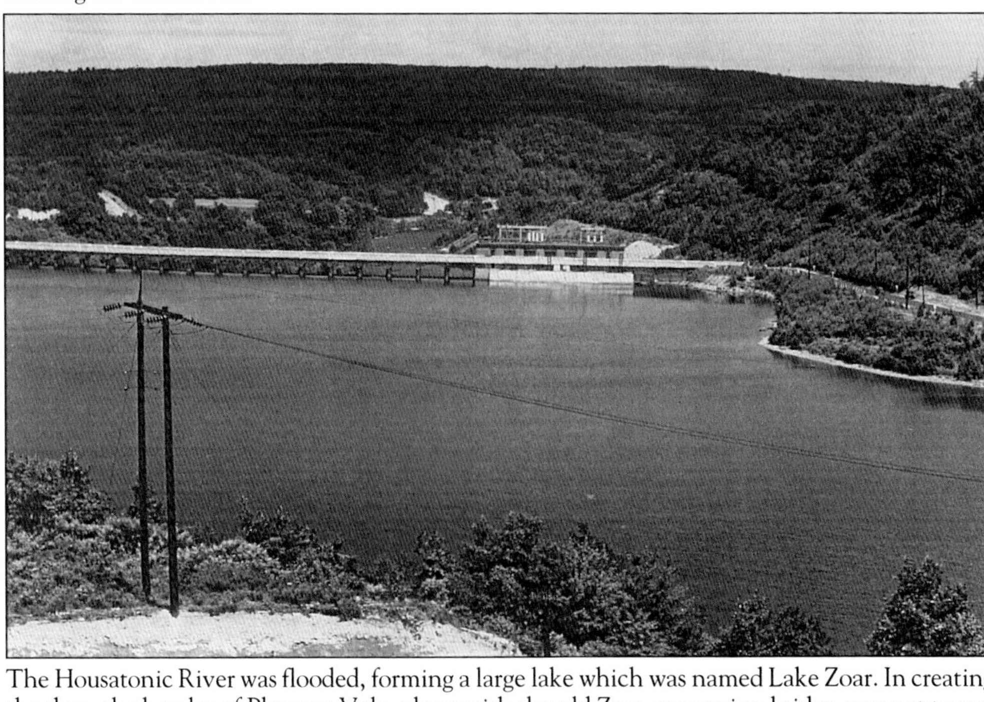

The Housatonic River was flooded, forming a large lake which was named Lake Zoar. In creating the dam, the hamlet of Pleasant Vale, along with the old Zoar suspension bridge, was put to rest at the bottom of the lake.

Eight

A Town for All Seasons

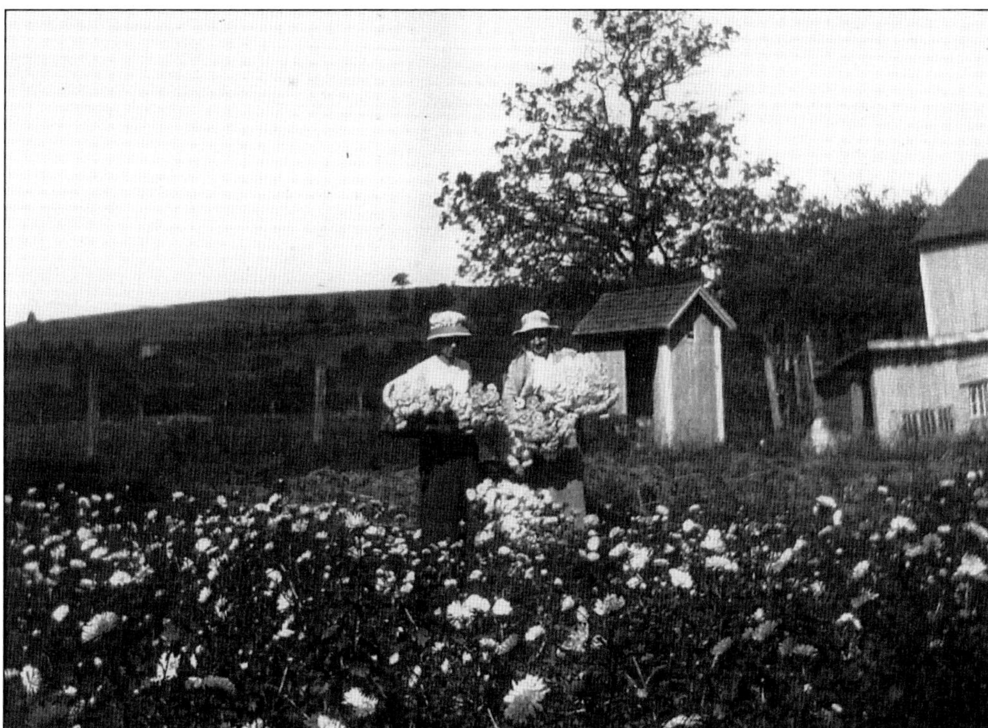

These gardeners in the early 1900s are enjoying their summer harvest of flowers. The best flowers, fruits, and vegetables would proudly be displayed at the Grange Hall in hopes of being awarded a blue ribbon.

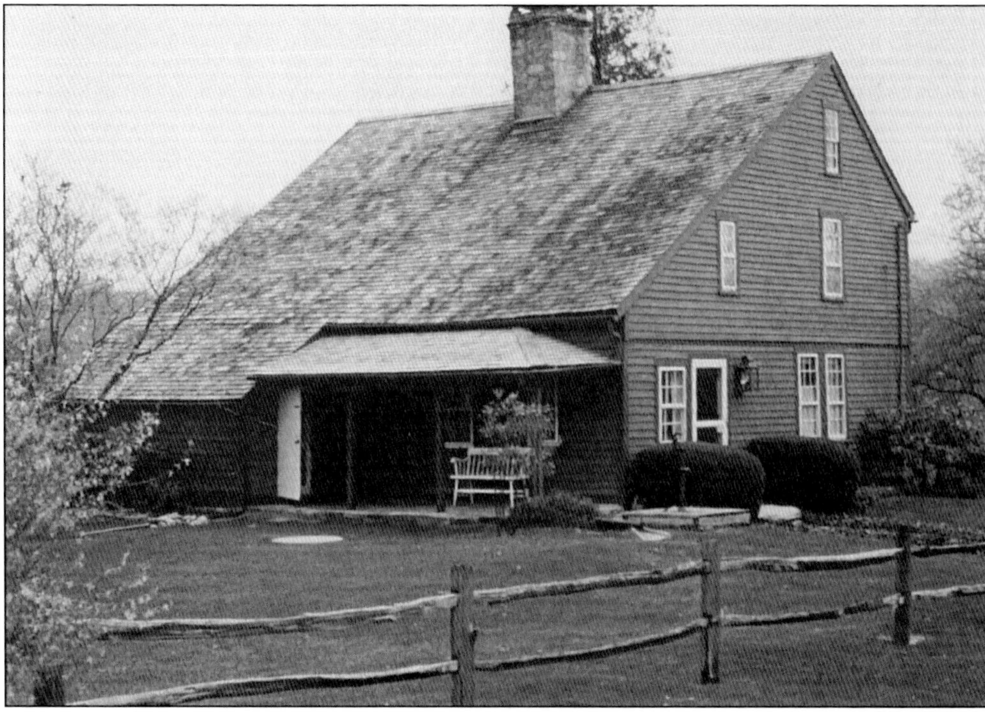

This charming eighteenth-century residence, originally the home of Elisha Mills, is one of Monroe's finest examples of the famous saltbox style of architecture. From the rear lawn, one can truly appreciate the handsome roof line and the massive chimney. Interesting features include a well with a working hand pump and four fireplaces, one with a beehive oven.

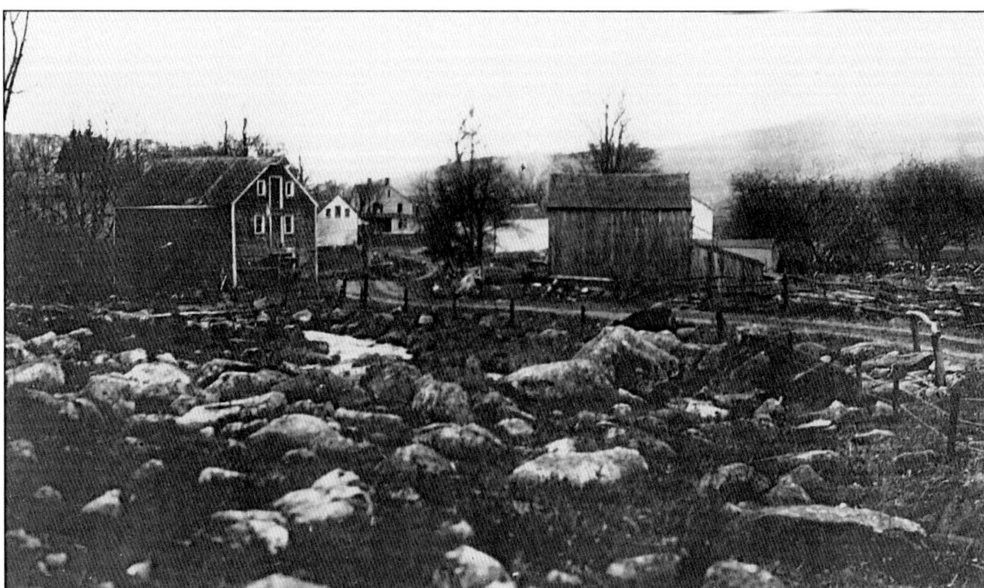

There are too many stones here to convert this into a crop-producing field, but the raw material available will build beautiful New England stone walls, the most back-breaking of all farm work.

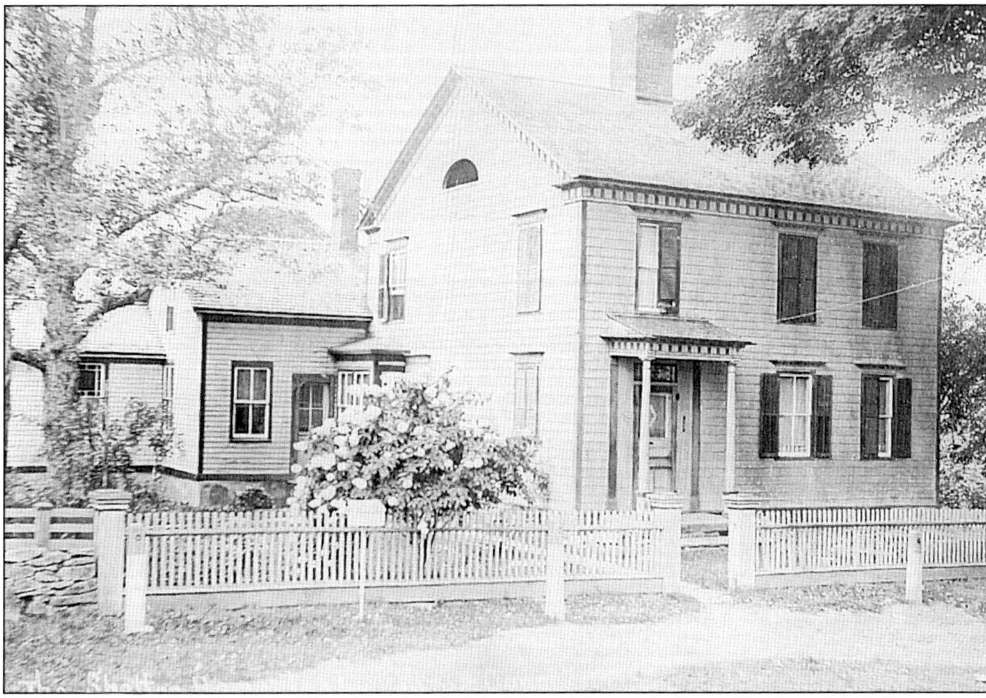

Built in 1823 by the Shelton family, this Federal half house is located on Barn Hill Road. It is the only house left in town that has been continuously owned by the same family. This photograph was taken *c.* 1900, before its present Victorian veranda was added.

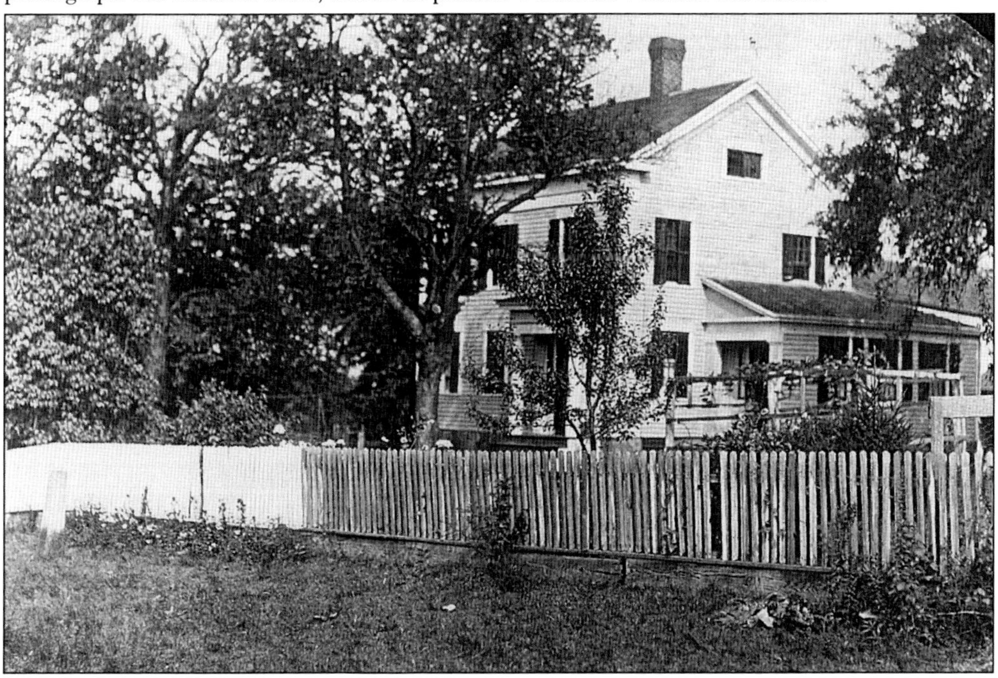

During the summer, while the crops grew, farmers could turn their attention to improving their property. The Nolan house, at what is now Purdy Hill and Farm View, has a fresh coat of paint. Another more pressing project, no doubt, has halted progress on the fence.

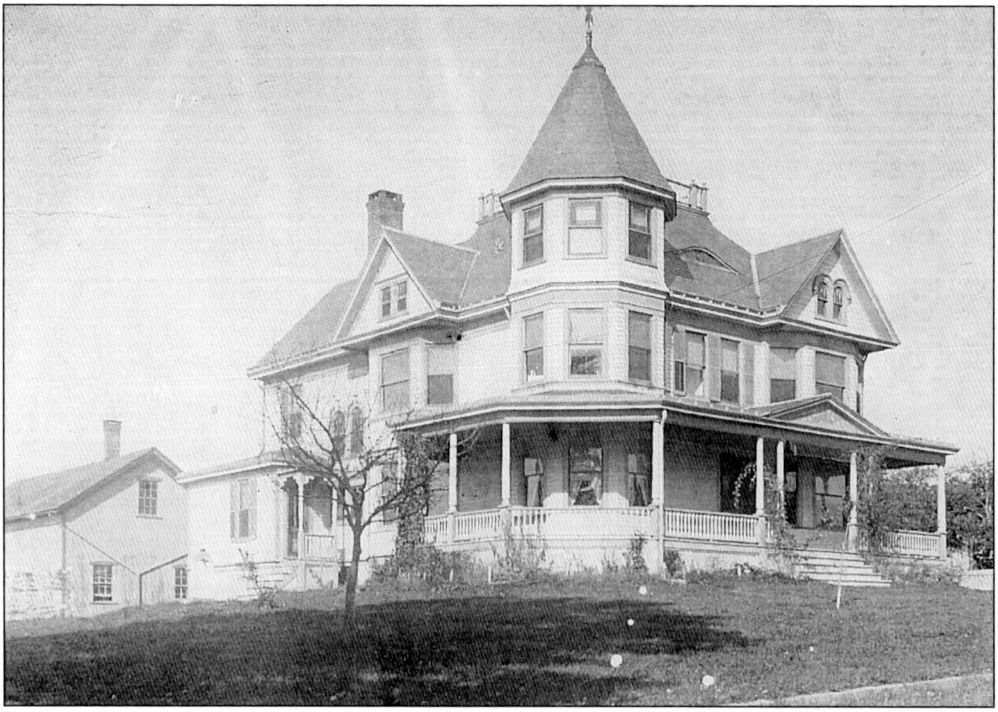

After his earlier home burned in 1896, James Johnson built this handsome Sears Victorian residence on Elm Street. During this period, nearly every house had a Victorian veranda added to its facade. The Johnson house was unique because Monroe's only windmill was on this property.

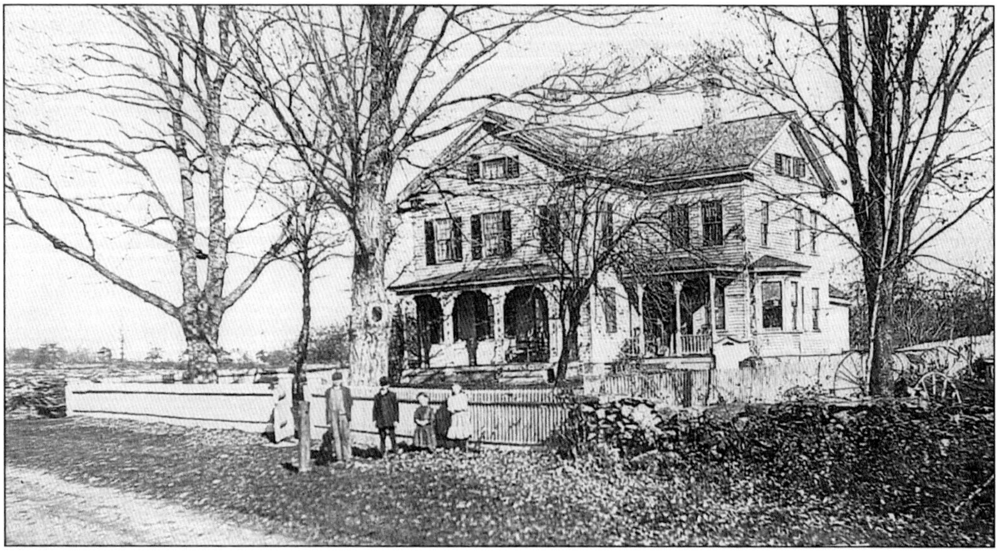

The Witkowski children stand in front of a fence they helped to whitewash. The Victorian porch and fence were added in the 1890s to this *c.* 1840 homestead.

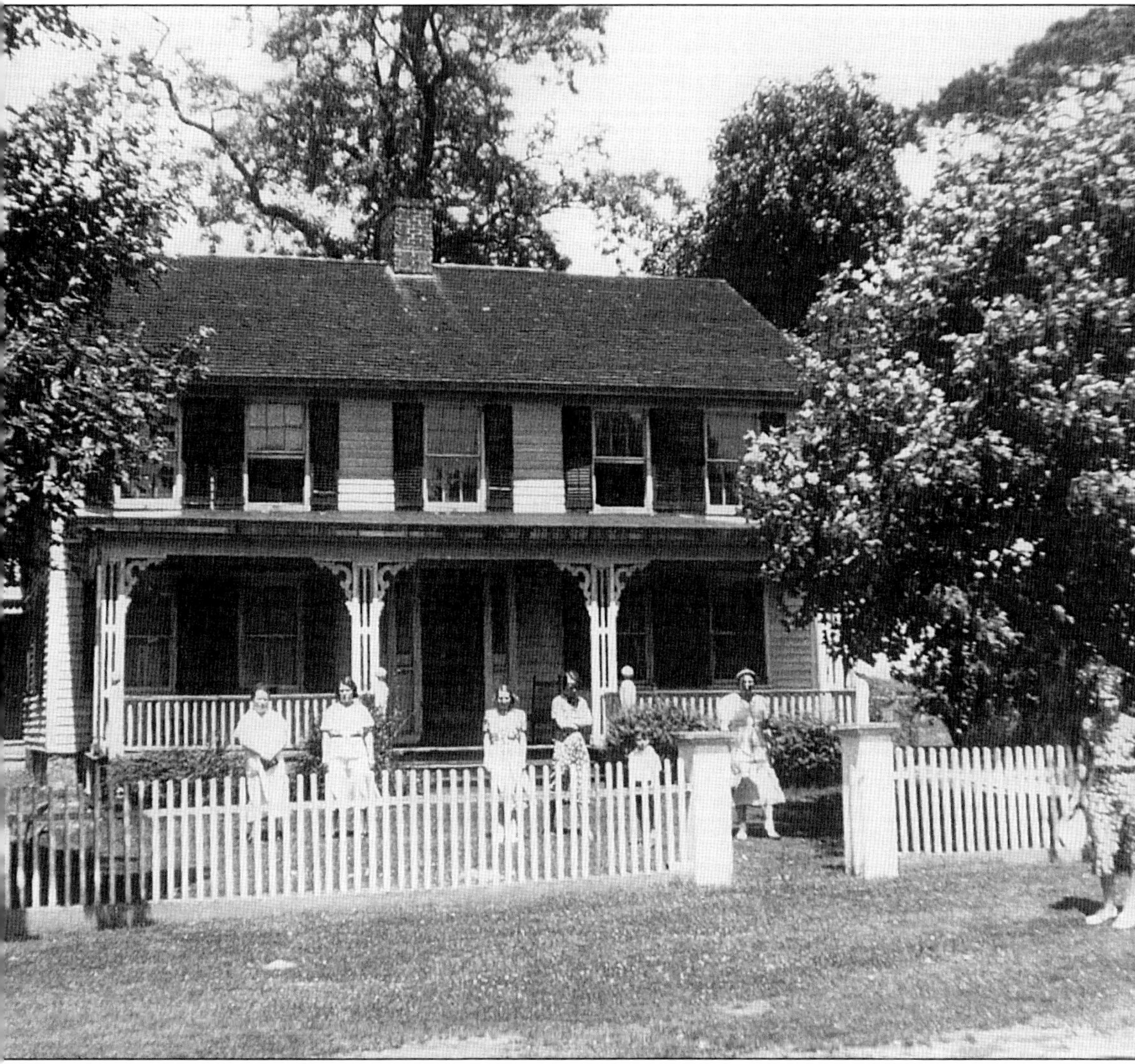

The Monroe Post Office has replaced the Henry Sherman home at "Five Corners" (Monroe Turnpike and Purdy Hill). Many games of horseshoes, volleyball, and croquet were played here by the Emmons family and their friends. This structure was taken down in the 1980s and moved to a nearby town.

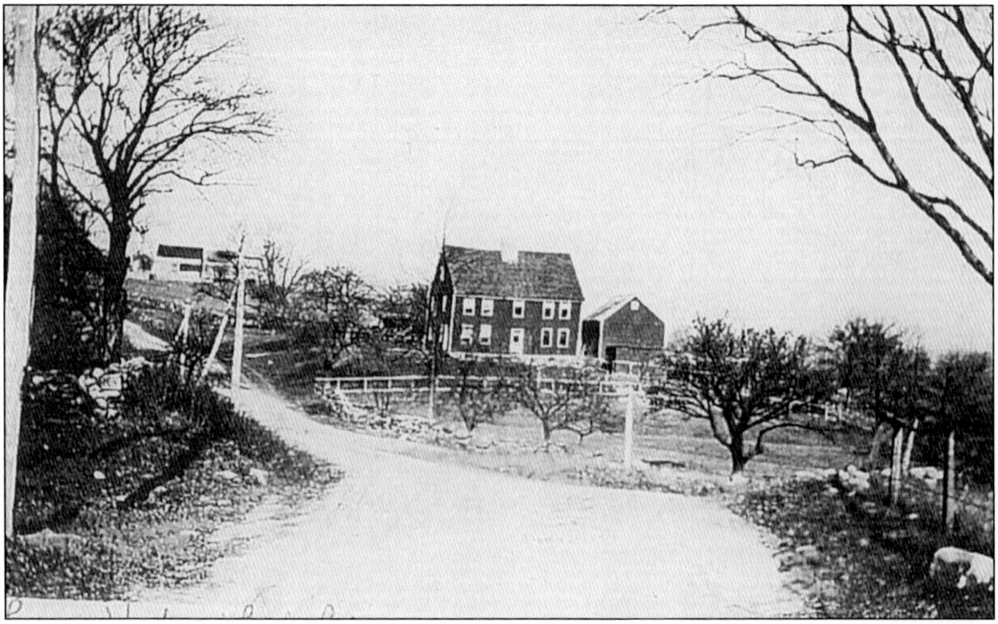

Through most of this century, this house by the side of Barn Hill Road has been known as the Miles Percival Standish house. Records designate this as the Milton and Hepzibah Hawley homestead. Built in the 1750s, it is believed to be one of the oldest houses in Monroe. Hepzibah herself was a poetess during the Revolutionary War and some of her writing has been preserved:

"Our fathers to this Continent;
They left the tyrant with disdain,
And ventured on the raging main;
And when they reached this western shore
The savage monsters round them roar,
But God diminished them, in haste,
And in their room our Fathers placed.
'Twas God's own hand we must confess,
That brought them to this wilderness,
And made it blossom like the rose,
In spite of all their cruel foes.
But when the ancient stock was dead,
And others raised up in their stead,
A British tyrant sought, again,
To load us with his galling chain.
But our brave sons, in freedom born,
Do proud, oppressive tyrants scorn;
Resolved to die, or ever be
From their tyrannic bondage free."

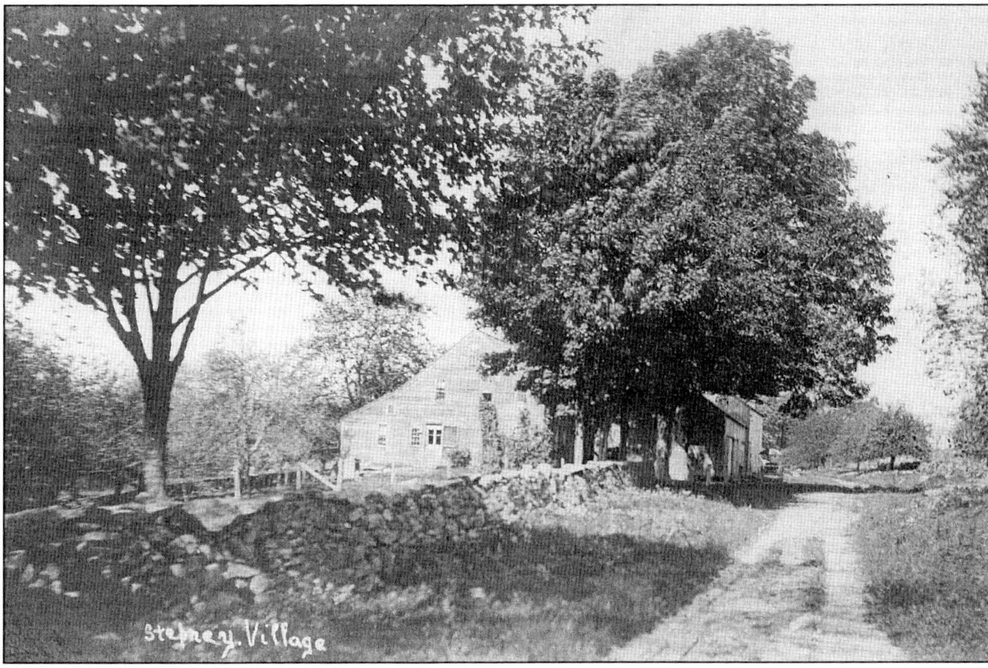

Winding lanes and picturesque roads characterized turn-of-the-century Monroe. Old Newtown Road and the Beard home are pictured here.

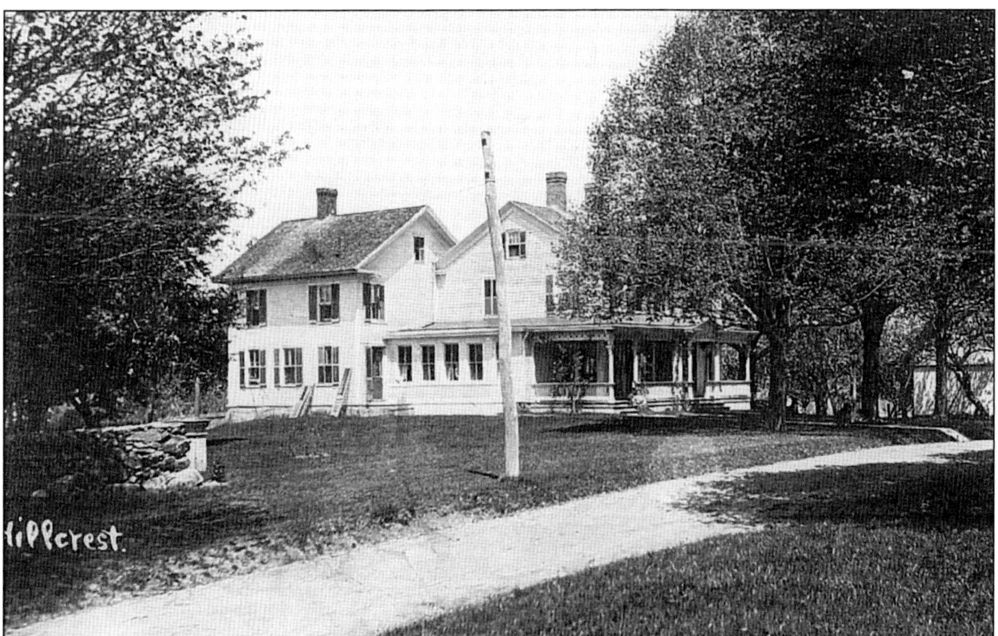

This old homestead, known as "Hillcrest," was built about 1827 and was separated into two parts in 1937 by Samuel Hurd. The rear section was detached and moved 100 feet north on Monroe Turnpike to become a residence for his son, Lewis Hurd.

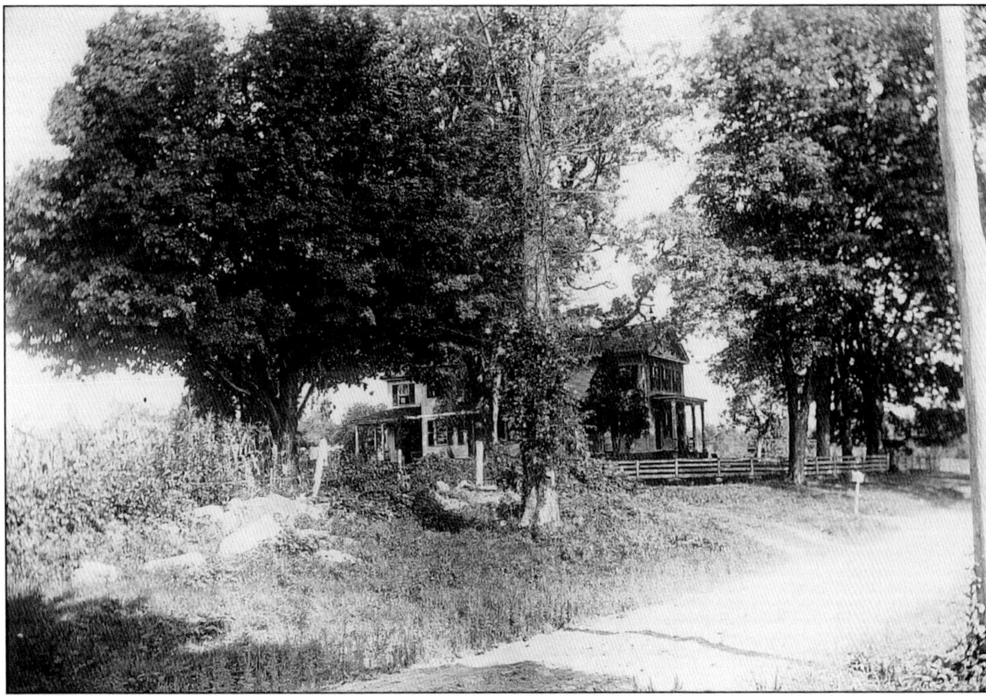

In 1900, large oak trees provided shade from the hot summer sun as it beat upon the Jacot home, a fine example of Greek Revival architecture. In 1866, Frederick Hollister purchased the house from the Bostwick family and later conducted Hollister's School for Fashionable Females here. It is located at the intersection of Hammertown Road, Old Zoar Road, and Monroe Turnpike.

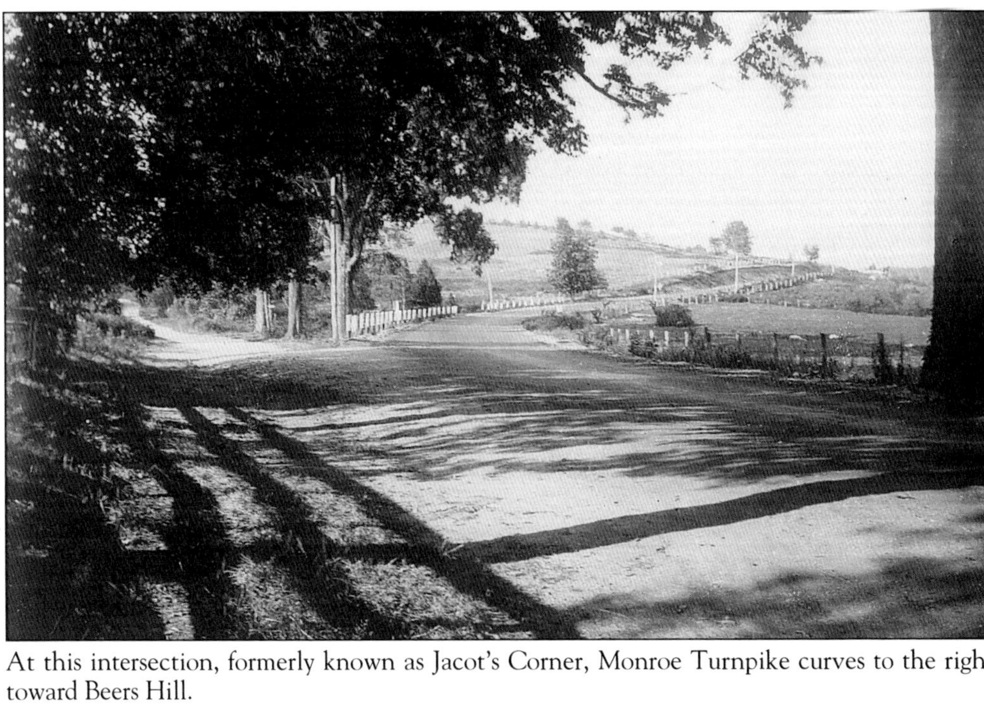

At this intersection, formerly known as Jacot's Corner, Monroe Turnpike curves to the right toward Beers Hill.

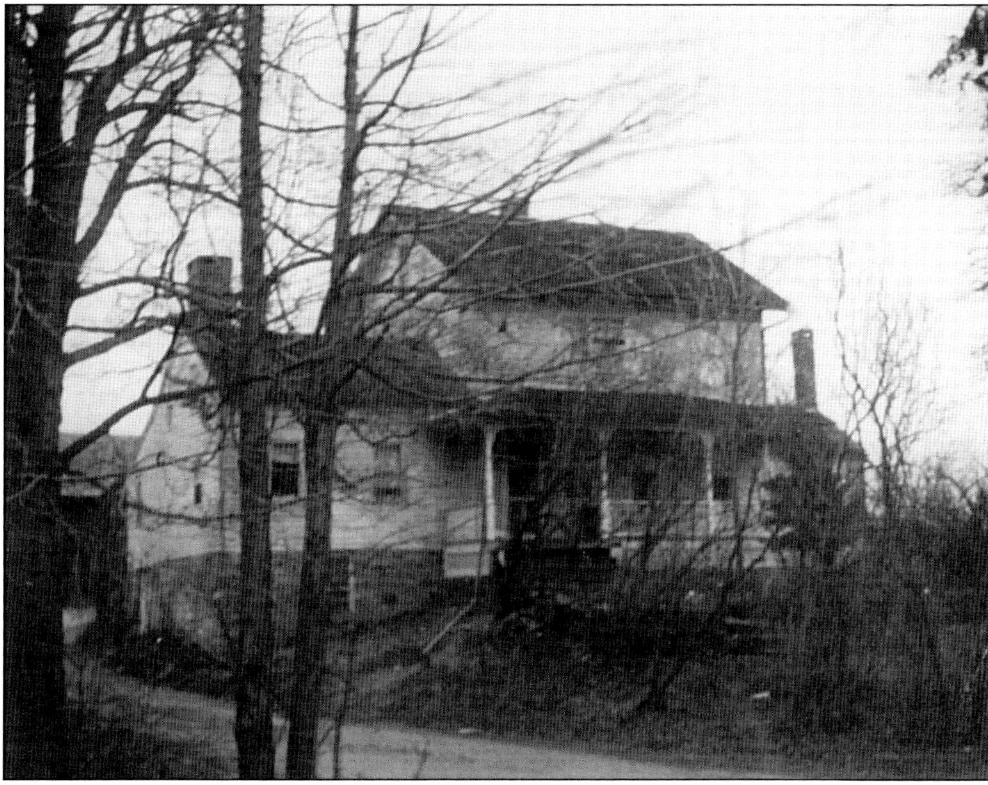

In late fall, after harvest, farmers had time to build additions to their homes and farm buildings. The smaller section, on the left of this farmhouse, is the original structure built by Isaac Burr. Located at the corner of Bug Hill Road and Cutler's Farm Road, this is now the Pulaski Farm.

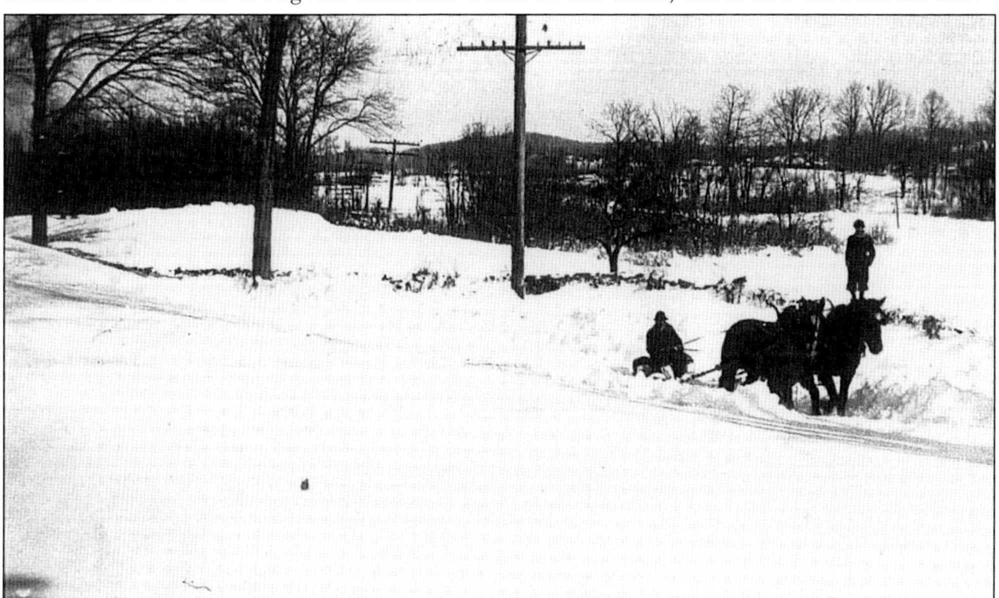

Snow was for children and sledding; otherwise it created a nuisance to be moved. Breaking through drifts on Pepper Street in 1930 required both manpower and horsepower.

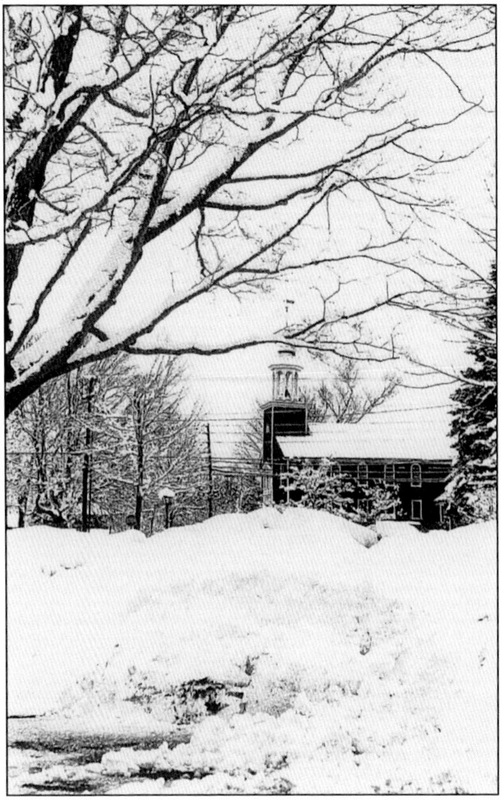

Two wood-burning stoves once kept St. Peter's Episcopal Church-on-the-Green warm when blanketed by snow.

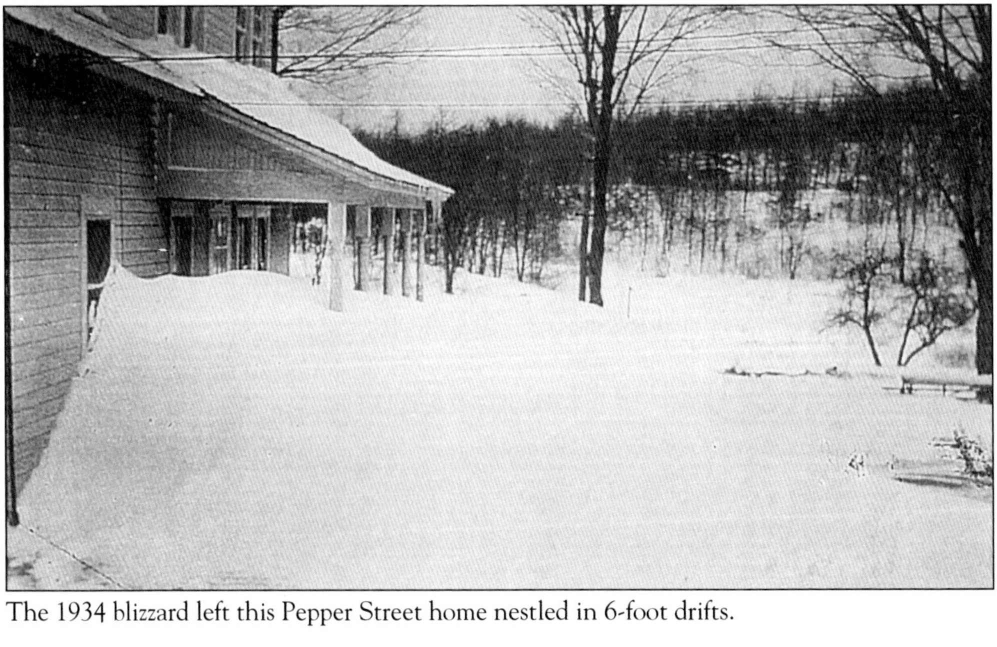

The 1934 blizzard left this Pepper Street home nestled in 6-foot drifts.

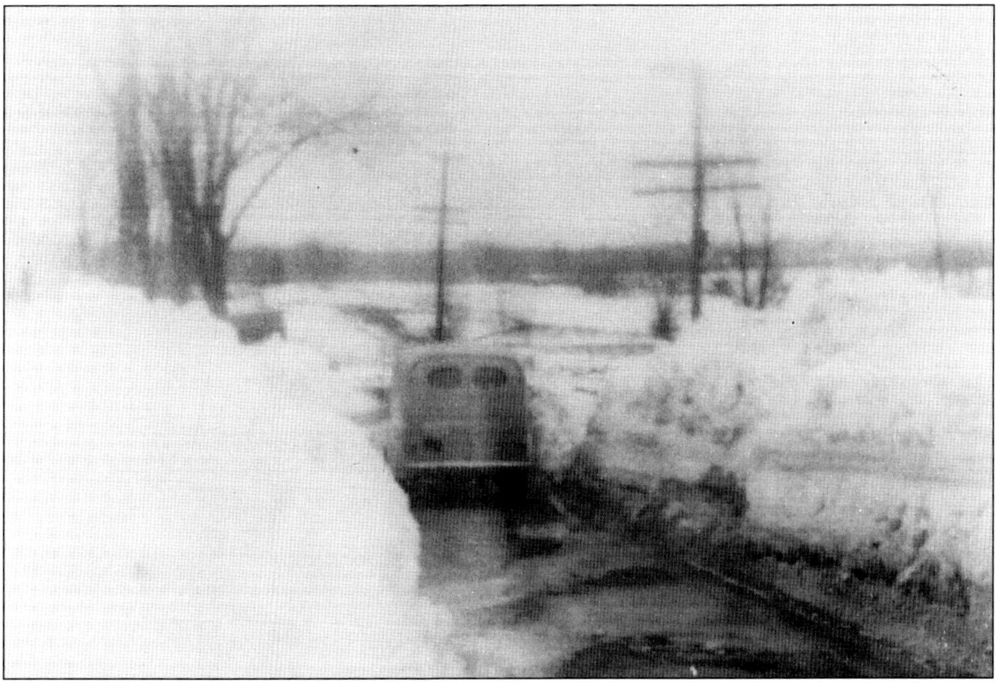

On the day after Thanksgiving in 1939, T. Raymond Reynolds's Home Pride Bakery delivery truck struggles with a snowbank on Shelton Road just below the Monroe Firehouse.

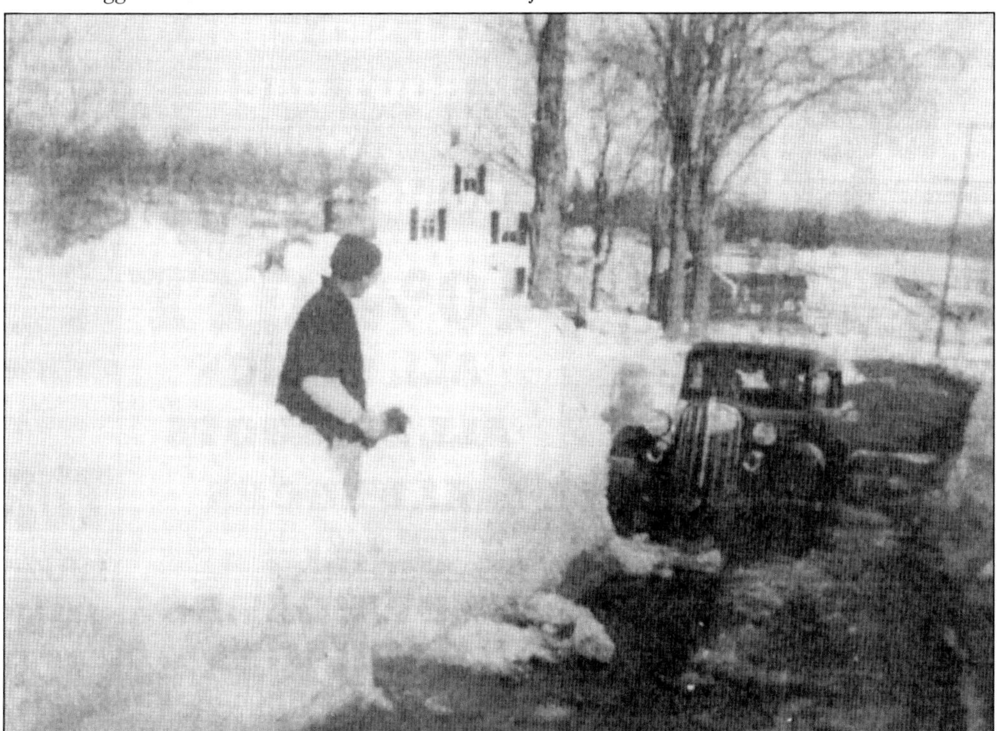

First Selectman George Hawley's car is dwarfed by huge snow banks on Purdy Hill Road after the Blizzard of February 14, 1940. Spring must have been eagerly anticipated that year!

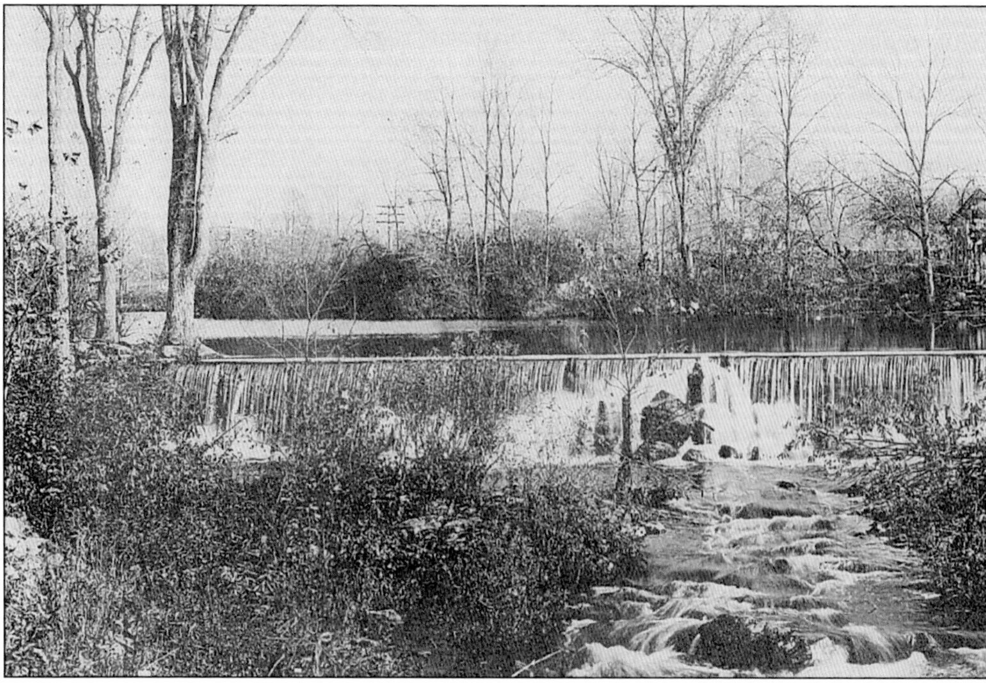

With thawing snow and spring rains, rivers and brooks ran rapidly. This millpond fed a plaster mill on the Barnum Curtis property in Stepney. It was located near the bustling area of town then known as "Times Square" off Maple Drive in the 1890s.

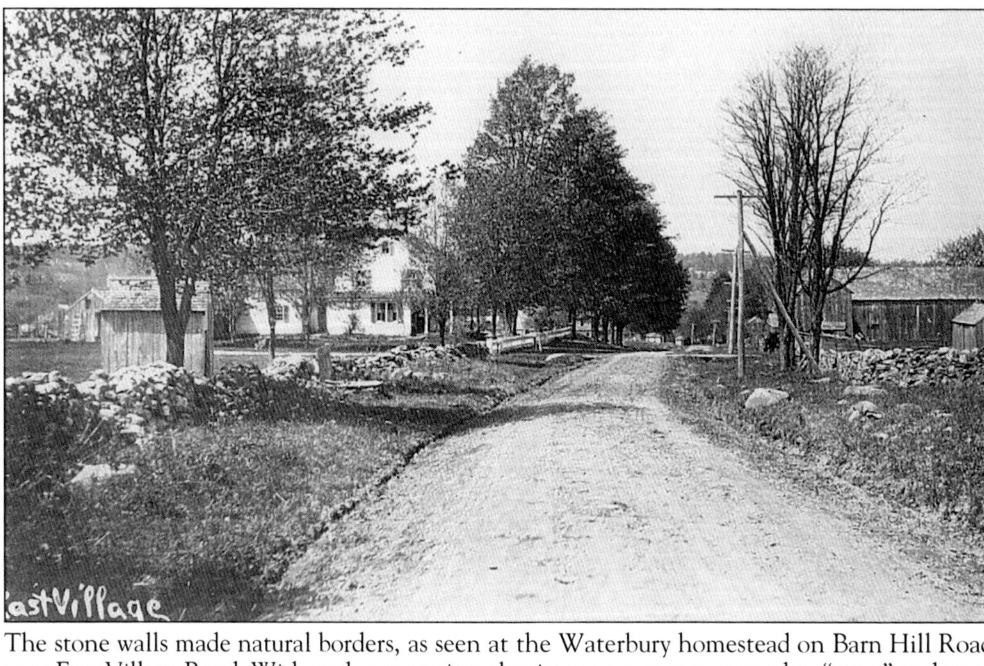

The stone walls made natural borders, as seen at the Waterbury homestead on Barn Hill Road near East Village Road. With each new spring plowing, more stones seemed to "grow" and were added to the stone walls.

Nine

Business as Usual

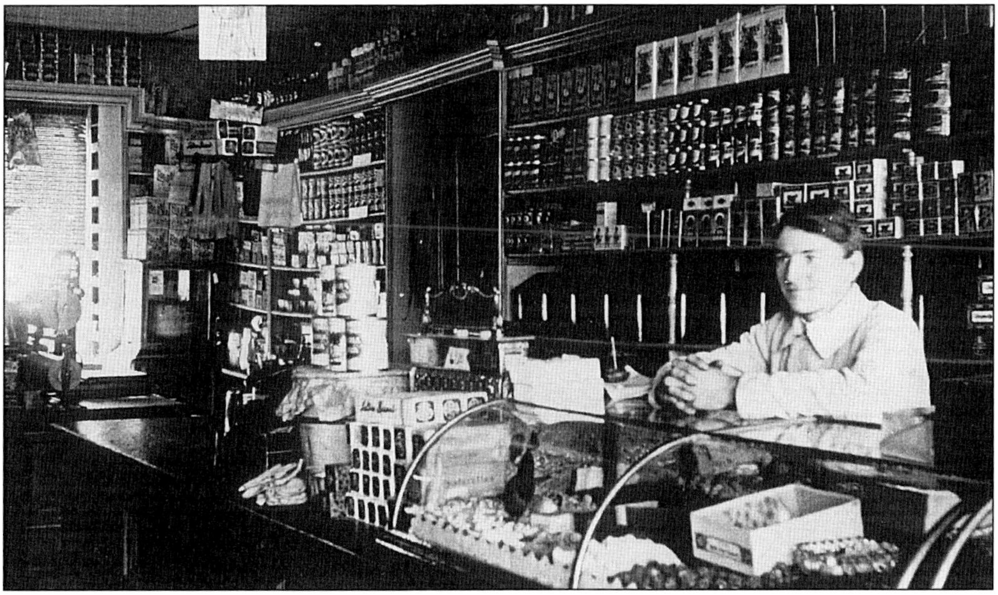

Fred T. Hunter awaits a customer at Burr Hawley's general store, Monroe's largest for 40 years. The store was located at the southwest corner of Main Street and Stepney Road in present-day Upper Stepney. This crossroads emporium carried everything from feed to lampblack, nails, and needles. Even Mark Twain of Redding is known to have stopped in for a chat around the wood stove.

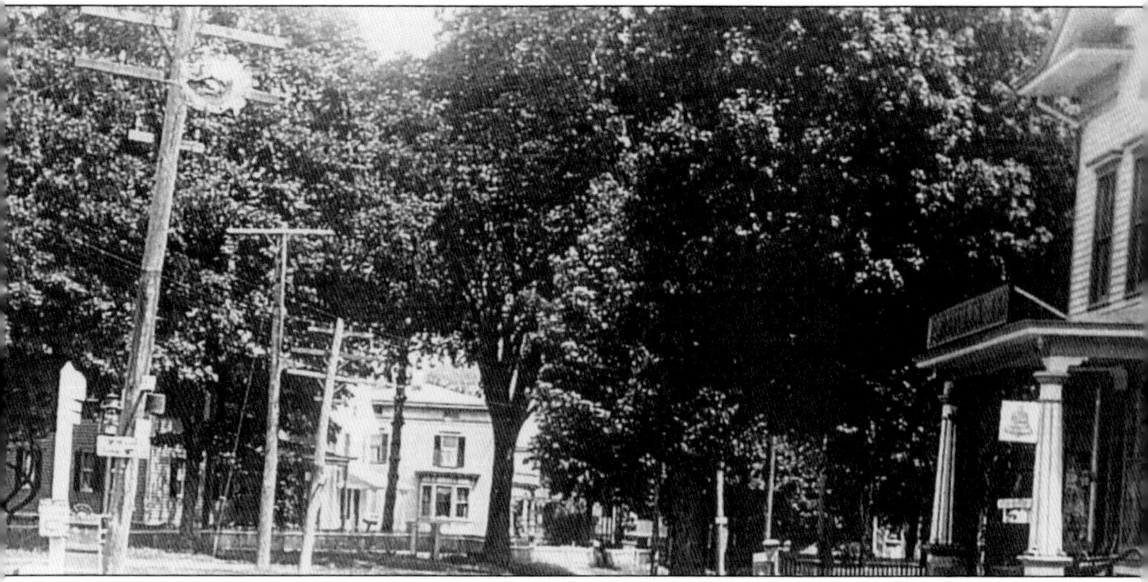

The Burr Hawley General Store was located north of the Stepney Baptist Church. Residents of the area were able to purchase a variety of goods including grain, hay, feed, and tack, as well as groceries, sewing supplies, and lumber. It was the "milk station" where farmers delivered their milk daily.

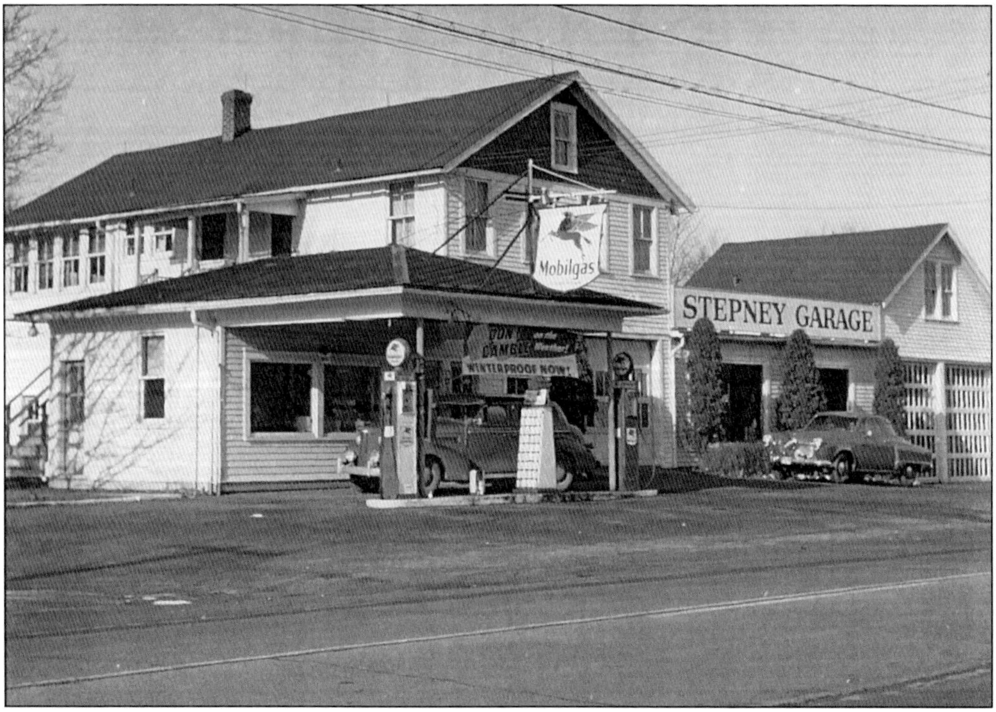

As the town grew, so did the needs for services. This garage, pictured previously on page 53, has expanded to meet the demands of a more suburban population.

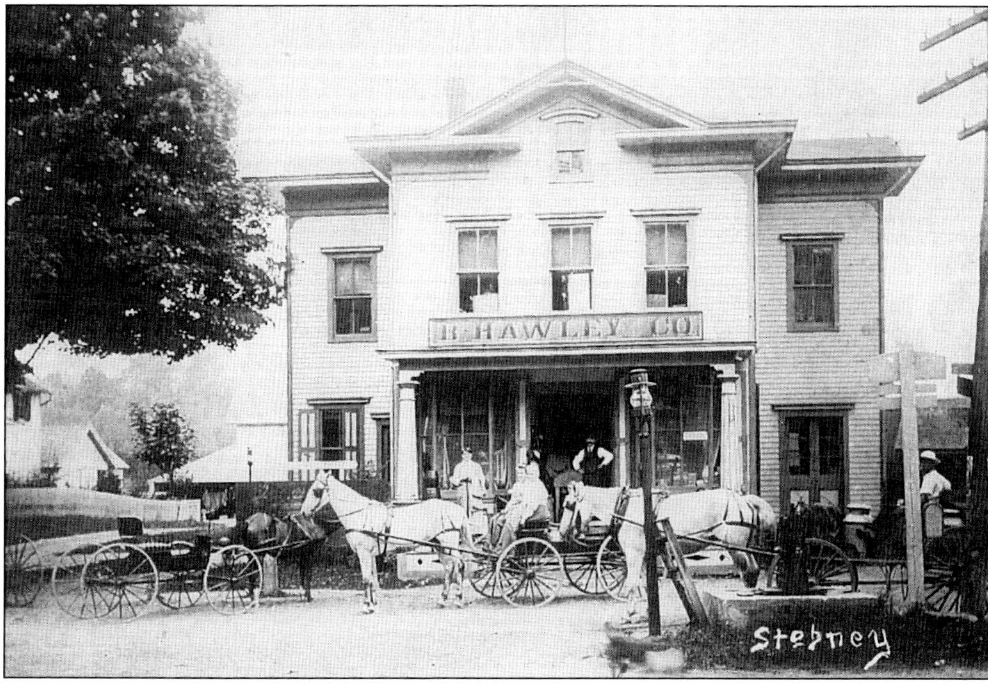

At Burr Hawley's store, farmers gathered their teams and wagons to bring milk to the milk station; to buy feed, hay, and grain; to shop in the store; and to swap news. The only motor-driven grain mill in town was located at the rear of the store.

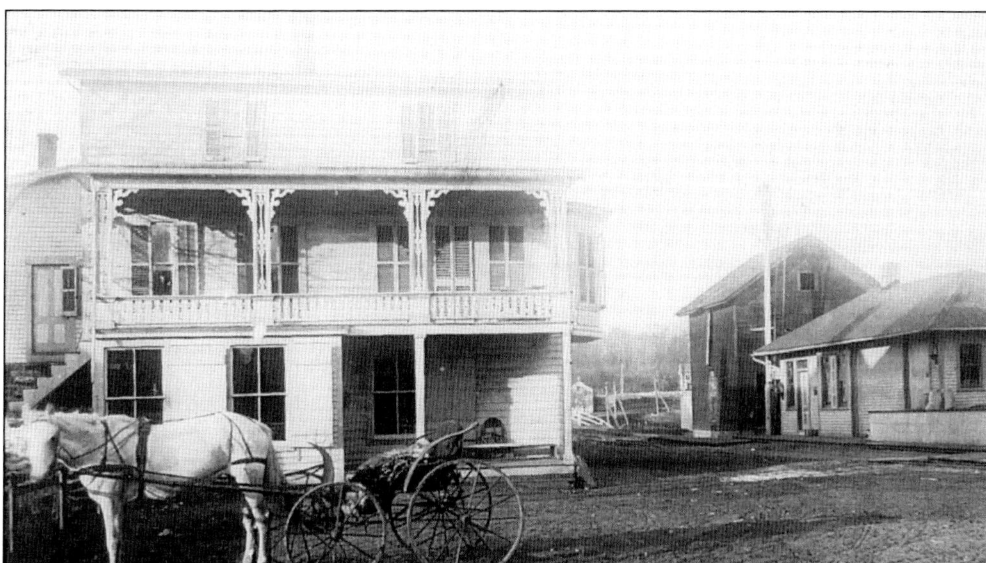

Stephen French's store and the old Stepney Railroad Station are pictured here. At the left side of the store (front addition) is the post office. The horse and buggy was available for rental from an attached livery stable.

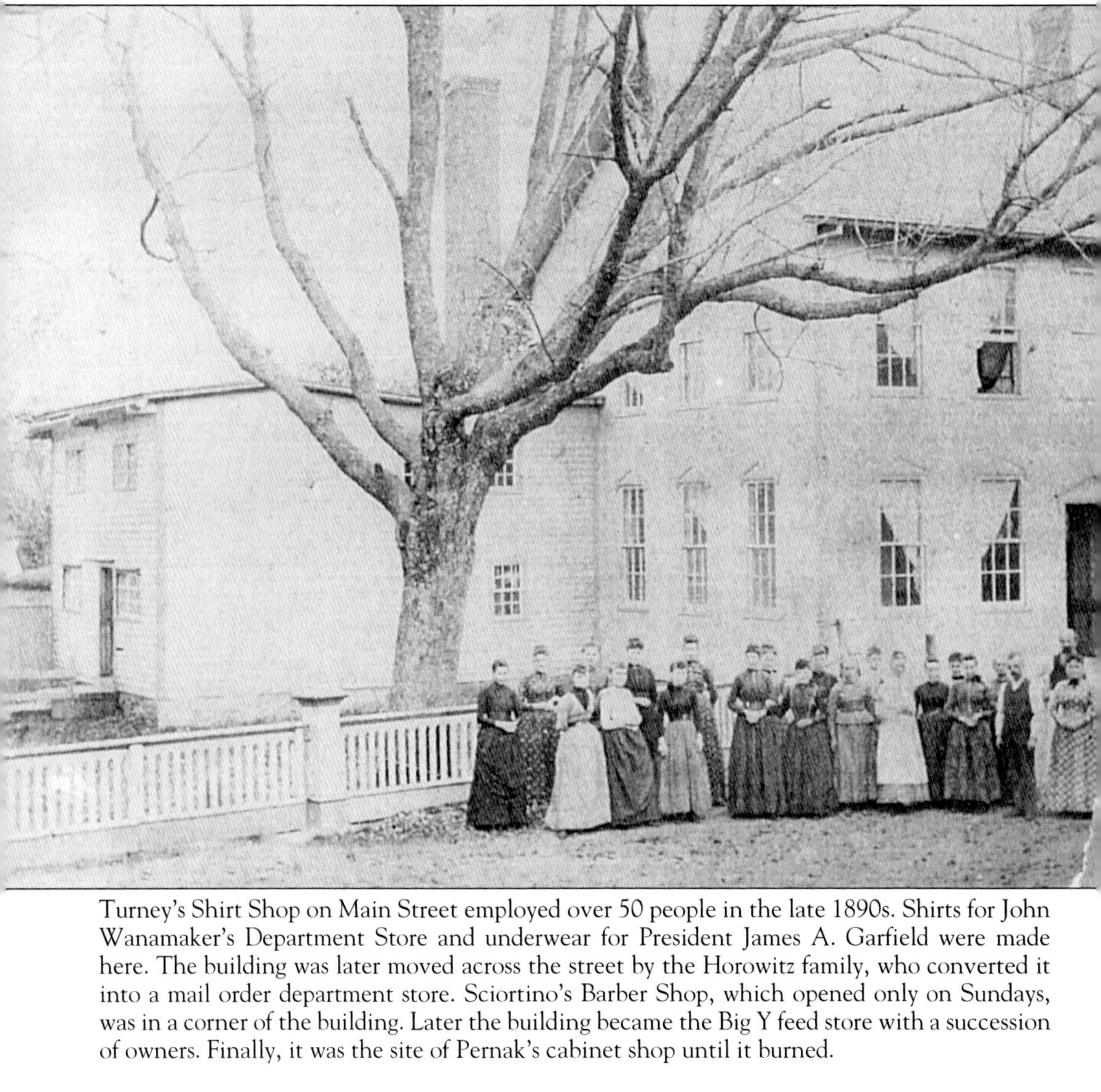

Turney's Shirt Shop on Main Street employed over 50 people in the late 1890s. Shirts for John Wanamaker's Department Store and underwear for President James A. Garfield were made here. The building was later moved across the street by the Horowitz family, who converted it into a mail order department store. Sciortino's Barber Shop, which opened only on Sundays, was in a corner of the building. Later the building became the Big Y feed store with a succession of owners. Finally, it was the site of Pernak's cabinet shop until it burned.

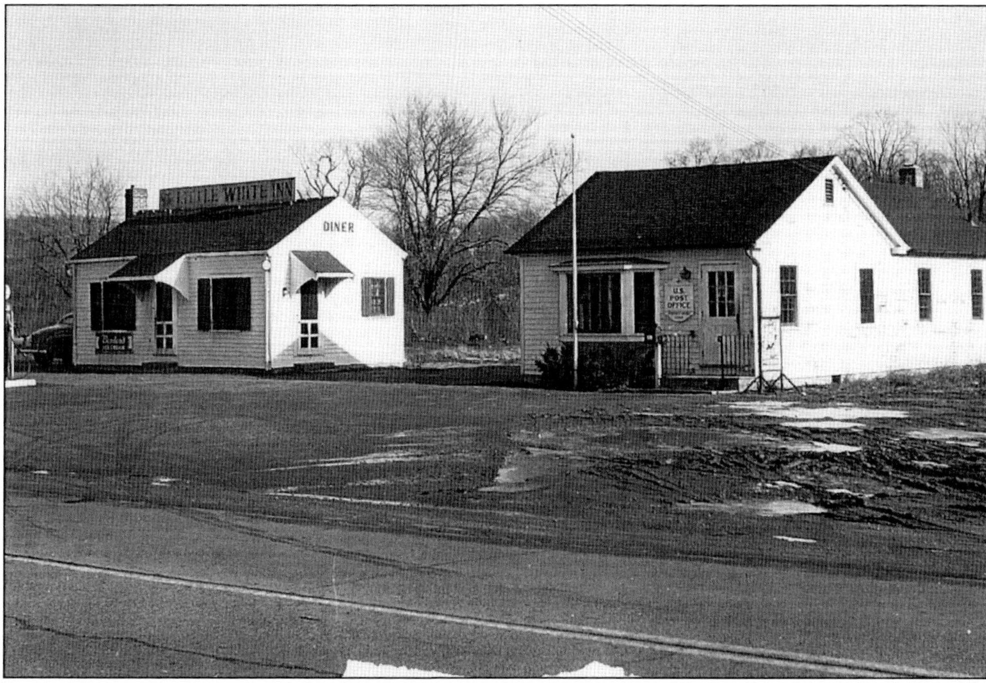

The Little White Inn (left) and the "new" Stepney Post Office stand along Main Street in the 1940s. Built by Ernest Williams, this was the first structure built exclusively as a post office. All previous Monroe post offices had been located in stores and in private homes.

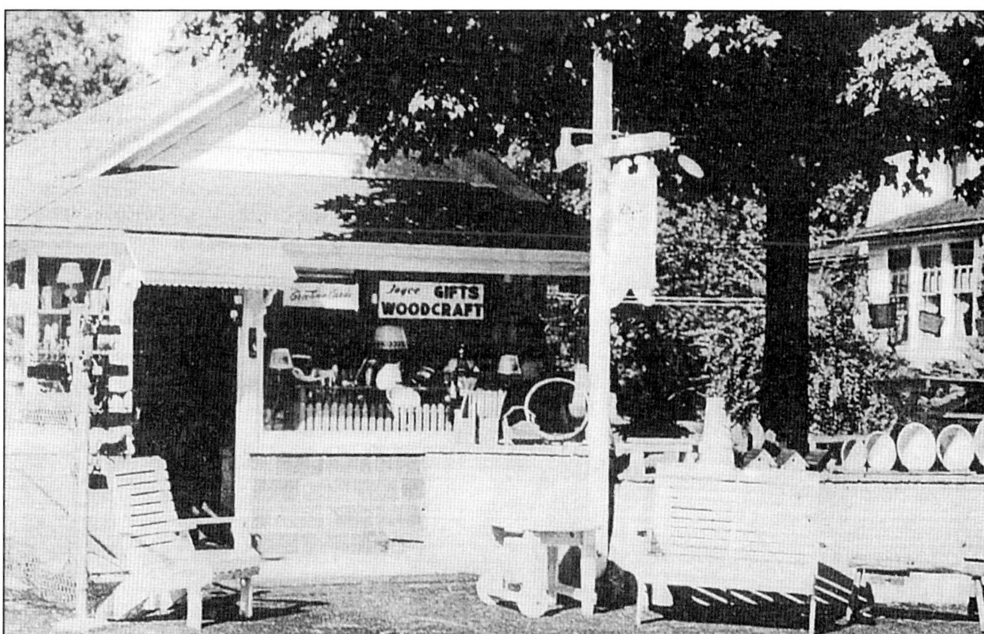

A variety of gift items made of brass, copper, and wood were sold at the Joyce family's Handee Gift Shop on Main Street in Stepney in the 1950s. The house on the right is presently the Smithy Restaurant.

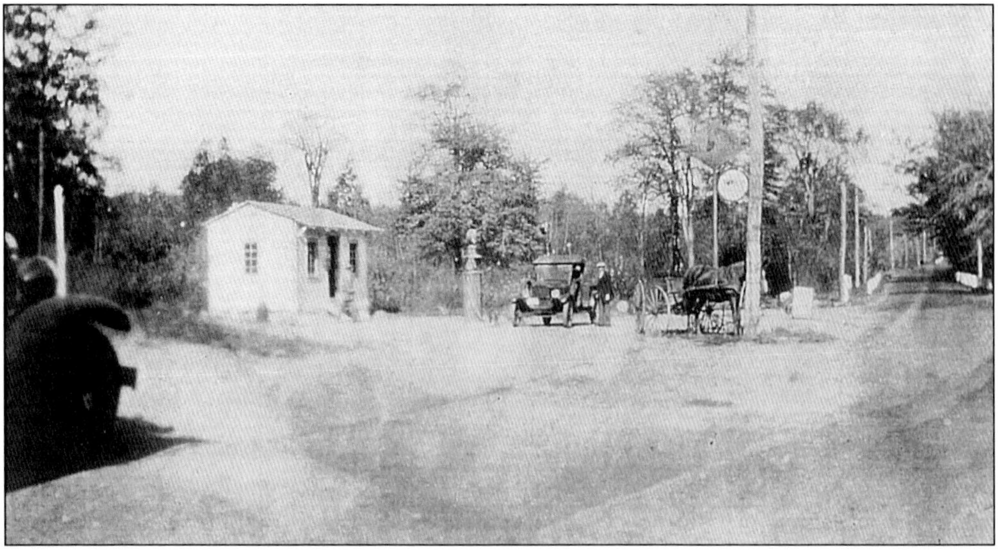

Monroe's first gas station was located next to Merrill's Modern Grocery. It is presently the site of Waite's Service Station and Garage. The single pump pictured here would hardly be adequate for today's commuter traffic.

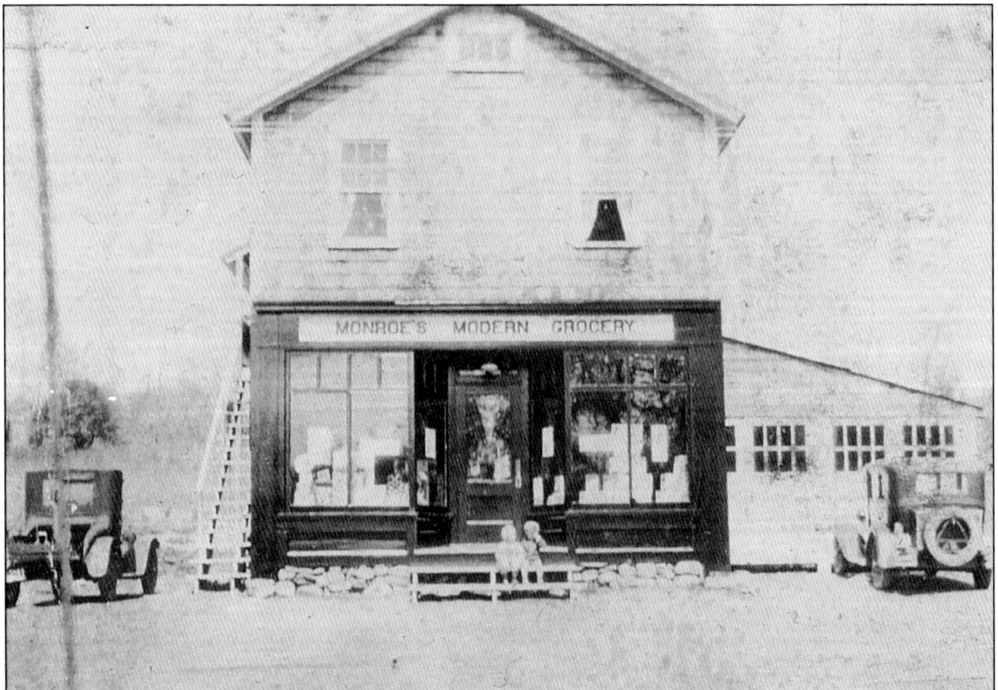

Merrill's Modern Grocery Store near the corner of Monroe Turnpike and Cross Hill Road was built and operated by the Merrill family in the 1920s. Monroe's most noted artist, David Merrill, called this his boyhood home.

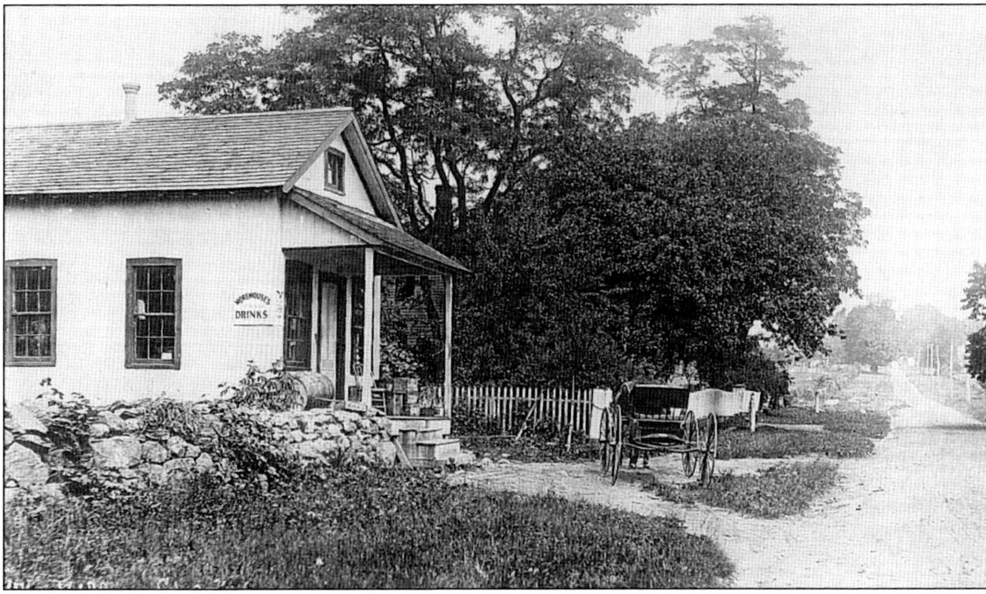

Earl Wales built and ran this village store on Elm Street near Bug Hill, serving the needs of the nearby residents. Notice there are no shopping carts abandoned in this parking lot! Now a private residence, it has been relocated to Cross Hill Road.

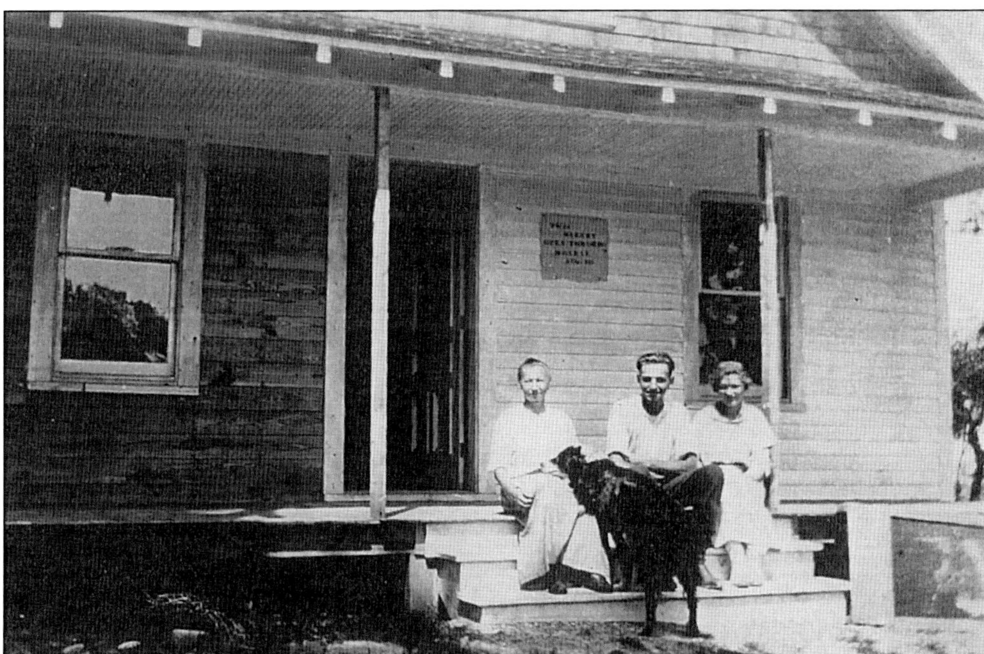

Old Tannery Road Bakery was an asset to the farming community. It is alleged that counterfeit money was made here at one time, which shocked the townspeople.

THE STEPNEY ELM HOUSE

MAX LOSS, Proprietor

POPULAR SUMMER AND WINTER RESORT

STRICTLY כשר KOSHER

ALL MODERN IMPROVEMENTS

MONROE, CONN. ....

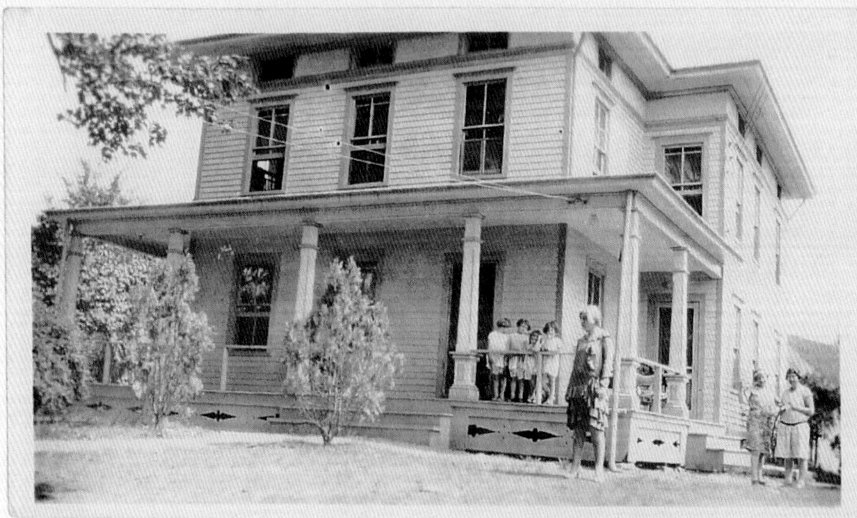

P. S. Reduced rail rates make your traveling inexpensive. Take New Haven Railroad to Bridgeport and call us on the phone upon your arrival. By Auto, with Merit Highway to Westport then on to Post Road to Bridgeport, then Route #25 to Route #111 on which turn left at Elm Street. When asking for us ask for MAX LOSS.

The Stepney Elm Hotel, a popular vacation destination of city folk, was located at the corner of Elm Street and Cross Hill Road. The Elm Street Crossing office complex is now on this site.

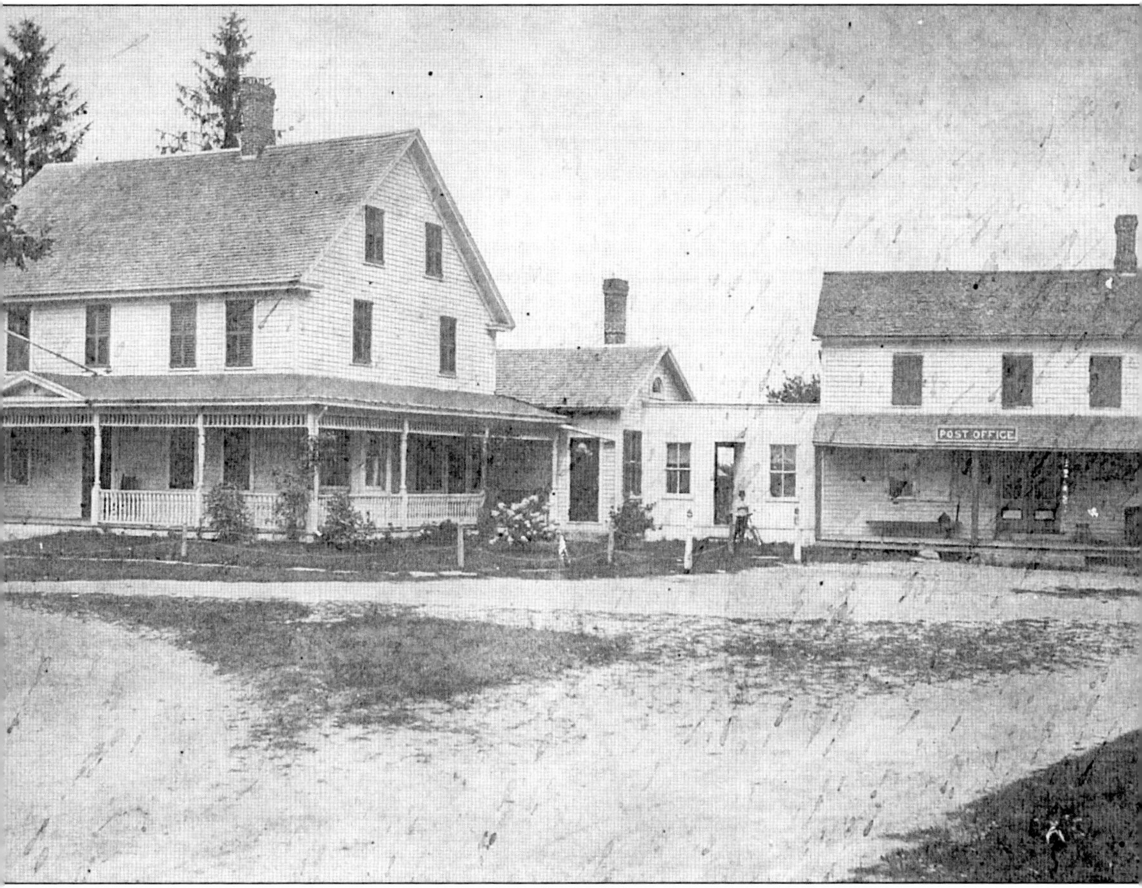

The Marshall Beach General Store and home was often the gathering place for our townspeople—whether coming to the post office (which was also located there), the general store, or just getting together on the veranda to see who could tell the tallest tale. The house and store date to the 1780s.

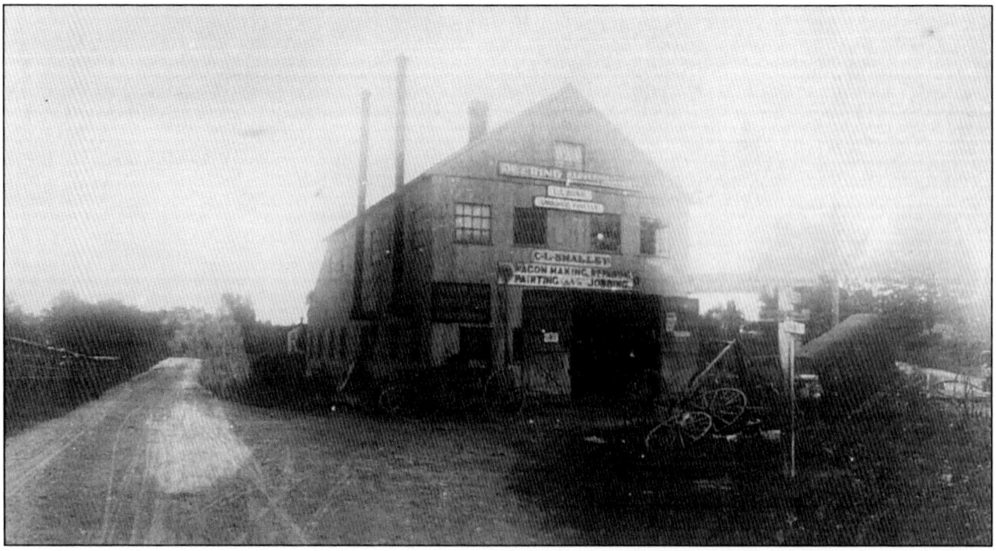

Smalley's Blacksmith Shop, across from the old Stepney Firehouse on Main Street, was famous for renovating and restoring farm vehicle wheels of all sizes and shapes. Iron rims were tightened, dished wheels put right, and horses shod.

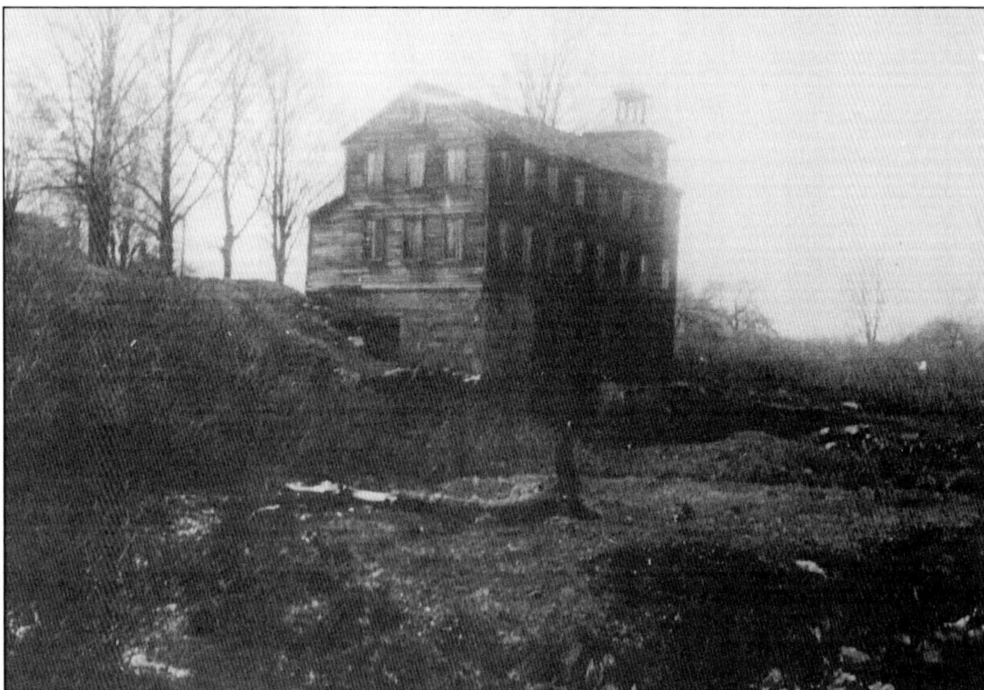

Foster Cargill's Hoopskirt Factory stood in East Village off Barn Hill Road. There, in the nineteenth century, hoopskirts, corsets, and twine were manufactured. This large wooden structure stood here until it was razed by the Bridgeport Hydraulic Company in the 1930s.

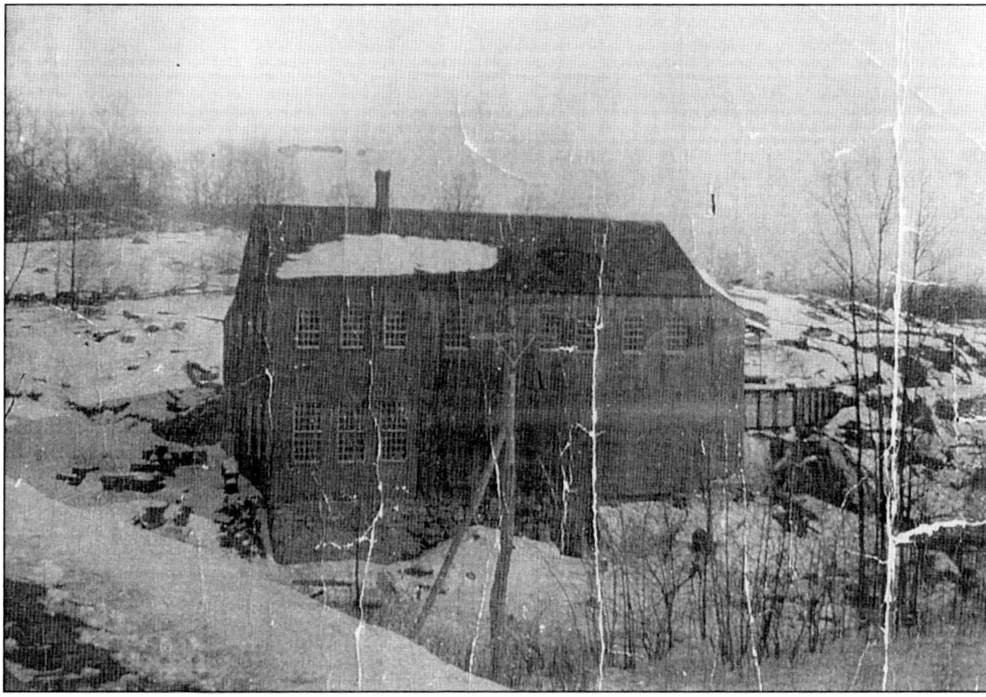

The Botsford Factory and Cider Mill on Hammertown Road was owned and operated by brothers Edward and Howard Botsford in the nineteenth century. They also had a lumber mill nearby.

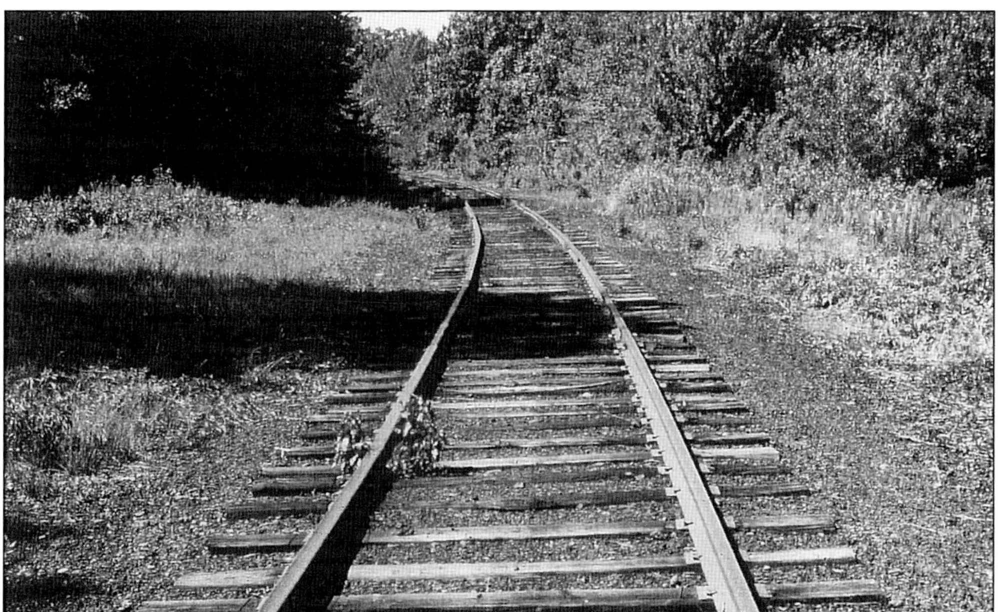

The Stepney Railroad spur near Pepper Street was active and served the William Benedict Agway business. Monroe's industrial era ended when this, part of the railroad to Stepney, was discontinued.

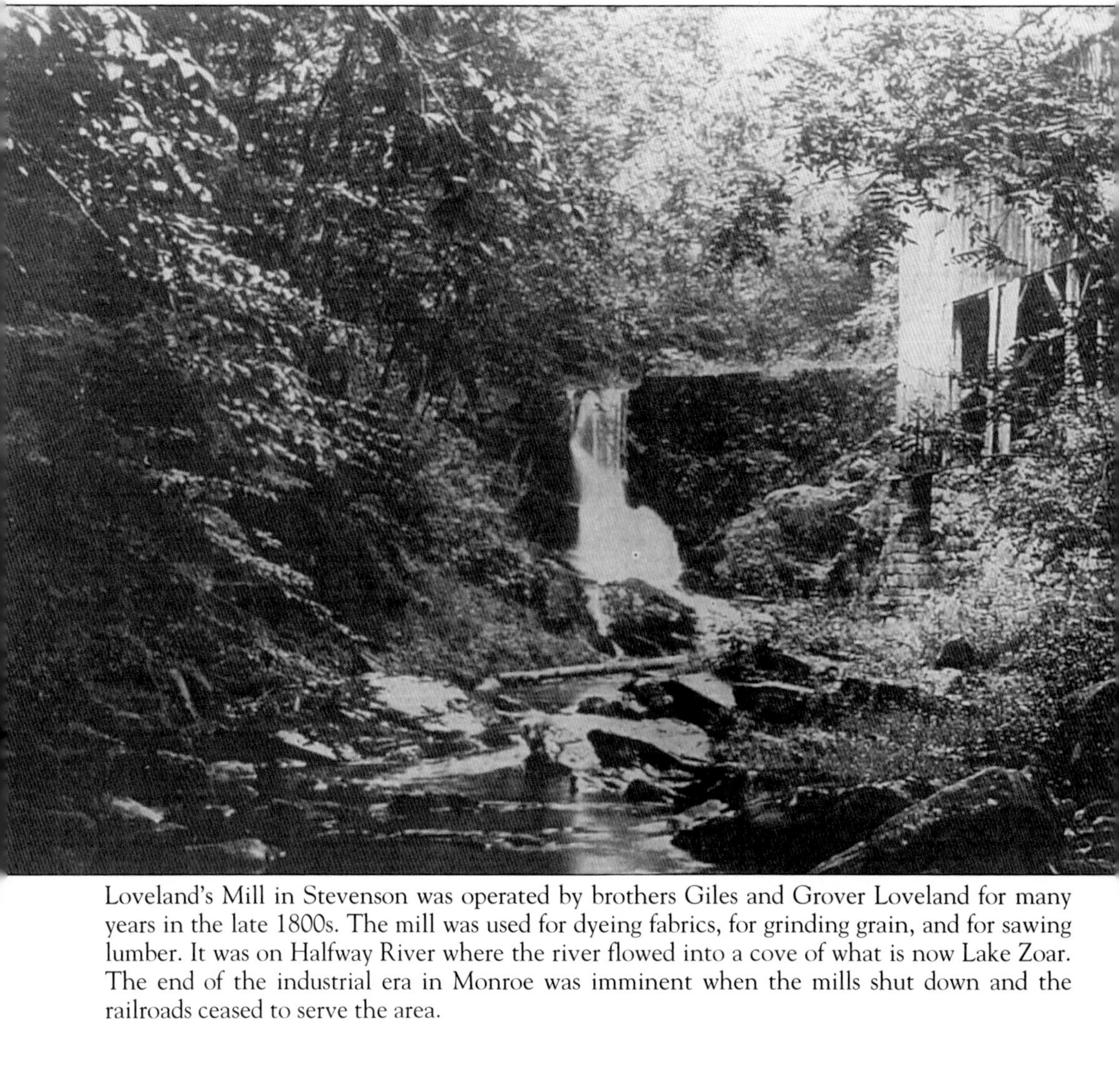

Loveland's Mill in Stevenson was operated by brothers Giles and Grover Loveland for many years in the late 1800s. The mill was used for dyeing fabrics, for grinding grain, and for sawing lumber. It was on Halfway River where the river flowed into a cove of what is now Lake Zoar. The end of the industrial era in Monroe was imminent when the mills shut down and the railroads ceased to serve the area.